*Corel*DRAW!™ 3

SELF-TEACHING GUIDE

Wiley SELF-TEACHING GUIDES (STG's) are designed for first-time users of computer applications and programming languages. They feature concept-reinforcing drills, exercises, and illustrations that enable you to measure your progress and learn at your own pace. Other Wiley Self-Teaching Guides:

DOS 5 STG, Ruth Ashley and Judi N. Fernandez
INTRODUCTION TO PERSONAL COMPUTERS STG, Peter Stephenson
OBJECTVISION 2 STG, Arnold and Edith Shulman, and Robert Marion
QUATTRO PRO 3 STG, Jennifer Meyer
LOTUS 1-2-3 FOR WINDOWS STG, Douglas J. Wolf
PARADOX 3.5 STG, Gloria Wheeler
Q&A 4 STG, Corey Sandler and Tom Badgett
FOXPRO 2 STG, Ellen Sander
ALDUS PERSUASION FOR IBM PC'S AND COMPATIBLES STG, Karen Brown and Diane Stielstra
PFS:Publisher for Windows STG, Sean Cavanaugh and Deanna Bebb
PERFORM STG, Peter Stephenson
NOVELL NETWARE 2.2 STG, Peter Stephenson and Glenn Hartwig
MICROSOFT WORD 5.5 FOR THE PC STG, Ruth Ashley and Judi Fernandez
MICROSOFT WORD FOR WINDOWS 2 STG, Pamela S. Beason and Stephen Guild
WORDPERFECT 5.0/5.1 STG, Neil Salkind
WORDPERFECT FOR WINDOWS STG, Neil Salkind
SIGNATURE STG, Christine Rivera
MICROSOFT WINDOWS 3.0 STG, Keith Weiskamp and Saul Aguiar
WINDOWS 3.1 STG, Keith Weiskamp
PC DOS 4 STG, Ruth Ashley and Judi Fernandez
PC DOS 3.3 STG, Ruth Ashley and Judi Fernandez
MASTERING MICROSOFT WORKS STG, David Sachs, Babette Kronstadt, Judith Van Wormer, and Barbara Farrell
QUICKPASCAL STG, Keith Weiskamp and Saul Aguiar
GW BASIC STG, Ruth Ashley and Judi Fernandez
TURBO C++ STG, Bryan Flamig
SQL STG, Peter Stephenson and Glenn Hartwig
QUICKEN STG, Peter Aitken
CORELDRAW! 3 STG, Robert Bixby
HARVARD GRAPHICS 3 STG, David Harrison and John W. Yu
HARVARD GRAPHICS FOR WINDOWS STG, David Harrison and John W. Yu
NORTON DESKTOP 2 FOR WINDOWS STG, Gerry Litton and Jenna Christen
AMI PRO 2 FOR WINDOWS STG, Pamela S. Beason and Stephen Guild
EXCEL 4 STG, Ruth K. Witkin
QuarkXPress for Windows STG, Kim and Sunny Baker

To order our STGs, you can call Wiley directly at (201)469-4400, or check your local bookstores. "Mastering computers was never this easy, rewarding, and fun!"

CorelDRAW!™ 3

SELF-TEACHING GUIDE

Robert Bixby

John Wiley & Sons
New York ▲ Chichester ▲ Brisbane ▲ Toronto ▲ Singapore

Library of Congress Cataloging-in-Publication Data:

Bixby, Robert, 1952–
    CorelDraw! 3 : self-teaching guide / Robert Bixby.
        p. cm.
    ISBN 0–471–57925-4 (pbk.)
    1. Computer graphics. 2. CorelDraw! I. Title. II. Title:
CorelDRAW! three.
T385.B562 1993
006.6'869—dc20   92–27827

Printed in the United States of America
10 9 8 7 6 5 4 3 2 1

Contents Overview

Contents

Introduction

You are about to embark on learning the basics of one of the most powerful PC graphics packages ever conceived: *CorelDRAW!*. A list of the features of this program could go on for pages. During the course of this book, you will see each of these features in action.

CorelDRAW! belongs to a class of graphics packages that includes paint and draw programs, presentation programs, illustration programs, and computer-aided design (CAD) programs. The differences among these programs are most easily explained in terms of their products.

There are two basic approaches to creating an image on the computer screen. The first is painting to the screen, also known as *raster* or *bit-map graphics*, the approach used by *PC Paintbrush* and *Deluxe Paint*. Painting depends on the resolution of the computer screen itself. When you alter the color or shape of something on the screen, you are actually changing the *pixels*, or picture elements, that appear on the computer screen. (If you look closely at the image on the screen, you can see that it's made up of tiny dots of light. Each of these dots is a pixel.)

The other approach is called *vector* or *object-oriented graphics*. This is the approach used by draw programs like *DrawPerfect*, presentation programs like *Charisma*, and illustration programs like *CorelDRAW!*. Instead of etching a circle or other object in the pixels of the computer screen, the object exists in memory in a sort of idealized, abstract description from which a representation of a circle is rendered on the screen to the best of the computer's ability.

The difference is subtle in concept, but when it is time to print the artwork on paper, it becomes much more important because printers are capable of far higher resolution than computer screens. Most laser printers are capable of placing 300 dots per inch (dpi) on paper, resulting in very fine printing. By contrast, the computer screen typically provides for no more than 72 dots per inch. If you print a circle created with a paint program, the curves that make it up would be composed of "jaggies"—straight lines arranged to resemble a curve, as shown in Figure I.1.

▼ *Figure I.1. Circle Created at Screen Resolution.*

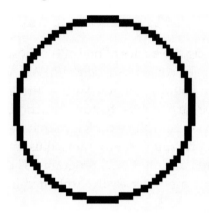

But a circle created with a draw program can be printed at the highest resolution the printer is capable of, as shown in Figure I.2.

Higher resolution devices, like Linotronic output devices, can create printouts with resolution over 2000 dpi. The circle in Figure I.1 printed on one of these machines would look similar to the circle you see in the figure, whereas a printout of the circle depicted in Figure I.2 would look perfectly smooth, even when magnified.

There are differences other than resolution. The product of a paint program like *Deluxe Paint II Enhanced* is a single layer of color. You can edit a painting, but the changes must be made pixel-by-pixel. In a painting of a boy and his dog, if you want to make the dog's ears longer, you must erase the existing ears and painstakingly repaint the ears. In the process, you could accidentally affect the part of the painting that contains the boy. Paint programs typically contain tools that make working with individual pixels simple: built-in microscopes called *zoom tools*, and an easily used palette.

By contrast, the product of an object-oriented draw program is a collection of independent objects. A drawing of a boy and his dog could consist of two objects or hundreds of objects carefully grouped. For example, the dog could be composed of a group of independent objects representing his body, his four legs, his neck, his tail, his head, and his two ears. To alter his ears, you would ungroup

▼ *Figure I.2. Circle Created at 300 dpi Printer Resolution.*

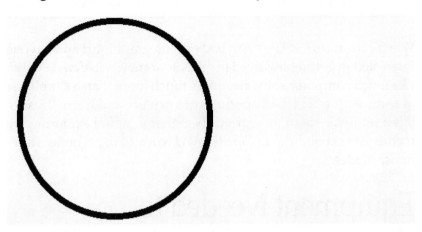

the dog (which means to "unstick" the independent objects so they can be manipulated), change to node-editing mode, move the control points that determine the size and shape of the ears, return to object-editing mode, and regroup the objects that compose the dog. During this process, there would be no way to accidentally damage any part of the drawing that was not related to the dog's ears.

The parallel between the shapes on the screen and a group of objects on a shelf is almost perfect. The objects are all arranged in order of precedence. They can be selected and moved, sized, colored, or deleted at will. You can even save items from a drawing and use them in other drawings. This is useful for commercial artists who spend much of their time creating nearly identical drawings for logos or for form design. It is this nearly perfect control that makes illustration programs so valuable.

With its ability to load bitmap graphics, turn them into vector graphics, and then save the graphics as bitmaps again, *CorelDRAW!* might be seen as a bridge between paint programs and vector graphic programs. In fact, the distinctions among the various types of programs in terms of power are becoming less important over time. Paint programs can exhibit a great deal of power, for example, providing scaling and perspective. But if you use a range of programs, you will quickly learn to recognize the superiority of illustration packages over paint and presentation programs.

Who Needs to Use *CorelDRAW!?*

Who needs *CorelDRAW!?* Anybody doing graphic art and anyone interested in getting involved in graphic art needs it. *CorelDRAW!*, like much computer software, offers much more than a simple list of features. It offers the opportunity to explore and learn. Because it is a professional tool, a curious beginner will find exploring the menus and capabilities of *CorelDRAW!* will add to his or her storehouse of ideas.

Equipment Needed to Run *CorelDRAW!*

The equipment required to run *CorelDRAW!* is very similar to the equipment needed for Windows operation. It can run on any PC-compatible with an 80286 or higher-numbered central processing unit, Windows, Hercules, EGA, VGA or higher-level video, and a mouse or similar pointing device. Naturally, the higher the level of your equipment, the more satisfied you will be with *CorelDRAW!* operation. Some users warn that the 80286 computer should be considered only the minimal platform. Hercules and EGA graphics should likewise be considered a bare minimum. If you want to use *CorelDRAW!* to its maximum power and flexibility, you will need a 386 and VGA graphics/ Better still, you should think about upgrading to a 486DX system with SuperVGA graphics.

How to Use This Book

Each chapter includes sections that cover specific topics and features. In addition, the following tools have been designed to make the most of your learning time:

    Check Yourself At the end of every major topic, you'll see a "Check Yourself" section where you can combine all of the detailed steps you have learned into one smooth procedure.

Practice What You've Learned Each chapter has one final "Practice What You've Learned" to enable you to review and practice the procedures you have learned in that chapter. It also integrates separate topics from the chapter into meaningful procedures.

Tip sections appear throughout the book, helping to draw your attention to special features and shortcuts. They also offer suggestions for using the features you have learned about. Incorporating these tips into your normal routine enables you to work at the most productive level and shortens the time needed to perform tasks.

Quick Summaries fall at the end of each chapter and review any shortcut keys, tasks, and procedures covered in the chapter.

Other Conventions

A few more conventions are used in this book. When DOS prompts you to do something, this will be shown in quotation marks, like "Copy another diskette (Y/N)?" Note that I will refer to all floppy disks as *disks* whereas DOS usually refers to them as *diskettes*.

When you are instructed to enter something at the command line, this will be shown all in uppercase letters. For example, to format a disk, you should type FORMAT A: and press Enter.

Using Keyboard Commands

We will assume that you are passingly familiar with the PC keyboard. Although *CorelDRAW!* as well Windows can be entirely mouse-driven, you will need to enter cetain commands.

In this book, you will occasionally be told to press a key combination like ALT + F4. This means that you should press and hold down the Alt key, simultaneously pressing and releasing the F4 function key. By coincidence, this is the command to close the currently active window. Within *CorelDRAW!*, you will issue certain commands from a menu bar arranged along the top of the screen (shown in Figure I.3). If you are told to press Ctrl-C, you should press and hold down the Ctrl, or Control, key and tap the C key. To activate the menu bar from the keyboard, press either the Alt key

▼ *Figure I.3. The CorelDRAW! Work Screen.*

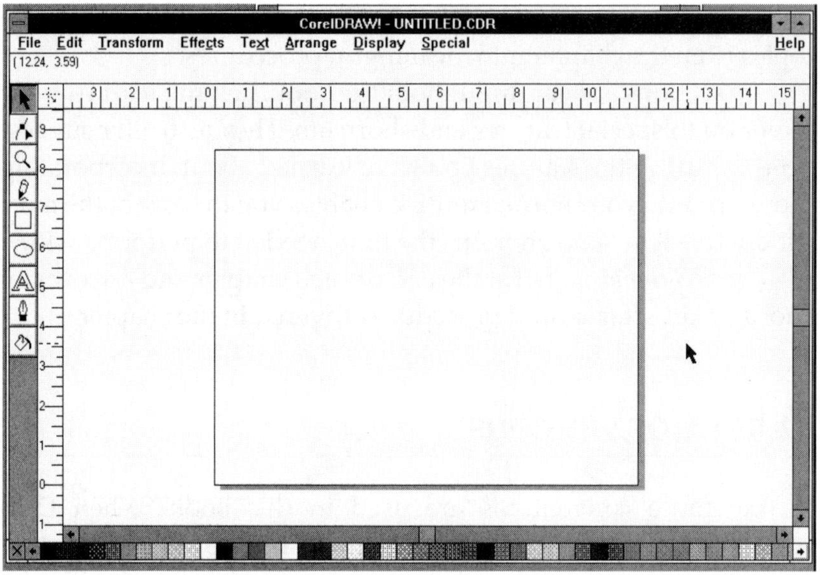

or the F10 key and then press the first letter of the menu you want to see.

Once the menu bar is selected, to pull down a menu from the keyboard, press the down-arrow key. Use the up- and down-arrow keys to move the highlight within a menu. To move to the next menu to the right or the left, use the right- and left-arrow keys.

If there is a dialog box visible on the screen, some part of that dialog box will be active. For example, in Figure I.4, the Open Drawing dialog box is open. The Files area of the dialog box is the active area. If you press the down-arrow key, you could move the highlight through all the CDR files in the current directory. To load the highlighted file, simply press Enter. (Note that a simple representation of the drawing in the file is shown in the large box at the right, just above the Cancel button.)

To move to the next area in the dialog box, use the Tab key. Tapping it once takes you to the File Name area where you can use the cursor keys to select a different directory.

Tapping the Tab key again takes you to the Directories area, where you can simply select the directory from which the files in the File Name are to be loaded.

▼ *Figure I.4. The Open Drawing Dialog Box.*

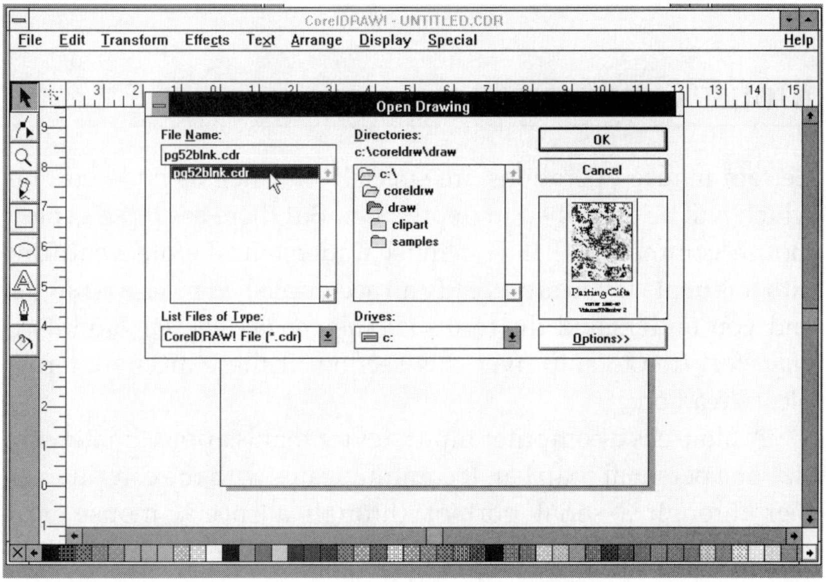

Pressing the Tab key again takes the selection to the List Files of Type box. Press the down-arrow key to see a list of filters representing the files *CorelDRAW!* can import.

Press Tab again and you are moved to the Drives box. Press the down-arrow key to see the list of drives you can access.

Press Tab again to highlight the OK button. If you press Enter right now, the highlighted file will be loaded into *CorelDRAW!*.

Press Tab again to highlight the Cancel button, which takes on a thick border to indicate that it's selected. If you press Enter at this point, the dialog box will close and no file will be loaded.

Press Tab to move to the Options button, which opens up a larger version of the Open dialog box, which allows you to specify the way files are sorted (by name or date), allows you to make use of Mosaic, to turn off the preview, and so forth.

Pressing Shift-Tab will make the highlight move in reverse order. All dialog boxes work this way, allowing you to maneuver either with the keyboard or the mouse. You will learn many keyboard shortcuts in this book, which are summarized in the appendix for easy reference. Some people feel more comfortable working with the keyboard and others prefer the mouse.

CorelDRAW! and Windows are flexible enough to allow you either option.

Mouse Commands

Certain mouse operations are specialized, such as node editing, which will be described in depth later. But there are three generic mouse commands that you must understand before venturing into this book. If you are already an accomplished mouse wrangler and you understand the terms *clicking, double-clicking*, and *dragging*, feel free to skip over this section. If these are new terms, please read on.

A mouse is a computer input device that is approximately the size of a personal soap bar. It communicates with the computer either through a serial port or through a special mouse port. Although there are cordless mice that operate like infrared VCR remote controls or by way of weak radio transmissions, most mice are attached to the computer by a wire. Mice for the PC usually have two or three buttons.

Generally speaking, we will concern ourselves with the left button. If you hold the mouse in the palm of your right hand, this button should be directly under your index finger.

Clicking

When you read the instruction to click on an item, you should move the mouse until the mouse pointer on the screen is located over the specified item and quickly press and release the left mouse button. Most mice have click switches under their buttons, so there should be an unmistakable clicking sound or tactile click inside the mouse. This action is typically used to select an item. It should be carefully distinguished from double-clicking, which will be covered next.

Double-Clicking

Double-clicking is an action used to start applications, open windows, and enter node-editing mode within *CorelDRAW!*. To double-click, place your index finger on the left mouse button and press and release it twice, in rapid succession. The speed of the click necessary to make a double-click is adjustable by using the control panel, which will be covered later.

Dragging

Dragging is a process used to move and size objects and windows. To drag, place the mouse pointer on the object you want to drag (*CorelDRAW!* requires that you place the mouse pointer on the *outline* of an object) and press the left mouse button. Hold the button down until you have moved the object to the position where you would like to place it and then release the button.

On to *CorelDRAW!* 3

As mentioned, *CorelDRAW!* is an object-oriented drawing program equipped with tools that multiply your drawing power. It's the appropriate tool for any illustration job, including lettering, and is particularly suited to publication graphics. It combines the features you would find in several competing packages.

If you are not a talented artist, you can still produce accomplished work with *CorelDRAW!* because it is shipped with hundreds of pieces of clip art and symbols. Many users will need only to select the appropriate components and arrange them in a pleasing composition to create the necessary graphic art. However, after you are finished with the lessons in this book, you will probably not be satisfied with this easy way out, and you may find yourself creating your own clip art for your own purposes.

Acknowledgments

I offer my thanks to Bill Cullen and Jennifer Poulsen of Corel Systems; Bill Gladstone and Matt Wagner of Waterside Productions, my literary agency; Laura Lewin, my editor at John Wiley & Sons; Positive for the use of a 486-33 PC; Chinon America and Caere Corporation, for the use of the scanners that produced the scanned images in this book; *COMPUTE* magazine and General Media International.; and most of all Kathy, Jennifer, and Steve.

Trademarks

Preparing to Use *CorelDRAW!*

Before we get started on learning how to use *CorelDRAW!*, you need to learn about the basics:

▲ Copying the disks onto backups and safeguarding work

▲ Setting up *CorelDRAW!*

▲ The basics of Windows operation

▲ Starting and exiting *CorelDRAW!*

▲ The elements on the *CorelDRAW!* screen and using menus

▲ Backing out of a decision with Cancel and Undo

Creating Backup Files

CorelDRAW! is shipped in two different versions. The versions are identical except for the way they are stored. One version is shipped on 1.2MB (megabyte) 5 1/4-inch disks and one is shipped on 1.44MB 3 1/2-inch disks. In either case, it's crucial that you pause before installing *CorelDRAW!* to make a complete backup of the disks.

Why make a backup? You should always have at least one copy of everything—programs and files. (One copy of a program is the most you can legally make. Don't share your copies because that is illegal and you can be prosecuted for copyright infringement. Always take time to read your software manufacturer's policies on copying program software.) Computer use is fraught with hazards. Hard disks die at distressingly unpredictable intervals. Disks are lost, damaged, and stolen. Fires and floods occur (if you have a modern sprinkler system in your office, they can both happen at the same time), neither of which is beneficial to computer disks.

The smartest way to start is to purchase a brand new box of disks designed for high-capacity or high-density data storage. It's possible to punch or drill an extra hole in some 720K 3 1/2-inch disks and format them at 1.44MB, but this practice isn't recommended. After all, the purpose of the backup is to safeguard your investment.

I'll make the assumption that you have a drive installed as drive A. If you are copying the disks with a drive designated as B, simply substitute the drive letter B where you see the letter A in the examples.

To format the disks:

1. Boot your computer (usually this involves simply turning it on and waiting a minute or two).
2. When the boot process is completed and you see the DOS prompt on the screen (which probably looks like C:\>) type FORMAT A: and press **Enter**.
3. DOS will prompt you with a message like "Insert new diskette for drive A: and press ENTER when ready . . ."

4. Put a new disk (*not* one of the *CorelDRAW!* disks, but a blank disk you have purchased) in the drive. When the disk is completely formatted, the formatting program will pause and ask you to enter a disk label. You can enter a disk name of up to 11 characters or simply press **Enter**. If there are any bad tracks, put the disk aside. You will want to return it to the manufacturer and request a replacement disk.

5. You will see a prompt that says "Format another (Y/N)?" Type Y and replace the disk in drive A with another new disk. Continue formatting until you have ten or more formatted disks.

6. When you are finished formatting the last disk and DOS asks you "Format another (Y/N)?" type N.

Creating Backup Files

Now that you have a supply of formatted disks, it's time to copy the *CorelDRAW!* disks.

To copy the *CorelDRAW!* disks:

1. Type DISKCOPY A: A: and press **Enter**. DOS will prompt you with "Insert SOURCE diskette in drive A:." Remember that the *CorelDRAW!* disks are the SOURCE disks and the blank disks you just finished formatting are the TARGET disks.

2. Place the *CorelDRAW!* disk marked Disk 1 in the drive and press **Enter.**

3. After a few seconds DOS will prompt you to "Insert TARGET diskette in drive A:." Replace the *CorelDRAW!* disk in drive A with one of the disks you just finished formatting and press **Enter**.

4. You will have to repeat this process more than once. Remember that *CorelDRAW!* Disk 1 is the SOURCE disk and you should continue to use the same newly formatted disk as the TARGET disk.

When the disk copying process is completed, you will see a prompt that says "Copy another diskette (Y/N)?" You do have a lot of disks to copy, but pause a moment to properly label the new copy you have just made. Be sure that the label doesn't cover any of the holes or notches in the disk, and that it is completely on the disk enclosure and clear of the disk itself. With a felt-tip pen, write the name of the *CorelDRAW!* disk you copied on the label you have affixed to the copy.

You should make copies of the rest of the disks, following the same steps outlined previously. Make sure to label each of the copies, and don't confuse the SOURCE disk with the TARGET disk. Put the original disks away and install *CorelDRAW!* with the copies of the disks to save wear and tear on the original disks.

If you use *CorelDRAW!* at work, you should keep the original disks at home. If you use *CorelDRAW!* at home, keep the original disks at work. If you work with a lot of expensive software, it wouldn't be out of the question to rent a safe deposit box at a bank for your disks. After all, if you paid $300 to $400 for *CorelDRAW!*, $600 to $700 for *Ventura Publisher*, a couple of thousand dollars for *AutoCAD*, and have a thousand or so tied up in word processors, that's a significant investment for a small pile of very fragile sheets of mylar.

Registering

You must register your software. This benefits both you and Corel Systems. Be sure to fill out the registration form completely, affix a stamp (remember that it is going to Canada, so it will require more than standard first-class postage.) The benefit to you is that you can upgrade at low cost, and (as perfect as *CorelDRAW!* 3 is) there may be minor upgrades and bug fixes between now and the next major version release. Generally, these improvements are provided at no cost to the user. Registration also makes you eligible to enter the design contest Corel is holding. If you are particularly talented, you stand to win thousands of dollars worth of prizes.

The benefit to Corel Systems is that it can keep track of its software. When a Justice Department investigation uncovers a pirate selling illegal copies of a product, Corel can trace the serial number of the copies back to the registered owner and, possibly, locate the person who committed the first copyright infringement and prosecute him or her. Copyright infringement is serious business. Don't get involved in the trafficking of illegal copies. A copy thoughtlessly passed to a coworker may be the beginning of a chain of events that can result in a stiff fine or even a prison sentence.

TIP

In years past, software piracy was dealt with relatively lightly. But lately there have been heavy fines levied. A construction firm in Chicago had to pay a fine in the hundreds of thousands of dollars for illegally copying and using software.

Safeguarding Work

As important as it is to safeguard your original disks, it's vital to protect your work files. Because hard disks transfer information so much faster than floppies, most people keep their work files on their hard disks. This is a dangerous practice because hard disks are as prone to destruction as any other PC peripheral. An earthquake or a hyperactive cat could jar an operating computer, causing a head crash—causing the read/write head to come into contact with the disk surface, planing off layers of the magnetic material that holds your information (word processor documents, databases, and graphics) in the form of magnetic code.

You could turn off your computer or suffer a power failure or brown-out while your computer is writing a vital file called the File Allocation Table, resulting in a bad byte of information that literally renders your hard disk unreadable. When mishaps occur, you have few options. A head crash may mean you need a new disk or that you will need to do a surface analysis with *Spinrite* or *PC Tools Deluxe* to set aside the damaged sectors on the disk—sectors that may contain important parts of other files, meaning that you may wipe out whole subdirectories full of files when you repair the damage. A scrambled disk resulting from a power failure will require that you reformat the disk, thus losing all data on the disk. Hard disk controller cards can fail, too. The hour or two a week it would cost to maintain a complete backup of your hard disk balances against weeks or months of lost work if you lose the disk to one hazard or another.

Setting Up *CorelDRAW!*

Before you can install *CorelDRAW!*, you must have Windows installed properly on your machine. This means that you must have the equipment necessary to run Windows—an AT-compatible or 80386-based PC with a hard disk, 640K or more of RAM, and a graphics adapter capable of high-resolution graphics (Hercules, EGA, VGA, or compatible; CGA is not supported). You will also need to have a mouse and you will want a printer, though a printer isn't necessary to Windows or *CorelDRAW!* operation.

Installation of *CorelDRAW!* is almost completely automatic.

To install *CorelDRAW!*:

1. Start up Windows and open the Main program group.
2. Insert the first installation disk in the floppy disk drive.
3. Double-click on the **File Manager** icon to start the File Manager.
4. When the File Manager starts, you will see a window with an icon at its top representing each of your disk drives. Click on the drive you will be installing from.
5. Check out the right side of the resulting dialog box. One of the files on the disk should be SETUP.EXE (if that file isn't in the window, you probably inserted the wrong disk in step 2). Double-click on the text SETUP.EXE to start the installation program.
6. You will see a screen containing a box informing you that you are in the *CorelDRAW!* installation program. Click on the button marked **Continue.** You will see a dialog box giving you the option of installing everything, installing a minimal version of *CorelDRAW!*, or a custom install. Click on **Full Install.** If you don't have the disk space for a full installation, the Setup program will warn you. Either clear some space on the disk or take one of the less-than-full-installation options.
7. You will be asked where you would like *CorelDRAW!* to be installed. The default is C:\CORELDRW. If that is where you want *CorelDRAW!* installed, press **Enter.** If you want it installed elsewhere, enter the complete path to where you want it installed, including the disk designation.
8. You will be asked the name of the program group you want to have the *CorelDRAW!* program icons placed in. If you want to use the default, Corel Graphics, click on **Continue.**

9. A dialog box will appear to confirm that you want to install at this time. Click on **Install.**

At this point the installation program begins unarchiving files and placing them on your hard drive. More informative than most installation programs, *CorelDRAW!*'s installation will tell you what files are being unarchived.

Don't abandon your computer at this point. Eventually, you will be prompted to replace the first disk with the next. Computers can do a lot of things automatically, but no one has yet successfully marketed an automatic system for changing floppy disks.

The Basics of Windows Operation

There is a good chance that at least a few people have bought Windows specifically to run *CorelDRAW!* or are coming to the PC for the first time. Therefore, although the true resource for your Windows questions should be the Windows manual, a few important matters will be discussed here.

To start up Windows:

▲ Enter WIN at the DOS prompt and press **Enter.** In Figure 1.1 you can see the Program Manager window in Windows. This is the starting point. Note some of the icons in the bottom of this window: Main, Corel Graphics, Games, and so on.

Each of the icons stands for a program group. It's wise to keep your related applications in the same program group. It's possible to create a new program group at any time by pulling down the File menu and selecting "New", then clicking on Program Group. Fortunately, it isn't necessary to create a new program group to install *CorelDRAW!*. The *CorelDRAW!* Setup program takes responsibility for creating its own program group.

Therefore, to keep this explanation as simple as possible, let's open the Corel Graphics program group icon.

To open the Corel Graphics program group:

▲ Double-click on the Corel Graphics icon. You will see the Corel Graphics program group.

▼ *Figure 1.1. The Program Manager Screen.*

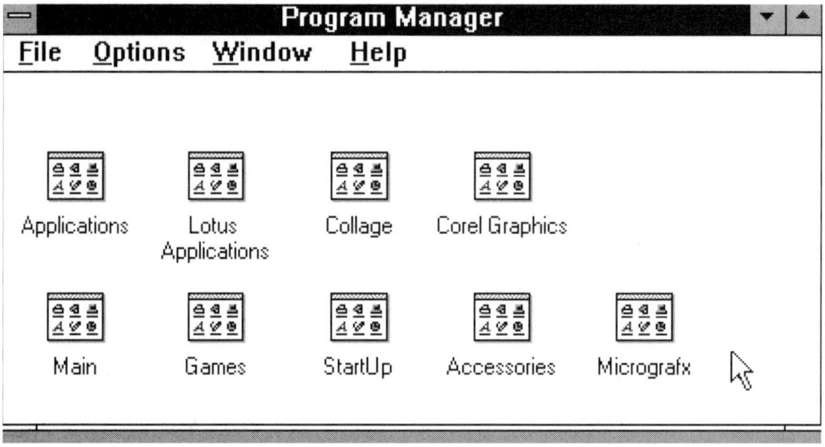

```
─                      Program Manager              ▼ ▲
 File   Options   Window   Help
```

Applications   Lotus   Collage   Corel Graphics
               Applications

Main   Games   StartUp   Accessories   Micrografx ⌖

Because the size of windows can be changed, the Corel Graphics program group on your screen—and, in fact, any window displayed in the figures throughout this book—may be of a different size or in a different position.

Note that all the major *CorelDRAW!* applications are accounted for: *CorelDRAW!*, *CorelMOSAIC!*, *CorelTRACE!*, *CorelSHOW!*, *CorelPHOTO-PAINT!*, and *CorelCHART!*. We'll talk about the other programs in later chapters.

CHECK YOURSELF

1. Drag the icons of the programs in the Corel Graphics program group so they are all mixed up in the window. Pull down the Window menu and select Arrange Icons.
    ▲ The icons shift into an orderly pattern in the program group.

2. Double-click on the *CorelDRAW!* icon.
    ▲ *CorelDRAW!* starts up.

Starting and Exiting *CorelDRAW!*

Let's explore Windows further by starting up the main application: *CorelDRAW!*.

To start *CorelDRAW!***:**

▲ Double-click on the *CorelDRAW!* icon.

The *CorelDRAW!* program will start. For a moment, you will see an introductory screen containing a hot-air balloon and the *CorelDRAW!* logo. Then you will see the *CorelDRAW!* screen shown in Figure 1.2 (see Figure 1.3 for explanation).

If you have any familiarity with *CorelDRAW!* 2.0 or 1.2 or earlier versions, you will see two new menus on the menu bar: Effects and Text. The Effects menu contains a number of new and exciting features for distorting a drawing. The Text menu contains specialized text commands, including a spell checker and a thesaurus. The palette along the bottom of the screen may also be new to you. In the past, you would have had to call up the pen or fill menu from the toolbox to effect a color change. Now you can simply click on the palette. Also a box has been added to the left end of the onscreen palette (marked with an X) that allows you to remove an object's fill without accessing any kind of menu. As you can see, in its latest version *CorelDRAW!* has become both more innovative and user-friendly.

Two items are of particular interest, if you are not very familiar with Windows. First are the scroll bars along the bottom and right-hand side of the screen that allow you to move through a zoomed

▼ **Figure 1.2. The CorelDRAW! Screen.**

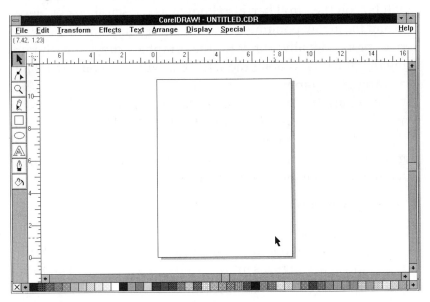

▼ *Figure 1.3. The CorelDRAW! Screen Explained.*

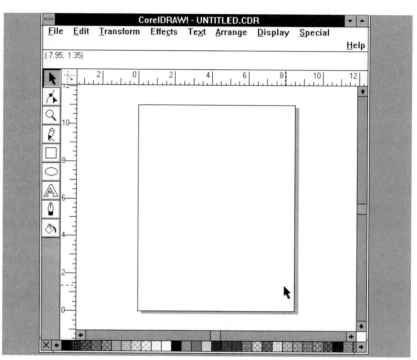

(magnified) screen easily. To move incrementally, click on the arrow in the direction you want to move. To move an entire screen in a given direction, click on the scroll bar between the *thumb* (the small box on the scroll bar, also known as the scroll box or elevator) and the arrow pointing in the direction you want to move. To move proportionally through the graphic, drag the thumb. Dragging it halfway along the scroll bar will take you about halfway through a graphic.

Second are the Minimize and Maximize/Restore buttons. In Windows, any window, including the *CorelDRAW!* window, can be one of three sizes: minimized (a very tiny icon), maximized (filling the whole screen), or in restore size. A restore screen can be sized to your liking by dragging its outline.

To size the window:

1. Click on the Maximize/Restore button.
2. Place the mouse pointer on the right edge of the *CorelDRAW!* window where it turns into a two-headed arrow. Drag it to the left until it won't move any farther.

3. Place the mouse pointer on the bottom edge of the screen where it turns into a two-headed arrow. Drag it upward until it won't move any farther.

4. You should be able to see a fragment of the window that contains the word "CorelD." Place your mouse pointer on it and drag it. You should be able to move it around the screen at will.

Starting and Exiting CorelDRAW!

When *CorelDRAW!* is in its restore size, the toolbox always remains visible, no matter how tiny the window becomes, and always retains its position relative to the upper left-hand corner of the window. Naturally, you can do little with *CorelDRAW!* in this state other than move it around the screen. To minimize the screen, click on the Minimize button.

To return the window to its restore size:

1. Double-click on the icon of the minimized window (these gravitate to the lower left-hand corner of the screen).

2. Drag the edges of the *CorelDRAW!* window to make it nearly fill the screen. Now click on the Maximize/Restore button. The window will expand to fill the screen.

To take a look at the system menu:

▲ You can click on the close button/system menu or press Alt-spacebar. The system menu is shown in Figure 1.4.

Note that you can select options on this menu to restore, move, size, minimize, or close the window. You can also use Switch To...

▼ *Figure 1.4.* *The System Menu.*

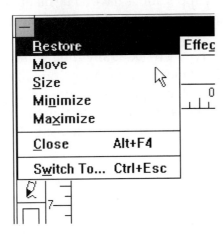

on this menu to switch to another Windows program. To get to this menu from a minimized window, click on the window's icon once. You can also shut down a program by pressing Alt+F4 (note in Figure 1.4, this key combination is on the same line as the Close option, to the right).

Finally, let's talk about closing the window. You can quit an application one of four ways: double-click on the close button; click on the close button and select Close (either by clicking on Close or by pressing the **C** key on the keyboard); press Alt+F4; or pull down the File menu and select **Exit**.

TIP

Never quit a Windows application by shutting off the computer or rebooting. It's simple enough to quit a program, as you have seen. All Windows applications have a File menu and an Exit option on that menu. You can quit any program by pressing Alt+F and then X, or by double-clicking on the Close box. Windows reads and writes your hard disk frequently and if you turn off the power or reboot at an inopportune moment, you could trash your hard disk.

Since you will need to understand how to use menus in *CorelDRAW!*, let's use the last option to quit the program.

To quit CorelDRAW!:

▲ Place your mouse pointer on the word File in the menu bar and click or press **Alt+F**. You will see the menu shown in Figure 1.5.

Most Windows applications have a File menu that is similar to this one. Note that *CorelDRAW!* offers yet another way to exit the program. On the Exit option, at the right, you can see ^X. This means that if you type Ctrl+X at any time while *CorelDRAW!* is running, you will exit the program. A key combination in the right side of a menu is a hotkey option—an option that you can access directly from the keyboard without selecting the menu. In the appendix of this book, you will find an exhaustive list of hotkeys.

To exit the program:

▲ Click on the word **Exit,** or type **X** on the keyboard. The window will close and the application will quit running.

▼ *Figure 1.5. The File Menu.*

If the graphic was named, it will automatically be saved under its current filename. If it was unnamed, you will be shown the *CorelDRAW!* Save As... dialog box. Using this box, you can specify the filename and the location of the saved file.

CHECK YOURSELF

1. Load or save a drawing. Which menu did you use?
   ▲ The File menu.

2. Draw something on the screen and select Exit from the File menu.
   ▲ *CorelDRAW!* prompts you to save your work.

The Elements of the *CorelDRAW!* Screen

There are several other items on the *CorelDRAW!* screen we haven't yet discussed. You might want to refer back to Figure 1.3 during this discussion.

The Toolbox

Like most graphics programs, *CorelDRAW!* offers the toolbox as a simple way to access the most commonly used tools. This is the part of the screen you will use most often. It contains the tools you will use for selecting objects, drawing lines and curves, magnifying sections of the screen, and performing other day-to-day tasks with your *CorelDRAW!* graphic.

The Pick Tool

The pick tool has three main purposes: selecting, moving, and editing objects. When you want to select an object, you have two options. You can click on the wireframe—the lines of the object on the page area—or you can drag a rectangle on the screen. To test these two operations, we need to have something on the *CorelDRAW!* screen, so we'll skip ahead briefly to the rectangle tool.

To draw a rectangle:

1. Locate the rectangle tool on the toolbox (fifth from the top, between the pencil tool and the ellipse tool). Click on the rectangle tool.
2. Place the mouse pointer somewhere in the upper left-hand quarter of the page area.
3. Press the left mouse button and drag the mouse pointer to the lower right-hand quadrant of the page area. Release the mouse button. A rectangle will be drawn there.

Note that the rectangle is selected as soon as it is drawn. You can recognize a selected item because its *nodes* are visible. A node is a tiny rectangle that appears at the corners of polygons and along the curves of curved objects. Nodes can be used to adjust the shape of an object. We'll cover that shortly.

To see the object's handles:

1. Click on the pick tool. Note that eight *handles* (tiny black squares used to control the size and shape of the rectangle) appear all around the rectangle.

2. Deselect the rectangle by clicking in the *CorelDRAW!* window away from the rectangle. Note that the nodes and handles disappear.
3. Move the mouse pointer so its point is on the very edge of the rectangle. Click on the outline of the rectangle. The nodes and handles should reappear. If they don't, you probably don't quite have the point of the mouse pointer directly on the outline.

The other method of selecting an object is to drag a selection rectangle around it. This method is less discriminating than clicking on the outline because you can select more than one object by dragging a selection rectangle. Any object that is completely enclosed by the selection rectangle will be selected. To demonstrate, draw an additional rectangle on the screen completely inside the first rectangle.

To draw an additional rectangle:

1. Locate the rectangle tool on the toolbox. Click on it.
2. Place the mouse pointer somewhere in the upper left-hand quarter of the first rectangle.
3. Press the left mouse button and drag the mouse pointer to the lower right quadrant of the first rectangle. Release the mouse button. A rectangle is drawn.
4. Click on the pick tool.
5. Deselect the rectangle by clicking in the *CorelDRAW!* window away from the rectangle. Note that the nodes and handles disappear.
6. Move the mouse pointer so its point is above and to the left of the first rectangle. Press the left mouse button and drag the mouse pointer until it is below and to the right of the first rectangle. When you release the mouse button, the handles should reappear around the large rectangle. If they appeared around the smaller rectangle, you probably didn't entirely enclose the larger rectangle in your selection rectangle.

You should now have handles all the way around the larger rectangle. So how do you know that both rectangles are selected? Note that each rectangle has a single node visible. This indicates that each is selected. But if you're still not sure, let's use the pick tool for sizing to show how having both rectangles selected gives you the power to affect both at the same time.

The Elements of the CorelDRAW! Screen

To size both rectangles at once:

1. With both rectangles selected, place the mouse pointer on the lower left handle. Note that when the mouse pointer is on a handle, it turns into a cross. This makes it easy to tell when your mouse pointer is in contact with a handle.
2. Press the mouse button and drag this handle up and to the right.

When you release the mouse button, you will discover that both rectangles have been made proportionately smaller. The corner handles always maintain the proportionality of the shape. This is called *scaling*. If you have a rectangle that is 4 inches long by 2 inches wide and you drag a corner handle so that the rectangle is 2 inches long, you have scaled the width to 1 inch.

What if you want to adjust only the length or only the width of a rectangle? That's what the handles on the sides are for.

To adjust just the width of an object:

1. Place the mouse pointer on the handle in the middle of the right side of the rectangle.
2. Press the mouse button and drag this handle to the right. When you release the mouse button, you will discover that both selected rectangles are proportionately wider, but their heights have not changed. This is called *stretching*.

To select certain objects within an area, but not all objects, hold down the Shift key and click on the outlines of objects you want to move or size. If you accidentally click on something you want to leave alone, click on that object again with the Shift key down. That will deselect the object.

TIP

If an object is filled with a color, you don't have to click on its outline to select it. Click on a rectangle and click on a color in the palette that runs across the bottom of the screen. The rectangle will change to that color. Click away from the rectangle so that it is no longer selected and click anywhere within the rectangle. The rectangle will be selected.

Finally, the pick tool can be used to rotate objects.

To rotate an object:

1. Double-click on the wire frame of an object and the handles will shrink to two-ended arrows. Place your mouse pointer on one of the corner arrows. The mouse pointer will turn into a cross when you are in the right position.
2. Drag the corner arrow to rotate the object.

Note that there is a dot with a circle around it at the center of the object. This is the *axis of rotation.* You can drag it to any position in the *CorelDRAW!* window and then rotate the object around it.

Skewing an object turns its selection rectangle into a parallelogram. This makes an object look as if it is being buffeted by a severe wind or is on a plane that is at a different angle from the plane of the screen. It's easier to see this effect than to explain it.

To skew an object:

1. Select the object, then click on it again to change its handles to rotate and skew handles.
2. Place your mouse pointer on one of the double-headed arrows located at the middle of one of the sides. The mouse pointer will turn into a cross when you are in the right position.
3. Drag the arrow and that side of the selection rectangle will follow your mouse movements while the opposite side remains fixed.

The pick tool has additional uses, which will be covered thoroughly in Chapter 2, but here's one that you might like to experiment with: If you grab a handle on the right side and move it to the left of the left side of the selected object, you can flip the object horizontally.

Although it would be pointless to ascribe higher or lower values to the tools in the toolbox, the pick tool is certainly one of the most essential tools, and the one you will probably find yourself using most often. If you are the least bit unsure of its use, go through the exercises again until you are completely confident of your mastery of the pick tool.

The Elements of the CorelDRAW! Screen

CHECK YOURSELF

1. Use the pick tool to select, move, size, and skew an object.
   - ▲ These actions are accomplished by clicking on the object for the first time (selecting), placing the mouse pointer on the outline of the object and dragging (moving), dragging a corner or side handle of the object (sizing), and clicking a second time, then dragging a side handle (skewing).

2. Create an object on your screen and click away from it so it isn't selected. Now click on the object's outline twice.
   - ▲ The rotate and skew handles appear. You can now rotate or skew the object. Note the arrows around its perimeter; these are the rotate and skew handles.

The Shape Tool

The shape tool is used to make more complex changes in a shape than simply changing its width or length or making it proportionately larger or smaller. You'll find a thorough discussion of the shape tool in Chapter 2.

The Zoom Tool

You will want to work on graphics in detail sometimes, and it can be difficult to see individual lines in complex drawings. The zoom tool will be very important in this work. To see what the zoom tool is capable of, let's select it. But first, there must be something on the screen to examine in detail. If there is anything on your page area, get rid of it. Click on the word File on the menu bar and then click on New. When *CorelDRAW!* pauses to ask whether you want to save the drawing to disk, click on the button marked No.

Now we must draw a squiggle on the page area.

To draw freehand:

1. Click on the pencil icon (the fourth icon from the top). Your mouse pointer will become a cross.

2. Place the mouse pointer on the page area and press the mouse button. Drag the mouse pointer in a random movement, making a squiggle on the page area.
3. Release the mouse button. *CorelDRAW!* will pause for a moment and your squiggle will be converted into a form called *Bézier curves* and it will be sprinkled with nodes.

The Elements of the CorelDRAW! Screen

TIP

There is another way to use the pencil tool. You can click in one location and then click again in another to create a straight line.

If your squiggle is very complex, it may be difficult to see various parts of it clearly. Use the zoom tool to see the squiggle in detail.

To see the zoom menu:

▲ Click on the zoom tool (it looks like a magnifying glass). You will see the menu associated with the zoom tool (Figure 1.6).

The magnifying glass with the plus sign will actually magnify part of the page area. The magnifying glass with the minus sign

▼ *Figure 1.6. The Zoom Tool Menu and the Squiggle.*

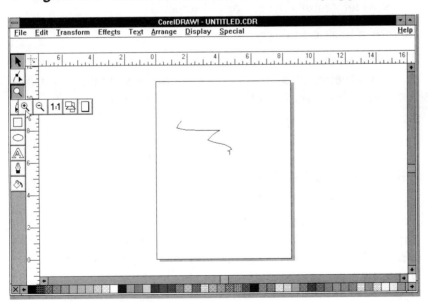

will make the page area smaller, less detailed. The section marked 1:1 will present the page area in approximately the size it will appear on the paper when it is printed. The section with a group of shapes on it will expand whatever is drawn on the page area to fill the screen. Finally, the section with a page drawn on it will cause the page area to appear as it has in all the figures up to now.

You will usually use the magnifying glass with the plus sign, and the page tool, which returns the page to its normal (default) size. Let's zoom in on the squiggle.

To see an object close up:

1. Click on the zoom tool. The zoom tool menu will appear.
2. Click on the magnifying glass with the plus sign. The mouse pointer will turn into a magnifying glass.
3. Place the magnifying glass at the upper left-hand corner of the area to be magnified and drag it to the lower right-hand corner of the area to be magnified. (This is the only tool in the zoom tool menu that uses a selection rectangle.)

When you release the mouse button, you will see the area within the selection rectangle expanded to fill the screen. How do you move around within the zoomed screen? Use the scroll bars at the bottom and right sides of the screen. This is called *panning*.

Now let's return to the normal screen.

To return to a normal screen:

1. Click on the zoom tool.
2. From the resulting menu, click on the item that represents a page. The page will return, as shown in Figure 1.5.

There is a limit to how close you can zoom, but you will undoubtedly find that the closest zoom is adequate for close work.

The Pencil Tool

You have already used the pencil tool. Basically, the pencil tool is capable of three different kinds of actions. It can create curves or straight lines or it can perform a powerful operation known as *autotrace*.

Let's draw a curve and a straight line. We'll leave autotrace for Chapter 4 in the section on importing art.

To draw a curved line:

1. Click on the pencil tool. The mouse cursor will turn into a cross.
2. Place the cross on the page area.
3. Press the mouse button and drag the pointer in a curve. A line will follow your mouse pointer.

When you release the mouse button, the curve that you have drawn will be reworked by *CorelDRAW!* and turned into Bézier curves. You will note when this happens by the appearance of nodes along the line you have drawn.

To draw a straight line:

1. Click on the pencil tool. The mouse cursor will turn into a cross.
2. Place the cross on the page area.
3. While holding the mouse perfectly still, click the mouse button.
4. Move the mouse pointer to another location.
5. Click the mouse button again.

A straight line will appear linking the two places where you clicked.

TIP

You can also draw polygons with the pencil tool. Instead of simply clicking at the terminus of a straight line, double-click and you will be ready to draw another line that begins where the previous line ended. Move the mouse pointer and double-click again at this new location. To close the polygon, finish the last side by clicking just once on the polygon's point of origin.

The Rectangle Tool

Most drawings are made up of normal geometric shapes like the square or rectangle and the circle or the ellipse. This tool and the next provide simple ways to draw these objects. First we'll cover how to draw a rectangle and then how to draw a square.

To draw a rectangle:

1. Click on the rectangle icon.
2. Move the mouse pointer to the page area. It will turn into a cross.
3. Place the pointer where the upper left-hand corner of the rectangle should be.
4. Press the left mouse button.
5. Drag the mouse pointer down and to the right. When the rectangle is roughly 1 inch by 1 inch, release the mouse button.

A rectangle will appear. This rectangle may be a square, but it's difficult to tell without printing it out and measuring it carefully. Sometimes that will be too much trouble. If you want to create a perfect square, you need a property called *constraint*. Constraint means that the shape is regularized, or more accurately, that it is prevented from deviating from the preferred shape.

To draw a perfect square:

1. Click on the rectangle icon.
2. Move the mouse pointer to the page area. It will turn into a cross.
3. Place the pointer where the upper left-hand corner of the square should be.
4. Press the **Ctrl,** or Control key.
5. Press the left mouse button.
6. Drag the mouse pointer down and to the right. When the square is about 1 inch by 1 inch, release the mouse button and the Ctrl key.

The resulting shape not only looks like a square; it *is* a square. You probably noticed that you didn't have to be careful when dragging the square. The shape remained a perfect square no matter where on the page you moved your mouse pointer.

You can perform a third action with the rectangle tool. Draw a rectangle while holding down the Shift key. Note that rather than drawing a rectangle from its corner, the place where you initially press the mouse button is the center of the rectangle. If you hold down the Shift and Ctrl keys, you can create a square from the center out. Try drawing a rectangle and alternately pressing and releasing the Shift and Ctrl keys, together or separately.

The Ellipse Tool

The other standard shape is the ellipse. As the name implies, you can create a rounded object of almost any width relative to its height using the ellipse tool. An ellipse can be constrained with the Ctrl key to form a circle.

To draw an ellipse:

1. Click on the ellipse tool.
2. Move the mouse pointer to the page area. The pointer turns into a cross.
3. Press the left mouse button.
4. Drag the mouse pointer down and to the right. An ellipse appears. You can create a very flat ellipse, even an ellipse that is indistinguishable from a line. But for the sake of this exercise, try to draw a circle.
5. When the ellipse looks roughly circular, release the mouse button.

Sometimes an almost perfect circle isn't good enough.

To see the difference between a carefully drawn ellipse and a perfect circle:

1. Click on the ellipse tool.
2. Move the mouse pointer to the page area. The pointer turns into a cross.
3. Hold down the Ctrl key.
4. Press the left mouse button.
5. Drag the mouse pointer down and to the right. A perfect circle appears. No matter how you move the mouse pointer, the ellipse that appears on the screen is a perfect circle.

You can perform a third action with the ellipse tool. Draw an ellipse while holding down the Shift key. Note that the place where you initially press the mouse button is the center of the ellipse. If you hold down the Shift and Ctrl keys, you can create a circle from the center out. This is useful for drawing, for example, wheels around an axle or gears around a pinion shaft. Try drawing an ellipse and alternately pressing and releasing the Shift and Ctrl keys, together or separately.

The Text Tool

Because Text is one of the most powerful parts of *CorelDRAW!*, it has its own chapter: Chapter 9.

CHECK YOURSELF

1. Click on the ellipse tool and hold down the Ctrl key. Drag the mouse pointer across the page area.
    ▲ You will create a perfect circle.

2. Create a perfect square and rotate it 45 degrees.
    ▲ Click on the rectangle tool, hold down the Ctrl key, and drag the mouse a short distance over the page area. Click on the already selected square and drag a corner rotate and skew handle until the number 45.0 degrees appears in the status line.

The Outline Tool

This tool, covered thoroughly in Chapter 7, is used to change the appearance of the outlines of objects.

The Fill Tool

This tool is used to change the appearance of the interiors of objects and also is covered in Chapter 7.

Palette

The palette can be seen along the bottom of the screen. In former versions of *CorelDRAW!*, you had to access the fill tool menu to make use of the palette. Having the palette visible onscreen is a tremendous convenience. Note that, like the scroll bars, the palette has arrows at either end. Click on the arrow at the right end to scroll through the huge palette. The arrow on the left end of the palette will scroll you back the other way.

Page Area

You've been using the page area in the earlier exercises in this chapter. It represents a page of paper. You can set up the page of paper to be tall or wide, or to be a different size than a standard sheet of typewriter paper by using the Page Setup command on the File menu. In Figure 1.7 the page is shown *wide* (or sideways to the normal orientation of typing paper, which would be called *tall*).

TIP

Although you can draw to the edge of the page area, that doesn't mean that your printer will be able to print to the edge of the paper. Most laser printers must leave a border of about a quarter of an inch around the sheet. If part of the drawing impinges on this margin, it will be left out of the printout. An option in the Print dialog box (accessed by selecting Print on the File menu) called Fit to Page will shrink the image enough that it will all print on the page. If your drawing is actually smaller than the page area when this option is selected, the drawing will be expanded to fill the page.

CorelDRAW! Window

You may note that your drawings sometimes run off the edge of the page area. Having the page area smaller than the entire drawing area (which includes the whole *CorelDRAW!* window) allows you to occasionally run off the edge and then size your drawing to fit on the page.

Status Line

You may have noticed the status line while you were doing the exercises in this chapter. It is located directly beneath the menu bar and it is a fount of information (see Figure 1.7).

The Elements of the CorelDRAW! Screen

▼ *Figure 1.7. The Status Line.*

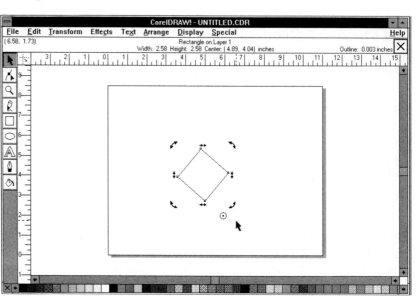

Note that the highlighted object is a rectangle and that the word "Rectangle" appears at the center of the status line, along with the layer number. The numbers that appear under the word tell you the size of the selected object (2.58 inches in width and 2.58 inches in height) and where its center can be found (at 4.89 inches from the left edge of the page and at 4.04 inches from the bottom of the page).

At the right edge of the status line is information about the outline (.003 inches thick) and the fill (none, as represented by the heavy X in the middle of the square at the extreme right of the status line).

At the left end of the status line is information about the location of the mouse pointer (6.58 inches from the left edge of the page and 1.73 inches from the bottom).

CHECK YOURSELF

1. Create a square with no fill. Look at the status line. How is it represented?

    ▲ At the right end of the status line you will see a rectangle with a large X in it, indicating no fill. At the center of the status line, you will see the word "Rectangle." Its width and height measurements will be identical.

2. Change the default outline (the outline used when no outline is specified) to the thickest line available on the outline tool menu.
   ▲ Click on the pick tool, then click away from any object so that none is selected. Click on the outline tool and click on an outline thickness from the menu that appears. A dialog box will appear that allows you to specify to what objects the new default applies. Click on OK. That outline will be used in all objects you create from then on.

The Elements of the CorelDRAW! Screen

Since this is a permanent change, you should reinstate the previous default before moving on. Click on the pick tool, click on the page area away from all objects on the screen to deselect all objects, and then click on the outline menu and select the third item on the top row (the one with two arrows pointing toward each other—the icon for the hairline). When the New Objects Outline Pen dialog box reappears, click on OK. The default is restored to its previous setting.

Title Bar

The title bar tells you the name of the graphic currently on the screen. If you haven't saved the drawing, the name will be UNTITLED.CDR. Use Save or Save As on the File menu to save your drawings.

Menu Bar

The menu bar offers a series of menus packed with commands. You have already seen the File menu in action.

Using Menus

To access a menu, place the mouse pointer on it and click. This will pull down the menu. When the menu is visible, place the mouse pointer on the item you want and click. The command will be issued.

Backing Out of a Decision with Cancel and Undo

Just about any mistake you make in *CorelDraw!* can be undone by selecting Undo from the Edit menu. There is a terrific advantage in this. Being able to undo an action takes a lot of the risk out of experimentation, which is the heart and soul of creativity. You need never fear doing the wrong thing if you save often and you have a powerful Undo option.

To see Undo in action:

1. Draw a rectangle on the screen.
2. Click on the pick tool. Handles should appear around the rectangle. If they don't, click on the outline of the rectangle.
3. Drag one of the handles, changing the shape of the rectangle.
4. Pull down the Edit menu and select **Undo.** Note that the rectangle snaps back to its previous shape.

Sometimes you will discover that you really liked the change better after all. Will you have to painstakingly re-create the change you made to have it back after using the Undo command? No way. Simply select Redo from the Edit menu.

To see Redo in action:

1. Draw a rectangle on the screen.
2. Click on the pick tool. Handles should appear around the rectangle. If they don't, click on the outline of the rectangle.
3. Drag one of the handles, changing the shape of the rectangle.
4. Pull down the Edit menu and select **Undo.** Note that the rectangle snaps back to its previous shape.
5. Pull down the Edit menu and select **Redo** (note that Undo is now gray and can't be selected). The rectangle will jump back to its previous shape.

By using these two commands, you can change the drawing back and forth between two states.

TIP

But using Undo works only on your last change to your drawing. If you make a mistake and then make any other change, selecting Undo won't help you. That's why it's important to save your work often, so that you will be able to return the drawing to a state before you made the mistake without losing too much work in the process.

You will often have need to use a command that calls up a dialog box. Almost all dialog boxes will have a Cancel button. For example, if you attempt to quit *CorelDRAW!* and you have made a change in your drawing that you haven't saved, *CorelDRAW!* will pause and show you a dialog box that gives you the option of saving the current graphic. It will say "UNTITLED.CDR (or whatever your graphic is named) Has Changed. Save Current Changes?" and it offers three buttons: Yes, which calls up the Save As dialog box; No, which shuts down *CorelDRAW!* without saving the graphic; and Cancel, which returns you to the program as if you had never selected Exit from the File menu. Always consider whether you want to cancel the action when you see the Cancel button. Someday it could save you a lot of work. Pressing the Esc key automatically selects Cancel from the keyboard.

QUICK SUMMARY

Task	Procedure
Cancel	Esc
Exiting the program	Alt+F4

PRACTICE WHAT YOU'VE LEARNED

Exercises in this section are intended to cement your knowledge of the topics covered in the chapter.

If Windows is currently running, shut it down. We're going to go from DOS to *CorelDRAW!* and back again. The exercise assumes that your computer is running in DOS, as if you had just started up the computer.

WHAT YOU DO	WHAT YOU'LL SEE
1. Type WIN and press Enter.	1. You computer should churn for a few seconds and the Program Manager should appear on the screen.
2. Pull down the Window menu and select Corel Graphics.	2. The Corel Graphics program group should open up and become foremost of the windows on your screen.
3. Double-click on the *Corel DRAW!* icon. It is the icon with a hot-air balloon all by itself.	3. Once again your computer will churn for a few seconds while the *CorelDRAW!* screen is constructed.
4. Click on the fourth tool from the bottom of the toolbox, the ellipse tool. Place the mouse pointer in the page area and drag diagonally down the screen. Then release the mouse button.	4. An ellipse will appear on the screen.
5. Place your mouse pointer on the edge of the ellipse and drag the mouse to a new position.	5. The ellipse will follow your mouse movement.
6. Drag to the left the tiny black rectangle in the middle of the left side of the selection rectangle.	6. The ellipse will become wider.
7. Click again on the ellipse.	7. The handles will change to little arrows.
8. Press Alt+F4 to shut down *CorelDRAW!*.	8. A dialog box will appear stating "UNTITLED.CDR Has Changed. Save Current Changes?" and you will see buttons marked Yes, No, and Cancel.
9. Click on No.	9. You will return to the Program Manager screen in Windows. *CorelDRAW!* is shut down.

WHAT YOU DO	*WHAT YOU'LL SEE*
10. Press Alt+F4 again.	10. You will see a dialog box warning you "This will end your Windows session" and providing an OK and a Cancel button. The OK button is highlighted, meaning that it will be selected if you press Enter.
11. Press Enter.	11. You will return to DOS.

Editing the *CorelDRAW!* Drawing

In this chapter we will spend some time creating a drawing with *CorelDRAW!*, saving it, loading it, and closing it. You'll need to work through the exercises in this chapter to familiarize yourself with some of these basic procedures before you'll be able to advance in *CorelDRAW!*. In this chapter, you will learn about:

▲ **Creating and saving a drawing**

▲ **Loading and closing a drawing**

▲ **Editing an object**

▲ **Drawing**

▲ **Open and closed objects and solid fills**

▲ **Editing nodes and cutting and pasting**

▲ **Using text**

Creating a Drawing

Let's begin with something simple. First, you'll need to start up your PC and *CorelDRAW!*. If you are at the DOS command line, you will first have to start Windows. If Windows is already running, skip to step 2. If *CorelDRAW!* is already running, skip the entire sequence that follows.

To start up *CorelDraw!*:

1. Type WIN and press **Enter**.
2. When the Program Manager window opens, there should be an icon or window visible called Corel Graphics. If it is an icon, double-click on it to open the window.
3. Identify the *CorelDRAW!* icon—the hot-air balloon with *"Corel-DRAW!"* written underneath it.
4. Double-click on the *CorelDRAW!* icon.

When *CorelDRAW!* is finished loading, and before you draw anything in the page area, pull down the File menu. Note that some of the options are in black (New, Open, Import, Page Setup, Control Panel, Exit, and About *CorelDRAW!*). Other objects are "grayed" and unavailable to you (these include Save, Save As, Export, Print, and Print Merge; *CorelDRAW!* prevents you from saving a drawing until you have created something).

Set up a sample text area:

1. Click on the text tool in the toolbox (it looks like a capital A).
2. Click on the page area somewhere in the lower left quarter.
    We'll cover text in greater depth at the end of this chapter and again in Chapter 9.
3. Type in a name, a phrase, a nonsense word—anything you like. Note that the text appears in the page just as you type it, a little like a word processor, but you aren't constrained to specific lines (except within an individual piece of text).
4. Pull down the Text menu and select **Text Roll-Up**. The dialog box is shown in Figure 2.1.
5. Click on the down arrow at the right end of the typeface box (it says Avalon in Figure 2.1). Scroll through the box and select a typeface (I recommend Arabia).

▼ *Figure 2.1. The Text Roll-Up.*

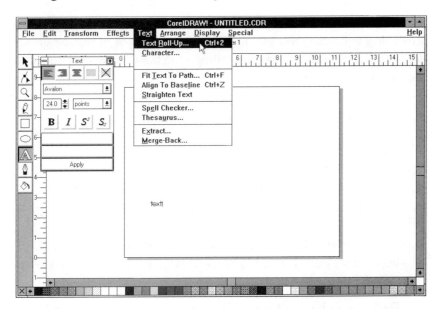

These are the names of fonts. To make the selected typeface apply, click on Apply at the bottom of the Text roll-up. Only the selected text will be affected. To select text, drag through it with the text tool. Other things you can select in the Text roll-up are justification (the icons across the top of the roll-up), size (the box that reads 24 in Figure 2.1), and style (the icons marked B, I, and so on, approximately in the middle of the roll-up). We'll talk about the other two buttons (Character Kerning and Frame) later on.

6. Once you have the text typed in and your style and justification selected, click on the button marked **Apply**.

   When you return to the page area, your text will be displayed. It's in 24-point type, which is about 1/3 of an inch high—pretty tall for text, but not easy to see on the screen. Let's enlarge it.

7. Click on the pick tool. Handles will appear around the text.

8. Place the mouse pointer on one of the corner handles and drag until the text is as wide as the page. Note that in the status line you can see the font name and the point size.

TIP

Although you can stretch text and it will probably work fine, if you are doing serious work, you should adjust the size of text by entering a text size either in the Text roll-up or in the Character Attributes dialog box.

Let's add one more enhancement to the drawing.

To draw a rectangle around it:

1. Click on the rectangle tool.
2. Place the mouse pointer above and to the left of the text.
3. Press the left mouse button and drag the mouse down and to the right.
4. When the resulting rectangle completely encloses the text, release the mouse button. This process is called *dragging a selection rectangle*.

Unless you have a far steadier hand than mine, you probably drew a rectangle that was a little off-center. Even if it looks well centered, the screen is so much smaller than the paper we will eventually print on that you can easily be fooled by appearances. Some people print out page after page, adjusting elements little bit at a time until they are perfect. You and I can save paper, however, by using the Align command on the Arrange menu.

To use the Align and Arrange menus:

1. Drag a selection rectangle to select the text and the rectangle: Click on the pick tool and place the mouse pointer above and to the left of the rectangle. Press the left mouse button and drag the pointer to a position beneath and to the right of the rectangle. When you release the mouse button, both items will be selected. The status line should say "2 objects selected."
2. Pull down the Arrange menu.
3. Select **Align**.
    You will see the dialog box shown in Figure 2.2. You want to center the image both vertically and horizontally.
4. Click on both center options. We'll talk more about aligning drawings, but you might want to look at your other options now. If you would like, select one of the other options. You can always realign it later. When you have the alignment the way

▼ *Figure 2.2. The Align Dialog Box.*

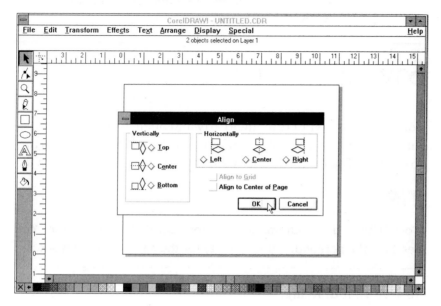

you want it, click on the button marked **OK**. The result is a perfectly aligned drawing.

Next we'll work with the drawing—saving it, loading it, and performing other tasks with it. If you would like, go through the last sequence of steps again, this time aligning the objects in some other way.

CHECK YOURSELF

1. Draw several items on the screen—circles, rectangles, lines— then select all of them and select Group from the Arrange menu. Try to move just one of the items on the screen.

   ▲ They all move. Grouping items is much the same as making all the grouped items into one item.

2. Draw a rectangle and an ellipse that overlap. Color them black by selecting them both and clicking on the black color in the palette at the bottom of the screen. Pull down the Arrange menu and select Combine. Pull down the Display menu and select Display Preview (if it isn't already checked). What do the shapes look like?

▲ The shapes are black, except where they overlap. Where they overlap, they are not filled and objects behind them will show through.

Saving a Drawing

You should save your drawings early and often. If you create something particularly pleasing, you can save it under a different name to use later. But let's start out by simply saving what we have so far.

TIP

CorelDRAW! **does automatic backups, but that isn't enough. You need to take personal responsibility for the safety of your work.**

To save your drawing:

1. Pull down the File menu. Note that all the selections that were grayed earlier are now black and available to you.
2. Note the text to the right in the Save option on the File menu: ^S. This means that if you wanted to save the drawing without pulling down the File menu, you could simply press Ctrl-S and the file would be saved. Click on **Save**. You will see the Save dialog box (Figure 2.3).

    In the Save Drawing dialog box, you have your path laid out (in Figure 2.3, it is C:\COLLAGE\DRAW*.CDR, but yours would probably be different). There are two CDR files (*CorelDRAW!* drawing files) in this subdirectory (their names are grayed and hard to read, but they are a pair of files I created earlier: JUNK.CDR and PG52BLNK.CDR). Their names appear in the File Name box. Your text cursor should be blinking in the File Name text box at the left of the dialog box. If you wanted to change directories, you could click on the name of a directory in the Directories box to the right of the File Name text box. In the Directory list box shown in Figure 2.3, the open file folders show the current subdirectory path (C:\, COREL-DRW, and DRAW are all open file folders, indicating where we are in the directory structure.) You can move around in the directory structure by double-clicking on the file folders.

▼ *Figure 2.3. The Save Drawing Dialog Box.*

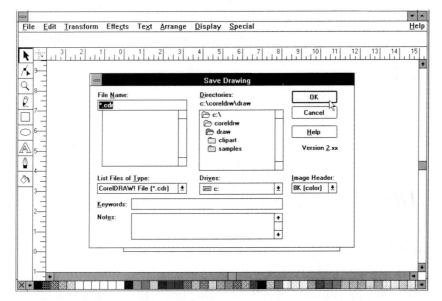

Double-click on an open folder to close it and move upward in the directory structure (toward the root directory); double-click on a closed folder to open it and move downward in the directory structure (away from the root directory). If you are not familiar with the directory structure DOS uses, you will need to refer to a book on DOS. Below, the Drives list box shows that we are logged to the C: drive. To access other drives, click on the down arrow at the right of this box and you will see a list of all of the available drives.

3. Once you have settled on which disk and directory to save the drawing, you should click on the **File:** text box and type a filename. A filename can be up to eight characters long. Filenames can use certain symbols beyond letters and numbers, but you should limit yourself to these and the hyphen and underscore character as a matter of style. *CorelDRAW!* will automatically add the CDR extension. I called my drawing SIGN.CDR, but you can use any filename you choose. I saved it in the C:\CORELDRW\DRAW directory by clicking on the Save button, saving the file to disk.

You will be returned to the page area. Note that the filename you gave your drawing now appears in the status line. Now if you make some changes and want to save the file, press **Ctrl-S**. The file will be saved without prompting you for a filename.

But suppose you want to save this preliminary drawing under the name SIGN.CDR and save your more complex drawing with some other name, like LTRHEAD.CDR. How can you do that, if *CorelDRAW!* won't ask you for a filename?

To save with a different filename:

1. Pull down the File menu and select **Save As**. You will see the familiar dialog box again, waiting for you to enter an alternative name. Note that in the File Name box, you can see the name of the file you just saved (in the figure, it's SIGN.CDR). Drag through the name SIGN and type LTRHEAD in its place.

TIP

Note that you can enter a keyword and notes in this dialog box (you also have this option in the Save dialog box, but you have to click on Options to see it). Entering a keyword will allow you to identify the drawing better than a filename can, with only eight characters. You can also enter some notes in the Notes field. These notes will help you to recall not only the content of the drawing but also the circumstances—who the drawing was created for, the date, the origin of any elements that you didn't create, and so forth.

2. Click on **Save** to save the file under the new filename.

Note that the name in the status line has changed to reflect the new name of your file.

Getting Rid of a Drawing

The next step is to clear the screen. This is very simple, but before you do it, you should always pause for a moment or two to make sure that you have saved your drawing, if it is an important drawing and if you have made any changes to it you don't want to discard. When you clear the screen, the drawing is gone.

TIP

Fortunately, *CorelDRAW!* is friendly enough to prompt you to save a drawing before it clears the screen. Pay heed to the prompt. It appears in the form of a dialog box that asks if you would like to save the drawing before moving on. If you want to discard it, click on No. If you want to save it, click on Yes. You can back out of the procedure by clicking on the button marked Cancel. This will take you back to the program with your drawing intact, as if you had never selected New.

1. Pull down the File menu.
2. Select New (it's the first item on the File menu).

   The drawing should now be gone.

CHECK YOURSELF

1. Click on the downward-pointing arrow at the right end of the Drive box in the Save Drawing dialog box. Scroll through the list, if necessary, and find the A listing. Double-click on it. What files are available to you?
   ▲ You are logged to the A drive; any files that appear in the Files list box will be files on the disk in the A drive.

2. Double-click on the last (bottom) open file folder in the Directories list box in the Save Drawing dialog box. What is the equivalent of this action in DOS?
   ▲ Clicking on this button will take you to the parent directory of the current directory. The two-dot designation always refers to the directory of which the current directory is a subdirectory. Therefore, clicking on the last open file folder is the equivalent of CD . . in DOS. To return to the previously open directory, double-click on the now-closed folder that you double-clicked on to close (it should be the DRAW folder).

Loading a Drawing

You now should have a couple of drawings saved to disk. (If you don't, back up to the section called "Creating a Drawing" and go through the steps in that section and the next section, "Saving a Drawing.")

To load your drawing:

1. Pull down the File menu. Look at the Open option. Note the text off to the right of the word Open: ^O. This means that if you want to call up the Open Drawing dialog box from the keyboard, you can simply press Ctrl-O.
2. Select Open.
3. When the Open dialog box appears, click on the **Options** button (lower right-hand corner) and click on **SIGN.CDR** in the File Name list box. You will see the dialog box shown in Figure 2.4.

You can see that this dialog box is virtually identical to the Save Drawing dialog box seen earlier in Figure 2.3. The current path is shown in the Directories box, the drawing files are listed in the File Name list box, the directories and disk drives immediately available are shown. There is a text box marked File Name where you can type a filename, if you wish. Also note that the drawing itself is displayed in an example box at right and that you could see the keyword and notes had we entered them earlier.

▼ **Figure 2.4. The Open Drawing Dialog Box.**

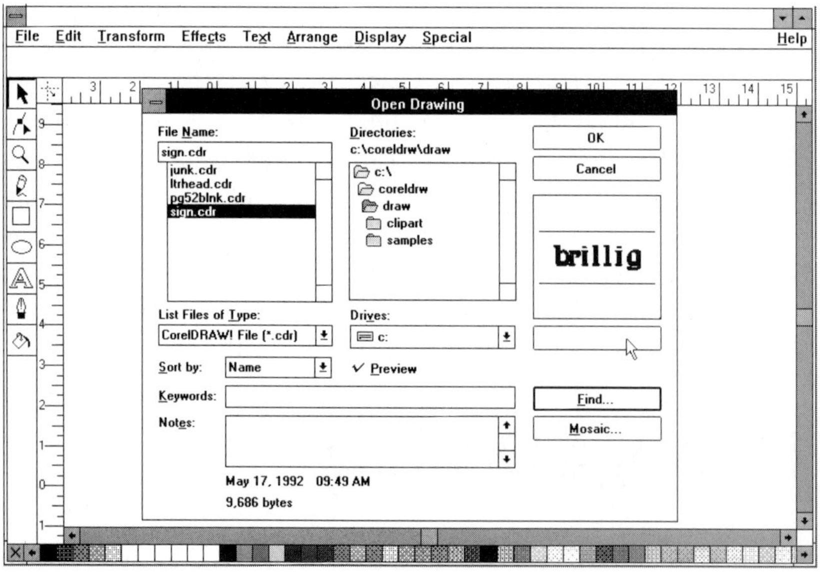

The simplest way to open a drawing is by double-clicking on its name in the File Name list box. Let's load a file that way. But first, given the DOS limitation of eight characters for a filename, how will you know which file you want to load? Now, it's easy to recall the two drawings we have saved so far in this chapter. But what if you had hundreds of drawings, or even a few dozen?

Eventually, you will use filenames like FACE1, FACE2, PIC1, and so on, because it is simply too difficult to come up with really descriptive terms for essentially similar drawings, given the eight-character DOS maximum.

But don't despair. You will be able to tell your drawings apart as long as you are using *CorelDRAW!*, because of a remarkable feature of the Open Drawing dialog that can be seen on the right side of the dialog box. In Figure 2.4, this box, called the display box, shows the selected graphic in thumbnail form (a small bitmap representation of the graphic).

To view an existing drawing:

1. Click on a different filename. Its thumbnail will appear.
2. A representation of the contents of LTRHEAD.CDR opens in the display box. To load this graphic, either click on its name in the File Name box and then click on the button marked **Open** or simply double-click on the filename (most people prefer this because it saves motion).

Now that you have a drawing on the screen, we can move into editing an existing drawing.

CHECK YOURSELF

1. Pull down the File menu and select Open. What do you see in the display box in the Open dialog box?
   ▲ The display box shows a thumbnail sketch of the drawing whose filename is currently selected. This eliminates most of the ambiguity in loading files.

Loading a Drawing

Editing an Object

As we go through the actions in this section, we will refer to many options that we may or may not use. The options that we bypass will be similar enough to the ones we cover that you should be able to use them yourself simply by applying the steps provided for other actions.

Editing an Existing Rectangle

This action applies to nearly any object you might have on the screen, but since we boxed our text with a rectangle, this is the object we will edit.

TIP

Note in some illustrations the page is "wide"—is wider than it is tall. I prefer this orientation because it's more in keeping with the appearance of the computer screen (which is about 133 percent as wide as it is tall) and with the *CorelDRAW!* window, which is even more sharply distorted.

Suppose that you have developed this letterhead for Brillig, maker of industrial solvents. The chair of the board has looked over the letterhead and determined that the rectangle looks too loose. He would like less white space between the text and the box.

To reduce the box:

1. Click on the pick tool.
2. Place the point of the mouse pointer on the outline of the rectangle and click. It is selected and you will see the familiar handles all around it.
3. Place the mouse pointer on a corner handle and move it toward the center of the rectangle. The rectangle will shrink but maintain its aspect ratio—the relative length and height.

If you don't want to maintain the aspect ratio, drag one of the handles in the center of the sides of the rectangle. When you have the rectangle the size you want, remember to use the Align command on the Arrange menu to center the name in the rectangle again.

TIP

Rounded rectangles are also possible with *CorelDRAW!*. Select a rectangle, click on the Shape Tool, and drag any corner of the rectangle toward the center of the rectangle. All the corners will become rounded.

Editing Multiple Objects

Now you take the graphic back to the chair of the board and he says that he likes it better, but it looks staid, uninteresting. Is there some way you could make it bend a little? How about making the rectangle into a parallelogram? Sure, you can do that. Before you do, though, you should save your drawing.

▲ Use the Save As command to save the drawing with a slightly changed name, like LTRHEAD1.CDR.

TIP

Always save a drawing-in-progress before you make a major change.

This is the best kind of insurance: It's free, it's convenient, and it's virtually guaranteed to save you time. You'll discover that even on a good day you will regret about a quarter to a half of the changes you make. Using Save As will allow you to go back many changes, whereas the Undo/Redo options only allow you to go back one change.

To change a rectangle to a parallelogram:

1. Select the entire drawing by dragging a selection rectangle: Click on the pick tool, place the mouse pointer above and to the left of the letterhead rectangle, press the left mouse button, and drag down below and to the right of the letterhead. When you release the mouse button, you will have selected the entire graphic.

▼ *Figure 2.5. The Skewed Drawing.*

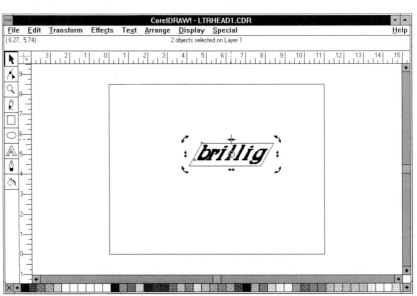

2. Click on the outline of any part of the drawing. The arrows will appear. These are special handles: the rotate/skew handles. You may recall from Chapter 1 that dragging the handles in the corners will rotate the drawing, and dragging the handles on the sides of the drawing will skew, or bend, the graphic.

3. Place the mouse pointer on the arrow in the center of the top of the drawing and drag it to the right. Your drawing will look like the drawing in Figure 2.5.

You may want to size the drawing slightly and drag it back to the center of the page area (or use the Align option on the Arrange menu and click on the box marked "Align to Center of Page").

Making Precise Adjustments

"This looks pretty good," the chair of the board says. "What angle, exactly, is this? We prefer things to be at 45-degree angles." Back at your computer, you could use a protractor to measure the angle. Or you could skew the object with the mouse and keep a careful watch on the status line, which will tell you the angle of the skew. But there is an easier way. Since you saved your work before skewing it, you can simply reload it. But first, save the current drawing as LTRHEAD2.CDR.

Editing an Object

1. Open the backup file you just saved as LTRHEAD1.CDR. Select the entire drawing. Now you need to specify the skew angle.
2. Pull down the Transform menu.

    The options are Move, Rotate & Skew, Stretch & Mirror, and Clear Transformations. Note that you can call up the first three options from the keyboard by pressing Ctrl-L, Ctrl-N, and Ctrl-Q. The Move option allows you to specify in a text box the exact location of a drawing on the page. The Stretch & Mirror option allows you to flip a drawing left-for-right or right-for-left or specify, in percentage, how much larger or smaller to make the drawing both vertically and horizontally. But our immediate concern is the Rotate & Skew option.
3. Select **Rotate & Skew** from the Transform menu. You will see the dialog box shown in Figure 2.6.

TIP

You can constrain an object to moving only in a vertical or a horizontal direction by holding down the Ctrl key while dragging an object.

▼ *Figure 2.6. The Rotate & Skew Dialog Box.*

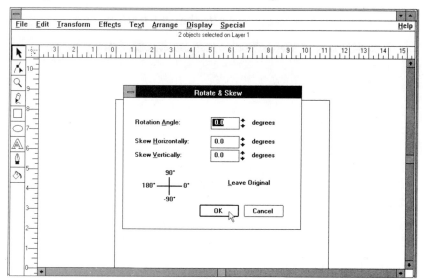

Note that you can rotate an object a specified angle or skew an object vertically or horizontally a specified angle. Arbitrarily, Corel Systems has determined that a skew to the left is a positive value and a skew to the right is a negative value. You want to skew your letterhead -45 degrees horizontally.

4. Click on the downward-pointing arrow next to the Skew Horizontally text box nine times, until the number -45.0 appears in the box. Or drag the mouse pointer through the text in the box and type -45.0.

Before leaving the dialog box by clicking on OK, note that you have the option of leaving the original. Although we won't use it now, this is a valuable option to use and we'll return to it in a moment. This leaves the currently selected object while rotating or skewing a duplicate. This option is also found in the other Transform dialog boxes.

5. Click on **OK** to skew the object exactly -45 degrees.

Creating a Drop Shadow

This time the chair of the board is pleased. But he wants a shadow. He says the shadow should make it look as if the letterhead is sitting on a horizontal plane. This is easily accomplished, again using the Rotate & Skew option.

▼ **Figure 2.7. The Skewed Letterhead Shadow.**

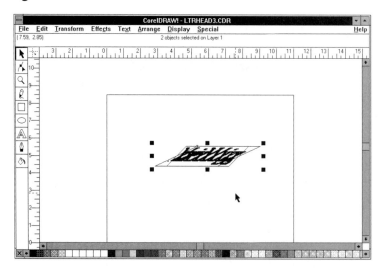

1. Save your work, then select the entire drawing and select **Rotate & Skew** from the Transform menu.
2. Click on the down arrow next to the Skew Horizontally text box until it reads -50.
3. Click on the box that says **"Leave Original."**
4. Click on **OK**. You will see the drawing shown in Figure 2.7.

*Editing an
Object*

It looks like a hopeless tangle, but it is actually two versions of the skewed letterhead—one at -45 degrees (the original letterhead object) and one at a greater angle (the shadow). There are some problems with the shadow. First, since it is newer than the original, it has a precedence that is above the original—that is, it will appear in front of the original. A shadow should never be between you and the thing that is casting the shadow. Second, the shadow is the wrong color (all drawing up to now has been in black). By changing the color of the shadow to a light gray, it will appear more shadowlike. And finally, the bases of the two objects are not the same. You will need to move the shadow so that its base coincides with the base of the letterhead.

Changing Precedence

Let's start by putting the shadow behind the letterhead object.

To create a shadow:

1. Select the shadow. The best thing to do be sure you have the shadow and only the shadow selected is to click away from the drawings to remove all selection, then hold down the Shift key and click on the text and the rectangle of the shadow.
2. Pull down the Arrange menu.
3. Select **To Back**. This moves the shadow text and rectangle behind everything else on the page. Note that you could accomplish exactly the same action by pressing **Shift-PgDn**.

CHECK YOURSELF

1. Draw a rectangle and click away from it to deselect it. Click on it twice and drag the upper left corner handle down and to the right. What happens to the shape of the rectangle?

▲ Nothing happens to the *shape* of the rectangle, but it rotates around its center.

2. Looking at the same rectangle, note the dot in the center. Place the mouse pointer on this dot and drag it to one of the corners of the rectangle. Drag the same handle as in the previous check yourself item. What happens?

▲ Instead of rotating around its center, the rectangle rotates around the corner where you moved the dot. This dot determines the axis of rotation.

Changing Outline Color

Next, we must change the color of the outline of the rectangle and text and the color of the fill of the text.

1. With the shadow still selected, click on the **outline** tool in the toolbox. You will see the outline tool menu as shown in Figure 2.8.

   The items along the top of the menu determine the thickness of the outline and the items along the bottom affect the color of the line. We'll explore these items in Chapter 7.

▼ *Figure 2.8. The Outline Tool Menu.*

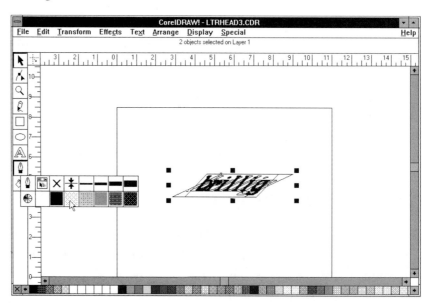

2. Select a light gray color from the bottom part of the outline tool menu, such as the shade of gray fourth from the right.

Changing Fill Color

Now we must change the color of the fill of the text. You won't want to have the rectangle selected for this action because if you fill the rectangle and the text with the same color, you will render the text invisible. Therefore, begin by deselecting the rectangle of the shadow.

1. Hold down the Shift key and click on the rectangle in the shadow. The status line should now read "Text: Arabia (Normal)," which should be the only selected object on the screen.
2. Click on the fill tool in the toolbox. You will see the fill tool menu as shown in Figure 2.9.

    The top part of the fill tool menu provides access to various patterns, which will be covered in detail in Chapter 7. The bottom part of the fill tool menu provides seven shades of gray. For now, select the same shade of gray as you used for the outline.
3. Click on the gray fourth from the right.

▼ **Figure 2.9. The Fill Tool Menu.**

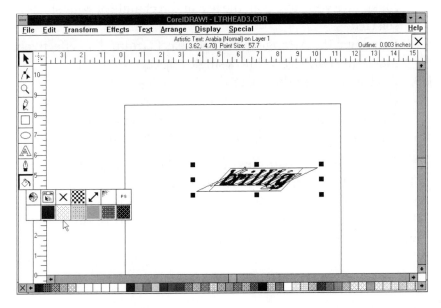

Aligning Objects

Finally, you must adjust the shadow so that its base coincides with the base of the original.

1. To begin, you must select the shadow rectangle again. Hold down the Shift key and click on the rectangle. The status line should now read "2 objects selected on Layer 1."
2. Place the mouse pointer on any part of the selected text or rectangle and drag the object to the right, being very careful to place its base visually on top of the letterhead's base.

After you have worked at this for a while, you will probably agree that it is not very efficient. Unless your hands and eyes are very well coordinated, you will probably leave the shadow at least a little distance from the letterhead. Even when they look perfect, they may not be perfect when the drawing is printed out. Remember, the resolution of your screen is about 72 dots per inch, while your laser printer is able to print at 300 dots per inch. That means that you can have four times as much error visible on the paper as you can see on the screen.

There are two solutions to the situation: snap and align. Either one will require that you group your objects.

To group objects:

1. Make sure you have both the text and rectangle of your shadow selected.
2. Pull down the Arrange menu and select **Group**. This effectively makes the two objects into a single object.
3. Click away from the selected object to deselect it.
4. Click on the outline of the text of the letterhead. Hold down the Shift key and click on the rectangle of the letterhead.
5. Pull down the Arrange menu and select **Group**.

You now have two groups of objects. You can treat the grouped objects as if they were two individual objects. Clicking anywhere on the outline of the rectangle or text of the shadow will now select the entire shadow. Rotating or skewing one part of the headline will rotate or skew the entire headline.

TIP

You may be wondering why we have waited until now to group the objects. If we had grouped them before changing the color of the shadow, we would have filled both components of the shadow—the text and the rectangle—with a solid, light gray. That would have made the text in the shadow invisible.

Now that the objects are grouped, you can use Align on the Arrange menu to align the two items.

To align items:

1. Select both objects either by dragging a selection rectangle that includes both of them or by holding down the Shift key and clicking on the outline of both groups of objects. Another option, since there are only two objects on the page area, is to pull down the Edit menu and highlight the option **Select All**.
2. Press **Ctrl-A** or pull down the Arrange menu and select **Align**.
3. Click on **Left** and **Bottom**, then on **OK**. This will perfectly align the objects at their bases. There will be no error on the screen, in a laser-printed rendition, or in a typeset version (errors that don't show in a laser printout will still show up in a typeset printout; by using Align, you have essentially eliminated error).
4. Save your work.

Using the Grid

Another option is to use the grid. Used properly, the grid can be a powerful tool. Basically, the grid forces you to place an object in a given position. Imagine arranging marbles on a piece of hardware cloth or very coarse mesh. You can move the marbles from place to place, but they will always maintain their relationship to the grid. If you move a marble a certain distance, it will fall into the next square in the hardware cloth with a snapping motion. The marble will line up with either one or another square in the grid and cannot be left halfway between.

To use the grid:

1. Pull down the Display menu and select **Snap to Grid** (or press Ctrl-Y, the keyboard equivalent).
2. Click on the outline of one part of the shadow outline toward the lower left corner of the shadow. Where you click on an object determines the part of the outline that snaps to the grid.
3. Drag the shadow toward the bottom part of the page area.

    You will want the shadow away from the letterhead so that you will be able to easily select the letterhead for the next step. Note that as you drag, the shadow jerks along. It doesn't move smoothly as it did in the past. This is the snap action we referred to.

4. Place the mouse pointer on the lower left-hand corner of the outline of the letterhead; drag the letterhead down and match its base to the shadow base. Now when they look as if they match perfectly, you can be assured that they do match perfectly.

Figure 2.10 shows what the final drawing looks like, printed out on a laser printer. Printing will be covered in Chapter 3.

This isn't all that you can do in editing a graphic, but we can only touch on the most creative aspects of *CorelDRAW!*. I hope that you will go back to the Transform menu and try out all the settings to see what they do.

CHECK YOURSELF

1. Click on an object on the screen; click on the fill tool; click on the first item in the top row of the fill tool menu.

▼ *Figure 2.10. Letterhead Printout.*

▲ A color mixing dialog box will appear, with which you can adjust the current color. Click on Cancel. We'll cover mixing colors in a later chapter.

2. Turn on the grid and drag an object by its upper left corner.
   ▲ The upper left-hand corner will snap to the grid as the object is dragged.

Drawing

So far, we have been satisfied with working and reworking shapes provided with *CorelDRAW!*, but there is no reason for you to stop there. Though we all have some limitations on our artistic abilities, everyone can create interesting drawings with *CorelDRAW!* and any line you create can be changed.

Let's draw a cartoon face by way of illustration. You can follow the steps exactly and create a drawing radically different from the results you see in the figures, so don't worry about the appearance of your drawing; the whole point is to get used to using the pencil tool.

To draw an oval:

1. With *CorelDRAW!* running and the page area cleared, click on the pencil tool.
2. Generally, drawings of faces begin with ovals, so place the mouse pointer on the page area, press and hold down the left mouse button, and draw a rough oval (Figure 2.11). Make sure the place where you lift your finger from the button is at some distance from the place where you started or the next section won't make much sense.

   OK, maybe that oval is too rough even to call an oval. But notice the tiny boxes on the perimeter of the oval. These boxes are called *nodes* and they can be edited. You're going to read about nearly a dozen high-powered commands that relate to nodes in the next section, but for now, let's just drag them so our oval looks more uniform.
3. Click on the shape tool (second from the top in the toolbox).

▼ *Figure 2.11. Rough Oval.*

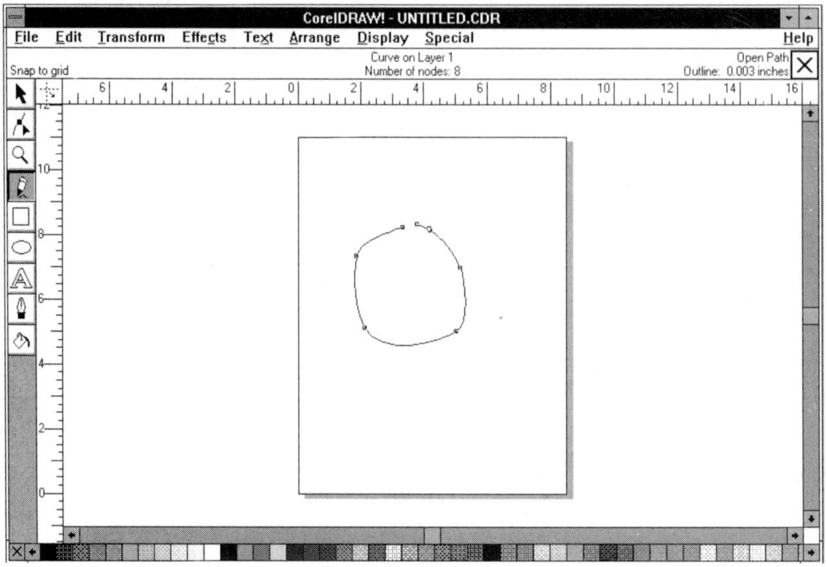

4. Place the point of the mouse cursor on any node that seems a little out of line. Press the left mouse button and drag the node into a better position, then release the mouse button.

    You need to fill this shape with some kind of coloring, but first, because only closed shapes can be filled, we need to close up the shape.

Open and Closed Objects

As you have surmised, there are two different kinds of objects: open and closed. An open shape has a gap between two of its nodes. You can draw a shape that crosses over itself, but unless all the nodes are connected in a complete circuit, the shape will still be open.

    Why is it important to have a closed shape? It isn't, if you don't care about filling the shape. Many times you will leave shapes open and use them as accent lines, or contours. But the shape we have begun must be closed to create a cartoon face.

To close a shape:

1. Click on the shape tool.
2. Hold down the Shift key and click on both end nodes—the two nodes that are unconnected. Another way to select both end nodes would be to drag a selection rectangle with the shape tool. Just make sure you don't accidentally include more than the two end nodes in the selection rectangle.
3. Double-click on one of the selected nodes. You will see the dialog box shown in Figure 2.12.

    You'll be seeing a lot more of this dialog box later in the chapter. For now, however, we are only concerned with one of its 11 buttons: Join.
4. Press the **J** key on your keyboard (when you see a letter underlined in a button, it means that pressing the key with that letter has the same effect as clicking on the button) or click on the **Join** button.

A more convenient and intuitive way to make closed shapes is to draw your shape with the pencil tool, making sure your mouse

▼ *Figure 2.12. The Node Edit Dialog Box.*

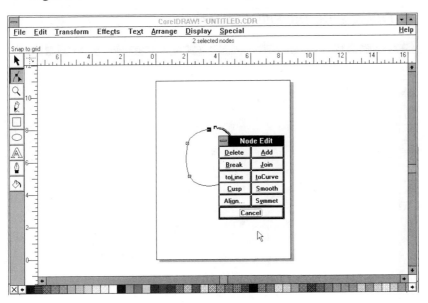

pointer is exactly on top of your starting point when you lift your finger from the button. *CorelDRAW!* will automatically close the shape and you can fill it immediately without node editing.

The end nodes will be joined into one and you will have a closed shape. Now you can apply fills to the closed shape, including color and patterns, which will be covered in a later chapter. For now, however, we need to apply some color to the face. Let's make it green.

Solid Fills

To color a closed shape green, you can take the easy way out and pick a green color from the palette you see running along the bottom of your screen, or you can go into the fill menu and mix a custom green. When you fill an object, it becomes opaque in the printout—that is, it completely covers all objects that coincide with it that have a lower precedence.

1. If the oval isn't currently selected (if the nodes or handles aren't visible), click on the pick tool and click on the oval.

▼ *Figure 2.13. The Filled Shape.*

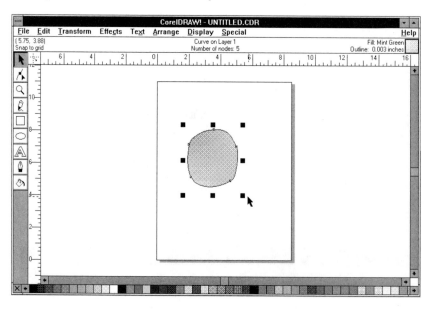

2. Click on one of the green shades on the onscreen palette. You will see the oval in the preview screen turn green (Figure 2.13). Because we are restricted to black and white printing, the shape in the figure may appear dark gray or black, but onscreen it is green.

   Solid Fills

   Let's finish the face.
3. Click on the pencil tool and give our cartoon lips, two or three noses, and an eye. Color them as you see fit.
4. Save your work.

When you create something with curves that aren't regular, or with straight lines where curves should be, you should use node editing to make the curves correct.

Editing Nodes

As you drew in the last section, perhaps you noticed something about the way *CorelDRAW!* handled your drawing. You would create a curve, then when you released the mouse button, *CorelDRAW!* would pause a moment and return the same curve with nodes sprinkled along it. *CorelDRAW!* operates entirely within the realm of a handy little item known as the Bézier curve. Everything you draw in *CorelDRAW!* is composed either of straight lines or Bézier curves.

Bézier

A Bézier curve, named after a French mathematician, is composed of five parts: two nodes, or end points; a connecting line; and two control points that determine the shape of the connecting curve. To illustrate, let's create a curve on the screen.

To draw a curve:

1. With *CorelDRAW!* running and the page area blank, select the pencil tool.
2. Place the mouse pointer on the left side of the screen. Press the left mouse button and drag to the right side of the screen.

When you release the mouse button, you will have a curve. You may recall that to draw a straight line, you should click in two positions on the screen. I'd like for you to do that now, so you will have a straight line to contrast with the Bézier curve (and also for ulterior reasons that will be apparent in a moment).

To draw a straight line:

1. Click on the page area an inch or so beneath the left end of the curve you created.
2. Click again on the page area an inch or so beneath the right end of the curve.

Your screen should now resemble Figure 2.14. Your curve may have more than two nodes. You will need only two.

To get rid of unwanted nodes:

1. Click on the shape tool.
2. Click on any node that appears between the nodes at the end-points of the curve.
3. Press **Del**.

Repeat steps 2 and 3 until all the unwanted nodes have been eliminated. Now you have two nodes.

▼ *Figure 2.14. A Curve and a Line.*

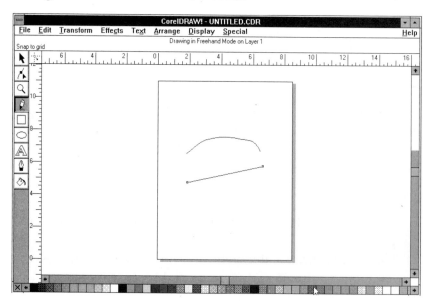

▼ **Figure 2.15. The Right Control Point Above the Node (Top) and Below (Bottom).**

Editing Nodes

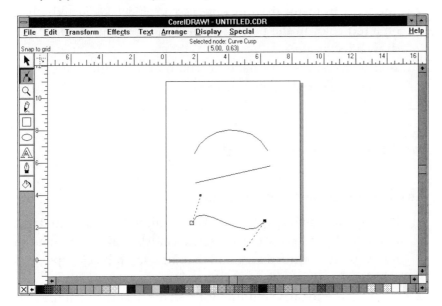

While the shape tool is selected, click on either of the remaining nodes to select it. Note the lever like devices that project from the nodes. On my screen, these levers are blue and at their ends are tiny squares called *control points*. The position of these control points determines the shape of the connecting line. Take a look at Figure 2.15. In the top of the figure, you can see the effect of moving these control points above the nodes and in converging directions. At the bottom of Figure 2.15, the right control point has been dragged below the nodes (unfortunately, it's impossible to show control points on two different objects at the same time).

You can draw any possible curved line between these points by making the appropriate change in the control points.

Now try doing that with the straight lines. When you click on the nodes of a straight line, no control points appear. The only adjustments you can make are in the length and angle of the straight line.

CHECK YOURSELF

1. Create an open object. Fill it with a blue color from the palette at the bottom of the screen.

▲ You can't fill an open object. *CorelDRAW!* wouldn't know where to stop filling. Only closed objects can be filled.

2. Click away from any existing object so no object is selected. Click on a red color in the palette at the bottom of the screen. Now draw a rectangle.

▲ The rectangle will have no color, and no fill, unless you have selected a default color.

Straight Line to Curve

To change a straight line into a curve:

1. Double-click on the right end of the straight line. Note that one of the node edit buttons says toCurve. Also take a moment to notice which buttons are available for use (in black type) and which are restricted to you (grayed type).
2. Click on the **toCurve** button or press the **T** key. When the dialog box disappears, the line will still be straight, but you will be able to see the control points (they will be right on the line, defining a straight curve).

Curve to Straight Line

To change a curve into a straight line:

1. With the shape tool selected, click on the top curve to select it.
2. Double-click on the node at the right end of the curve.
    Now when the Node Edit dialog box appears, toLine is available and toCurve is grayed.
3. Click on **toLine**.

Note that when the dialog box disappears, the curve has become a straight line. Its control points were stripped away.

Other Node-Editing Tools

You have probably noted that you have to double-click on the terminating node to edit a line segment with the Node Edit toolbox.

Try double-clicking on the point of origin. The dialog box appears, but the only button available is Delete. Since you may not know which node is the terminating node, you can simply double-click on the segment you want to edit. That will always select the terminating node and call up the Node Edit dialog box.

The tools in the Node Edit dialog box we haven't discussed are Delete, Break, Cusp, Align, Add, Smooth, and Symmet.

Delete

As you might suspect, selecting Delete causes the selected node to disappear. If it was the terminating node of a curve and the next segment along was a line, the next segment is made a curve. If you delete one of the ends of a line with only two nodes, the line is deleted.

Break

Break is the opposite of Join, which you used earlier. Join connects two nodes, making segments into a single line. Break separates the segments, making two lines out of one.

Editing Nodes

▼ *Figure 2.16. The Node Align Dialog Box.*

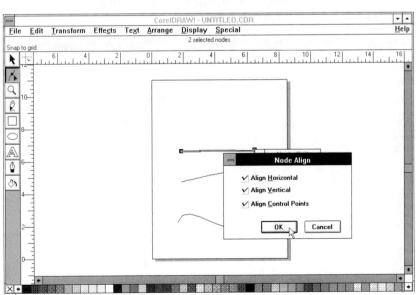

Align

If you want to place one node directly above or on exactly the same level as another node, Align is the button to use. To use this command, you will need to select two different nodes.

1. Hold down the Shift key and click on two different nodes on a line so they are both selected.
2. Double-click on one of the nodes. You'll see the dialog box shown in Figure 2.16.

Note that all the check boxes are selected. If you click on OK at this point, both of the selected nodes would be moved so they occupy the same place on the screen. If you leave Align Control Points selected, any curve in the line segment will be eliminated and a single line will emanate from the nodes. If you click on Align Control Points (turning it off), the curve in the line segment will remain. This is a little difficult to describe. In Figure 2.17, the top curve has been duplicated twice. In the middle example the nodes have been aligned with Align Control Points checked, and in the bottom example, the nodes have been aligned with Align Control Points turned off.

▼ *Figure 2.17. Aligning Control Points (Center) and Leaving Them Unaligned (Bottom).*

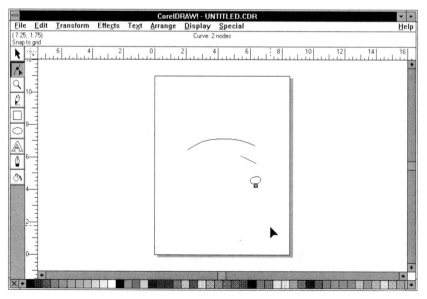

If you click on the Align Horizontal check box, it will no longer be selected and Align Control Points will also be deselected. The nodes will be aligned so that they are at the same distance from the bottom of the page area, but they may be at different distances from the left edge of the page area.

If you click on the Align Vertical check box, it will no longer be selected and Align Control points will also be deselected. The nodes will be aligned so that they are at the same distance from the left edge of the page area, but they may be at different distances from the left edge of the page area.

Add

Sometimes you need to add control points to a line segment to increase the amount of control you have over it.

1. Clear the screen by selecting **New** and use the pencil tool to create a curve onscreen with only two nodes. If additional nodes appear, click on the shape tool and press **Del** until only two nodes are left—one at either end of the curve.
2. If the shape tool isn't selected, click on it. Double-click on the curve you just created.
3. When the Node Edit dialog box appears, click on **Add**.

When the Node Edit dialog box disappears, you will see a new node in the curve. Having additional nodes makes it possible to create jagged lines with curves. You can also add nodes to a straight line.

Now try this.

1. Double-click on one of the selected nodes (all three should be selected).
2. In the Node Edit dialog box, click on **Add** again.

What happened? You should now have five nodes on the line. Do it again. Now there are nine. Each time you Add a node, you will add nodes between all the selected nodes on the curve or line segment.

Smooth

Sometimes you want control points on either side of the node to function independently and sometimes you want them to act in concert. To understand this command, we need to create a set of jagged curves.

1. Clear the page area by selecting **New** from the File menu.
2. Click on the pencil tool and draw a curve like a sine wave. If there are more than three nodes on the screen, eliminate all but the ones at the ends and one in the center.
3. Click on the center node to make the control points visible.
4. Place the mouse pointer on one of the control points attached to the center node and drag it up and down.

Note that although you can change the distance of the control point from the node so that it is different from the distance of the control point on the other side of the node, the line formed by the handles going through the node is always straight. This is because this node is *smoothed*. Note that this is indicated in the center of the status line: "Selected node: Curve Smooth."

Cusp

Start with the same sine wave as before.

1. With the shape tool selected, double-click on the center node to call up the Node Edit dialog box.
2. Select **Cusp** or press **C**.

    When the dialog box disappears, the node doesn't look very different from before, but the status line now reads "Selected node: Curve Cusp."
3. Now try dragging one of the control points attached to the center node.

The control points are now completely independent. You can drag either control point in a 360-degree arc around the node without affecting the other control handle or the curve on the other side of the node.

Symmet

Finally, you can cause the line through the node to be straight and both control points to be an equal distance from the node by selecting Symmet (for symmetrical).

1. With the shape tool selected, double-click on the center node of the sine wave.
2. When the Node Edit dialog box appears, click on the button marked **Symmet**.
3. Drag either of the control points up and down. Note that the other control point follows your motions exactly.

Cutting and Pasting

**Cutting and
Pasting**

CorelDRAW! uses cut, copy, and paste like many other Windows programs. To see all your options, pull down the Edit menu.

Cut (Shift-Del) removes any selected objects from the screen and places them in a temporary storage area known as the Clipboard (when something is cut, you would say that it's "on the Clipboard"). If you cut something else, it replaces the contents of this temporary storage area. You lose whatever was on the Clipboard.

Copy (Ctrl-Ins) places a copy of any selected objects on the Clipboard. If you cut or copy something else, it replaces the contents of the Clipboard and whatever was there is lost. If you are trying to get an image from *CorelDRAW!* to some other Windows graphics program, this is the quickest and easiest way to do it:

1. Click on the pick tool.
2. Select the object or objects you want to copy to another program.
3. Select **Copy** from the Edit menu.
4. Minimize or close the *CorelDRAW!* window.
5. Start the other graphics program.
6. Pull down the Edit menu in the other graphics program.
7. Select **Paste**.

This procedure is a powerful way to import graphics into *CorelDRAW!* from programs like *Designer* or *Arts & Letters*.

Paste (Shift-Ins) places a copy of whatever is on the Clipboard on the page area.

Paste Special places a special kind of link in with the pasted object. When you use this command, you paste not only the object but also the program that created or edited that object. Paste Special an object created with Windows Paintbrush and it's like having Paintbrush in your *CorelDRAW!* drawing. Double-click on the object and you automatically call up Windows Paintbrush with that object in it, ready to be altered. This is called Object Linking and Embedding (or OLE).

Delete (Del) is similar to Cut, with one important difference. When you select Delete, it removes any selected objects from the screen, but it doesn't place them on the Clipboard. This is a handy way to get rid of unwanted objects when you don't want to disturb the contents of the Clipboard. It's also a very natural thing to press the Del key to get rid of unwanted objects. Remember, though, that the only way to return something removed with Delete is by selecting Undo from the Edit menu immediately. If you issue any other command in between Delete and Undo, you will lose the option of undoing the Delete.

Duplicate (Ctrl-D) is a command you will use often. It has the same effect as selecting Copy and then Paste. Duplicate will cause a copy of any selected objects to be placed on the screen.

Copy Style From is a special kind of copy command. It doesn't copy an object but specific attributes of an object. Take a look at Figure 2.18.

If you want to make the circle look like the rectangle, you could guess what color it is and how thick its outline is, or you could simply copy the attributes from the rectangle.

1. Create a rectangle and circle like the ones shown in the figure. Use any attributes you like, so long as the circle and the rectangle have radically different attributes.
2. Make sure the circle is selected.
3. Pull down the Edit menu and select **Copy Style From**. The Copy Style dialog box will appear, as shown in the figure.

▼ **Figure 2.18. A Rectangle and a Circle with Different Styles and the Copy Style Dialog Box.**

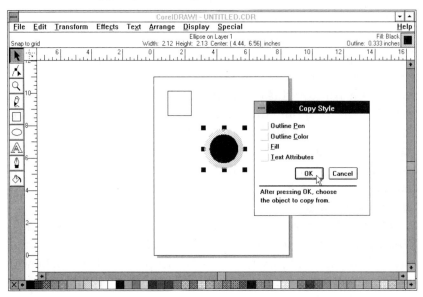

4. Click on the attributes you want to communicate from one object to the other: Outline Pen, Outline Color, Fill, or text attributes. Click on the **OK** button.

When you have clicked on the OK button, the dialog box will disappear and the mouse cursor will be changed to an arrow with the word "From?" written in it.

5. Click on the outline of the object whose attributes you want to copy: the rectangle. When you click on the rectangle, the circle will be redrawn so that it shares all the attributes of the rectangle.

This command doesn't just work from one object to another. If you have dozens of objects and you want them all to have the same fill as one object on the screen, select them all and then go through the preceding procedures, starting with step 3.

Edit Text is the next item on the Edit menu, but it doesn't quite fit in with the rest of the cut, copy, and paste commands. We'll talk about it in a moment in the section called "Using Text."

Select All is an important way of selecting objects on the screen. You've seen a couple of ways to select objects individually (clicking on their outlines) and to select objects in groups (dragging a selection rectangle or holding down the Shift key as you click on the outlines of all the objects you need to have selected). But Select All goes beyond these methods. It allows you to select every item on the screen at once, whether there is one or whether there are hundreds of objects.

TIP

If you want to select everything onscreen except for one or two items, it's very expeditious to use Select All to select everything on the screen, then hold down the Shift key and click on the objects you don't want selected. The more objects there are on the screen, the more efficient this method is.

Edit Object has the same effect as double-clicking on the OLE object: It calls up the program that created the object.

Links is used with Paste Special to specify the link between an object and its program of origin.

Using Text

You've already seen some text used in *CorelDRAW!*. Dozens of different typefaces are included in the *CorelDRAW!* package, ranging from the ultra modern to the informal to the calligraphic to the classic. There are also symbol libraries like Musical_Symbols.

To select a typeface:

1. Click on the text tool (the tool in the toolbox with a capital A on it).
2. Click on the page area where the text should appear.
3. Type the text.
   If you want to make changes, you can select Text Roll-Up or Character from the Text menu.
4. Choose any necessary settings in the dialog box.
5. Click on **OK** to place the text on the screen.

▼ *Figure 2.19. The Text Spacing Dialog Box.*

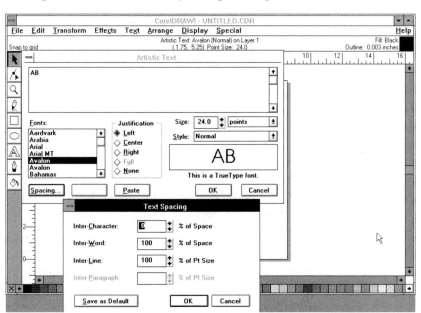

Editing Existing Text

Now that you have placed the text on the screen, you may discover that you have mistyped. How can you return to the Text dialog box and edit the text you have created? It's really very simple.

1. If the text isn't already selected, click on the pick tool in the tool box and click on the text to select it.
2. Pull down the Edit menu and select **Edit Text**.

The Artistic Text dialog box (Figure 2.19) will open up and you can use the mouse cursor and editing keys to make any corrections.

Adjusting Text Spacing

The Text dialog box contains a few specialized typographic tools. Let's begin with the Text Spacing dialog box.

1. To reach this box, the Text dialog box must already be open. Open the Text dialog box either by using the Edit Text command or by clicking on the text tool and then clicking on the page area.
2. Click on the button marked **Spacing**. The Text Spacing dialog box shown in Figure 2.19 will open.

The items in this box allow you to adjust the spacing between characters (intercharacter), between words (interword), between lines of text (interline), and between paragraphs (interparagraph).

The first two (intercharacter and interword) are in ems, a spacing based on the width of the capital letter M in a given typeface. The second two (interline and interparagraph) are based on a percentage of the point size of the current typeface. A setting of 100 percent (the default) is adequate spacing to prevent letters from becoming enjambed between the lines, and yet to provide visual cues that allow your eye to see that one line is conceptually connected to the next. But you may not want to use these settings. Sometimes you want to place a warning label on your ad so that customers will have less basis to sue when your product explodes, melts, or runs away. You could create a statement like, Warning: This product has been known to burst into flames at random intervals and for no known reason.

Naturally, you won't want that information to be as big and obvious as the headline of your ad or the picture of young adults enjoying your product at a fancy health spa. Therefore, you would use a tighter interline setting—perhaps 75 percent.

1. Return to the page area by selecting **Cancel** in the Text Spacing dialog box and the Text dialog box.
2. Click on the text tool in the toolbox.
3. Place your cursor near the bottom of the page area.
4. Press the left mouse button and drag a rectangle about two inches wide and two inches high. When you release the mouse button, the Text dialog box will reappear.
5. Enter the warning label as it appears (or make up your own).
6. Click on the button marked **Spacing**. Set the interline setting to 75 percent. Click on **OK** in the Text Spacing dialog box and the Text dialog box.

   When you return to the page area, your warning will be just legible enough to satisfy a Senate subcommittee.

Making Your Text Fit in the Text Rectangle

You may discover that your text rectangle wasn't long enough to contain all the words. Therefore, you must proofread these text rectangles very carefully. Text that doesn't fit simply doesn't appear on the page area.

1. To lengthen the text rectangle, click on the outline of the rectangle. The eight familiar handles will appear.
2. Drag any of the handles to adjust the size of the rectangle to show all the text.

An alternate way of making all the text fit is to adjust the point size of the text (a point is approximately $1/72$ inch, and it is the standard measurement for type size) or the interline space. You already know how to adjust the interline measurement.

To adjust the size of the text:

1. Select the text rectangle by clicking on its outline, then select **Edit Text** from the Edit menu.

When the Text dialog box appears, note the Size: text box about midway down the right-hand side of the dialog box. You can change the form of measurement by clicking on the box to the right of the Size: box, which normally says "points." You will cycle through measurements in inches; millimeters; and picas, points (a pica is roughly ⅙ inch or 12 points, so 24 points translates into 2 picas, 0 points).

2. Either type in a smaller point size by dragging through the value in the Size: box or click on the downward-pointing arrow at the right of the text box to reduce the value in the box.

If you reduce the point size enough, you will be able to fit the text in the box. Be conscious of the legibility of the text in the box. Text that is smaller than seven or eight points will begin to strain eyes older than 35 years and smaller text may be completely illegible when printed on a 300 dpi laser printer because of the limited resolution of these machines.

You have now seen two ways of placing text on the page: You can click on the text tool and then click on the page area or you can click on the text tool and drag a text rectangle. Using the first method puts the responsibility for aligning text on your shoulders. When you're typing a line of text in the Text dialog box, you have to watch your line length and press Enter when you think a line should "wrap," or return to the left margin. Using the second method makes the text wrap automatically to fit the box.

Text wrap brings up the whole issue of alignment. Text can be aligned in one of five different ways, each of which is provided in the Text roll up and in the text dialog boxes.

▲ Pull down the Text menu and select Text Roll-Up. The Text roll up will appear on the screen.

In the center of the box, beneath the text box in which you enter the words that should appear on the screen, are five icons representing left, right, center, full, and none. The effect of these icons is described by the illustrations on their faces.

Left justification is the standard arrangement of text you would see on most typed documents: The left margin is smooth and the right margin is rough (this alignment is often called ragged-right justificaton). *Right justification* makes the right margin smooth and leaves the left margin ragged (sometimes called ragged-left justification). *Center justification* makes the text ragged on both margins. Each line is centered within the text box or relative to the place on the page where you clicked the mouse cursor.

Full justification is only available for text typed into a text rectangle. It causes *CorelDRAW!* to carefully insert space between letters and words in a line to make it fill the rectangle, left-to-right. In this way, both the right and left margins are made smooth. Although you might think this would be the most desirable alignment because having no ragged margins results in a very neat-looking paragraph, in fact full justification can lead to some headaches. Sometimes so much white space has to be pumped into a line that the line begins to look disconnected, like a collection of characters rather than words. Sometimes line after line has so much white space pumped in between the words that these white spaces form channels of white space moving vertically through the text. These are particularly a problem when your lines are very short.

As long as you are aware that these problems can occur, and as long as you are alert to the potential problems, feel free to use full justification. If you have these problems, move to left or right justification.

The *None* justification button retains the justification that was set before, but it "disconnects" the individual characters on the screen, allowing you to position them individually without respect for the bounds of the text rectangle.

Getting Text from the Clipboard

Let's return to the Text dialog to see what else it has to offer. But first, let's create some text in the Windows Write word processor that was shipped with Windows.

1. Minimize *CorelDRAW!* by pulling down the system menu and selecting **Minimize** or by clicking on the Minimize button (second button from the right on the upper right corner of the *CorelDRAW!* window).
2. Open the **Accessories** program group by clicking on it.
3. Double-click on the *Write* icon.
4. Write the poetry: "Over one arm the lusty courser's rein/ Under her other was the tender boy,/who blushed and pouted in a dull disdain,"

5. Select the text by dragging the mouse through it. The text will be in reverse type, white for black. Pull down the Edit menu in *Write* and select **Cut**.

6. Double-click on the **Close** box in the upper left corner of the *Write* window. A dialog box will appear asking if you want to save your work. Click on the **No** button.

7. Restart *CorelDRAW!* by double-clicking on its icon in the bottom left corner of the screen (if it's hidden by another window, close or minimize that window to make *CorelDRAW!* visible; if the window hiding the *CorelDRAW!* icon is the Program Manager, just minimize it—closing it will end your Windows session!).

8. If the text on the screen isn't selected, click on the pick tool and select it.

9. Pull down the Edit menu and select **Edit Text** to open up the Text dialog box.

   Note that the word "Paste" appears on a button. This refers to the same cut and paste operation discussed in the previous section. Windows is a multitasking operating system shell that allows you to have several different applications going at the same time. The text you selected and cut in *Write* is still on the Clipboard.

10. Drag the mouse pointer through the text in the Text box that contains your warning. It should turn into reverse type—black-for-white.

11. Click on the **Paste** button. What happened?

If all went well, your warning text should have disappeared and in its place the text you created with the word processor should have appeared.

Getting Text from a File

1. Once again minimize *CorelDRAW!*.
2. Open the **Accessories** program group by clicking on it.
3. Double-click on the *Write* icon.
4. Write the concluding words to the famous stanza from Venus and Adonis: "With leaden appetite, unapt to toy;/She red and hot as coals of glowing fire,/He red for shame, but frosty in desire."

5. Pull down the File menu and select **Save**. The Save dialog box will appear.

6. Type in "VENUS" as the filename.

7. There are three check boxes in the dialog box marked Make Backup, Text Only, and Microsoft Word Format. Click on the button that says **Text Only**. This will prevent any formatting commands from being saved with the text—you don't want them.

8. Click on the **OK** button. *Write* automatically appends an extension, so the file will actually be saved under the name VENUS.WRI.

9. Double-click on the Close box in the upper left-hand corner of the *Write* window.

10. Restart *CorelDRAW!* by double-clicking on its icon in the bottom left-hand corner of the screen.

11. If the text on the screen isn't selected, click on the pick tool and select it.

12. Pull down the Edit menu and select **Edit Text** to open up the Text dialog box.

Now you should be back at the familiar Text dialog box. Our goal is to replace the first half of Shakespeare's stanza with the second half.

1. If there is no I-beam flashing in the text box, click at the end of the text to place the I-beam there (the I-beam indicates where your typing will appear.

2. Click on the button marked **Import**. This is the button you use to pull in text from a file.

    The Import Text dialog box will appear. Look at the Path box. It should read something like "C:\CORELDRW\DRAW\ *.TXT." That means it's going to look in the specified directory for a file with the extension of TXT. That won't work. You need to enter a different path into this box. Your VENUS file was saved in the same directory that contained the *Write* program, which was probably your Windows directory (unless you've made radical changes in your Windows setup). Usually this is on the C: drive. If yours is elsewhere, you're on your own. I will assume that you saved VENUS.WRI in the WINDOWS directory directly under the root directory on your C: drive.

3. Click on the file folder marked **Windows** in the Directories box.

4. Click on the **File Name** text box, type C:\WINDOWS*.WRI, and press **Enter**.

    Your file, VENUS.WRI, should appear in the Files list box.

5. Double-click on VENUS.WRI.

    You will be returned to the Text dialog box and the first part of the poem will be replaced with the second. Want to unite the two? If you have been following directions to the letter up until now, the text you placed on the Clipboard should still be there.

6. Click in the text box ahead of the first letter that appears there.

7. Click on the button marked "**Paste**."

    The material on the clipboard will appear.

TIP

CorelDRAW! is not a desktop publishing program, though its output can be used in *Ventura Publisher* and other programs specifically developed for desktop publishing. There are severe limits on the amount of text that can be added at one time. If you have simply clicked on the screen with the text tool, you can only enter 250 characters. This is called a *text string*. If you have dragged a text rectangle, you can enter up to 4,000 characters (around 600 words). This is called *paragraph text*. Although the individual strings and paragraphs are limited in size, there is no set limit on the number of strings or paragraphs you can place on the screen (though memory would probably serve as a practical limit).

CHECK YOURSELF

1. Create a text file with several pages of text in it. Drag a small text rectangle in the page area. Import the text you just created to *CorelDRAW!* via the Text dialog box.

    ▲ The excess text simply doesn't appear in the text rectangle.

2. Create a narrow text rectangle (about two inches across) and type in some text with large words in it (you can simply type *typewriter* several times). Click on the **Full (Left & Right)** radio button in the Justification area of the dialog box and click on **OK**.

    ▲ In justified text, particularly when the words are long and the column narrow, the spaces between letters and words can become excessive, ruining the appearance of the text. This is less of a problem with certain fonts and with text in extremely long lines, but if you can't solve the problem any other way, consider using left alignment for your text.

Changing the Appearance of a Block of Text

CorelDRAW! offers four standard type styles: Normal, Bold, Italic, and Bold-Italic. You can select these styles for an entire block. It also offers superscript and subscript, but these are typically applied to individual characters.

1. Click on the text tool in the toolbox and either click on the page area or drag a paragraph rectangle.
2. Type in some text.
3. Select the text by clicking on it with the pick tool. Press **Ctrl-T** to call up the Text dialog box. Note the Style list box. Click on the downward-pointing arrow to make the list of styles appear.
4. Click on the various typefaces available.

    Note that when the Avalon typeface is selected, all four styles are available, but when you cick on Aardvark, only bold is shown in black, indicating that bold is the only available style. In the Arabia typeface, only Normal is available.
5. Select a typeface and a style and click on OK to return to the page area.

Changing the Appearance of Individual Characters

Say you have entered the text,

SALE: BLACK BEAUTY AND

THE BLACK STALLION

$14.95 EACH

in the text box. Good style requires that you italicize the names of the novels. This is easily accomplished.

1. Click on the text tool in the toolbox and click on the page area.
2. When the Text dialog box appears, type in the text written above.
3. Select a typeface that has both a normal and an italic style. I used Casablanca (use the scroll bar at the right side of the typeface list box to scroll down to Casablanca).
4. Make sure the point size is 24, the style is Normal, and the alignment is Center.
5. Click on OK to return to the page area. You may need to drag the text to the center of the page. Make any necessary adjustments.

    Now you need to set the two novel titles in italic.
6. Click on the shape tool.
7. Drag a selection rectangle that completely encloses BLACK BEAUTY. Pull down the Text menu and select **Text Roll-Up**, if it isn't already visible. You can change the typeface, adjust the point size, change the style (including two additional options—superscript and subscript), shift the selected text in any direction, or angle the characters.
8. Click on **Italic**. This is not the same as changing character angle, because italic characters generally have a completely different appearance from roman characters of the same type family (compare lowercase e's and a's between roman and italic types to see the sharpest contrast), whereas characters changed with character angle simply rotate the characters without changing their appearance otherwise.
9. Perform the same task on THE BLACK STALLION.

Using the Zoom Tool

Let's zoom in on the price for the next action.

1. Click on the zoom tool (third from the top) in the toolbox. You will see the zoom tool menu.
2. Click on the zoom-in selection—the magnifying glass with the plus sign in it.
3. Drag a selection rectangle that includes the price—$14.95 EACH—in the page area. When you release the mouse button, you will see the price in very large type.

The zoom tool is a powerful tool that we will cover briefly here. You know now how to zoom into a section of the screen. You can zoom in far closer, if you want, simply by repeating the steps above. The other option on the zoom menu is zoom out (the magnifying glass with the minus sign), which takes you to a previous level of magnification.

TIP

When sizing an object, you can constrain the size to full multiples of the object's current size by holding down the Ctrl key while dragging a corner handle on the selection rectangle. There are three other tricks having to do with sizing an object.

Hold the Ctrl key while dragging a side handle, and the length (or height) of the object will change in multiples of the object's size. The Shift key in combination with dragging a handle will cause the opposite handle to move the same distance as the handle you are dragging, whether it is an end handle or a corner handle. Using the Shift and Ctrl keys together will cause the opposite handle to move in such a way that the object increases in full multiples of its current size. This may sound a little complicated, but give it a try and you will instantly catch on.

The 1:1 option on the zoom tool menu makes the image on-screen about the size it will appear when it is printed on paper. The next option looks like a conglomeration of shapes. It displays whatever objects are on the page so that they fill the screen. The last option returns to the standard view, with the entire page area visible in the *CorelDRAW!* window.

What I want to do is reduce the size of the .95 part of the price and turn it into a superscript (superscripts are elevated above the normal text line; subscripts are lowered below the normal text line).

It is not necessary to zoom in on the screen to perform this action, but it is easier to pick out a few characters of text when the screen is zoomed in on them.

1. Click on the shape tool and drag a selection rectangle around the .95 part of the price.
2. Select the icon that shows an S with a small raised S next to it in the Text roll-up. There is no need to adjust the point size.

CorelDRAW! will automatically scale the type so it is about half the size of normal 24-point type.

3. Click on the zoom tool and select the page option (the last option on the right) to return to the standard page view.

QUICK SUMMARY

Task	Procedure
Open a file	Ctrl-O
Save a file	Ctrl-S
Call up the Move dialog box	Ctrl-L
Call up the Rotate & Skew dialog box	Ctrl-N
Call up the Stretch & Mirror dialog box	Ctrl-Q
Open the Align dialog box	Ctrl-A
Turn on snap to grid	Ctrl-Y
Cut	Shift-Del
Copy	Ctrl-Ins
Duplicate	Ctrl-D
Call up the Text dialog box	Ctrl-T

PRACTICE WHAT YOU'VE LEARNED

This exercise assumes that *CorelDRAW!* is running and a new, blank page area is visible. If you already have something on the screen, save it and select New from the File menu.

WHAT YOU DO

1. Click on the ellipse tool and drag your mouse diagonally on the page area. Release the mouse button.

2. Click on a color in the palette at the bottom of your screen.

3. Press F9.

WHAT YOU'LL SEE

1. An ellipse will be drawn in the page area.

2. The status line will show that you have an ellipse on the screen and will display the color you have selected.

3. The full-screen preview will appear, showing the colored ellipse.

WHAT YOU DO

4. With the ellipse still selected, pull down the Arrange menu and select Convert to Curves.
5. Click on the shape tool. Click on the top node.
6. Drag the right control point of the top node two inches to the right.

7. Double-click on the bottom node and in the resulting dialog box, select Cusp. Drag the right control point of the bottom node two inches to the right.
8. Pull down the File menu and select Save.

9. Type the name DISTELLI in the box and click on the Save button.
10. Select New from the File menu.

WHAT YOU'LL SEE

4. In the page area, the ellipse will be shown with nodes at top, bottom, right, and left.
5. Control points will appear.

6. The ellipse will be distorted with an enormous bulge in the top left and right quadrants. The node is symmetrical.

7. This time only one quadrant of the ellipse is affected. The control points of the bottom node are in effect divorced from one another.
8. The Save Drawing dialog box will appear, with the cursor already in the File Name text box.

9. Your ellipse will be saved to disk under the name DISTELLI.CDR.
10. The screen will be cleared and the word DISTELLI.CDR in the title bar will be replaced with UNTITLED.CDR.

Printing

You may have noticed that when you installed *CorelDRAW!*, you didn't have to specify what kind of printer or monitor or extended memory you had. Most programs need to know in detail what kinds of peripheral devices they will be working with, but programs that run under Windows depend on Windows to communicate with the monitor, printer, and other peripheral devices. This chapter explains how to use Windows with your printer. In this chapter, you will learn about:

▲ **Installing a new printer**

▲ **Changing printers**

▲ **Printing with *CorelDRAW!***

▲ **Preparing files for a typesetter**

▲ **Merge printing**

You may already be all set to work with your printer. When you installed Windows, you probably specified what kind of printer you are using. If not, it can be easily set (or changed) by using a program called the Control Panel.

To set your printer using the Control Panel:

1. Start Windows. After you've started Windows, locate and double-click on the Main icon in the Program Manager window.

    This part of Windows takes care of file management, printer spooling, shelling out to DOS, the Clipboard you've seen in use, and Windows setup. You might think that you need to run Windows Setup to set or change the printer, but this program only sets the display type, keyboard, mouse type, network settings, and location of the swap file.

2. Double-click on the Control Panel icon.

    You'll see the program group shown in Figure 3.1.

    The options are Color, Fonts, Ports, Mouse, Desktop, Keyboard, Printers, International, Date/Time, 386 Enhanced, Drivers, and Sound.

▼ *Figure 3.1. The Control Panel Program Group.*

2. Double-click on Printers. You will see the dialog box shown in Figure 3.2.

    This is a complex dialog box. In the Installed Printers list box, you can see the printers you installed when you set up Windows. Just click on the printer name if you want to change to one of the printers shown. Additional printers may be available. Scroll through the list by clicking on the up and down arrows on the scroll bar at the right side of the list box.

Printing

TIP

As good as PostScript is, it isn't perfect. Printers often stall because *CorelDRAW!* can create complex graphics so simply; therefore, printer manufacturers have developed a standard list of actions to take with the Control Panel when you have problems printing to a PostScript printer.

First among these strategies is to turn off the Print Manager, which is a useful device that feeds Windows' printer output to the printer at the printer's speed while you are allowed to continue working (this is called "print spooling"). The advantage to turning off the Print Manager is that you avoid whatever incompatibilities

▼ *Figure 3.2. The Printers Dialog Box.*

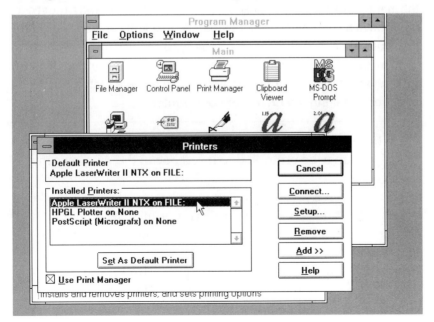

may occur. Each time you add a link, you risk weakening the chain. In the same way, each time you add a program like the Print Manager to the stream of input/output, you add to the risk of incompatibilities. The disadvantage in turning off the Print Manager is that when you send information to the printer, your program is unavailable to you until the printer is finished printing.

Other tips for improving compatibility will be introduced later in the chapter.

Installing a New Printer

You may want to select a printer that doesn't appear on the list. If you click on the button marked "Add", you'll be presented with a list of more than 260 printers.

TIP

Your printer may not be listed. Refer to your printer's manual. If your printer is similar enough to one of the listed printers to use its driver, this fact may be covered in your operator's manual. If it isn't, contact the manufacturer and ask for advice. The manufacturer will almost certainly have a suggestion for a compatible that you can use or will provide you with a disk containing a driver you can use for your printer.

The last item in the list of printers is Unlisted Printer. Click on this item and the Install button and you will see a dialog box to be used for installing the driver for your printer.

When you select a printer from the list of printers and click on Install, you may be prompted to insert one of the Windows installation disks.

You can have several printers installed, and I recommend that you take the time to install a PostScript printer (whether you own one or not), a PCL (Printer Control Language) printer (like the Hewlett-Packard LaserJet), and an Epson compatible (like the Epson MX–80) in addition to whatever printer you are using. These will place some 90 to 95 percent of all printers within your control. Even if you don't own a PCL printer or one of the others, there is a simple way to "print to disk" so that you can send a graphic on a disk for someone else to print. When you begin creating professional-quality graphics, you may want to proof on your dot matrix to get a general idea of the appearance of the drawing, then have those graphics printed on a typesetter or a laser printer.

It should be mentioned that many printers can't print graphics, most notably, daisywheel printers. If you have one of those, you will simply be unable to print your graphics unless you can borrow a graphics printer.

Installing a New Printer

Changing Printers

Many PostScript printers can be reconfigured to be PCL-compatible (which means that they will operate like a HP LaserJet). If you have problems printing to your PostScript printer, another way of dealing with this is to change to a PCL printer and change your printer's page-description language (PDL) to PCL. This leaves the interpretation to Windows instead of your printer. Surprisingly, Windows is often more capable at this task than your PostScript printer. You can expect the printout to take far less time, but there is a trade-off. Many *CorelDRAW!* fills won't print properly (or at all) on anything but a PostScript device. Also, you may see some degradation in the appearance of complex objects like letters in text.

To change printers:

1. Call up the Printer dialog box from the Control Panel window.
2. Find the printer to which you want to change in the list of installed printers (or install it as described in the previous section and then select it).
3. Double-click on the name of the printer you want to use.
4. Click on the **Connect** button. You will see the dialog box shown in Figure 3.3.

   When you install any printer you should check this box. You need to select the printer port to which the printer is connected (in this case, LPT1).
5. The next step in changing printers is to click on the Setup button in the Printers dialog box. This will call up the Setup dialog box shown in Figure 3.4.

▼ *Figure 3.3. The PCL Dialog Box.*

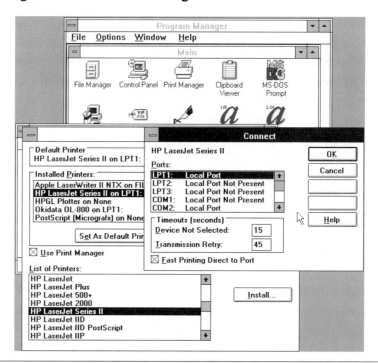

▼ *Figure 3.4. The Setup Dialog Box.*

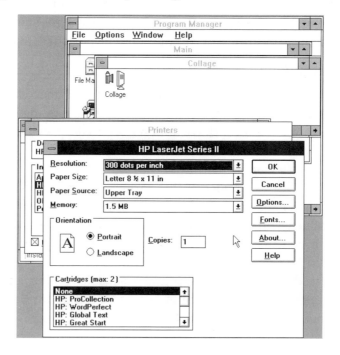

TIP

In the Printers-Connect dialog box, you have another setting that can help you deal with a recalcitrant PostScript printer. The Timeouts box at the bottom gives you settings for how long your printer can "time-out." A timeout is a period of time when the printer is signaling the computer that it's thinking or stalled for some kind of service. It isn't unusual for a PostScript printer to pause for half an hour to unravel a very complex set of PostScript instructions. Therefore, you should set the value in the Timeouts box to the maximum—999 seconds. Simply drag the mouse pointer through the value in the box and type 999.

You may still encounter problems with timeouts because, though 999 is the maximum setting, your printer may still need more time. Check a timed-out printer often. If you receive a dialog box with a message that Windows can't send any more information to the printer, click on the button marked "Retry" at least a few times to make sure the problem really is a printer that has stalled and not one that simply needs time to think. Faster RISC chips in laser printers may eliminate these kinds of problems in future printers.

In this box, you can make important determinations about the type of PCL printer that is installed.

The Resolution setting determines how finely your printout is rendered. A 300 dpi printout is the highest resolution that you can get with the HP LaserJet selected. Some laser printers can go to 400 or even 1000 dpi. A typesetter can produce even finer work.

Your PCL printer may be capable of printing at 300 dpi, but the setting may be for some lower resolution. This is because printing at a low resolution will speed the printing process. A 75 dpi printout takes a mere fraction of the time it takes to print a 300 dpi graphic. But you will want to print final drafts of your graphics at the highest possible resolution. Make sure the settings in the other boxes are correct. One setting that might give you pause is Orientation, which refers to the way the printing appears on the page, not to the way the paper is fed through the printer. The paper will always go through the printer "tall," or in portrait orientation. If you want to change to "wide" printing—or landscape printing in Windows parlance—Windows will take care of rotating the print so that it appears rotated 90 degrees on the paper. You will have the option of making this setting in *CorelDRAW!*, so there is no need to change the setting here. If you have cartridges installed in your PCL printer, you can make the appropriate selection in the Cartridges list box. If you want to print multiple copies, you can make this setting in the *CorelDRAW!* Print dialog box. It's best to leave the Control Panel Copies setting at 1. If you have soft fonts, proceed to install them by clicking on the button marked **Fonts.**

To exit from this chain of dialog boxes, click on the **OK** buttons that appear and then click on the close box of the Control Panel window and the Main program group.

CHECK YOURSELF

1. What can you do when your PostScript printer refuses to print your *CorelDRAW!* drawing?
    ▲ Turn off the print spooler.

2. If you opt to print to a PCL printer at 75 dpi, what will the printout look like? Why would you want to print out like this?
    ▲ The printout would look very blocky and coarse. You might use this setting if your printer won't accept any other setting, to see a draft printout, or just to get the idea of how objects in the drawing relate to one another.

Printing with *CorelDRAW!*

Let's start up *CorelDRAW!* and take a look at the process of printing.

To set up your document to print:

1. Start *CorelDRAW!* by double-clicking on its icon in the Program Manager window.
2. Pull down the File menu and select **Page Setup.** You will see the dialog box in Figure 3.5.

    Note that you can change the page orientation and page size in this box. Until now, you have seen the page in the portrait and landscape orientation. Now you'll see how the switch was made.
3. Click on **Landscape** and **OK.**

    Note that the page is now "sideways" in the *CorelDRAW!* window.

▼ *Figure 3.5. The Page Setup Dialog Box.*

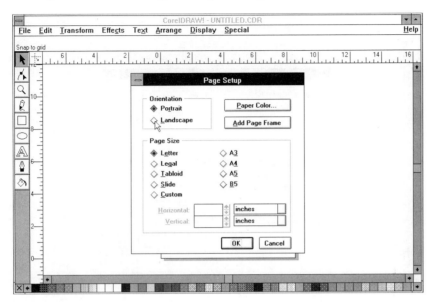

4. Return to the Page Setup dialog box and change the orientation back to Portrait. Click on **OK**.
5. Draw a rectangle on the page area. Click on one of the shades of blue in the palette at the bottom of the screen.
6. Pull down the File menu.
7. Select **Print**. You will see the dialog box shown in Figure 3.6. Most of the options are very easy to understand and apply only to PostScript devices. A PCL printer dialog box is much simpler.

TIP

If you have a PCL printer, you have easy access to PostScript. You can purchase a PostScript cartridge or a product like *Freedom of Press*, which is excellent software that turns any laser printer into a PostScript printer.

Let's go through the options quickly. Most apply to professional graphic design, so they may not be very useful to you now, but they're all interesting and well worth a look.

▼ *Figure 3.6. The Print Options Dialog Box.*

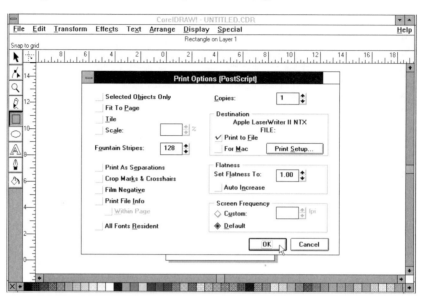

▲ Selected Objects Only. This option causes only selected objects to be printed.

▲ Fit to Page. This option allows whatever is on the page to be scaled to fill the page. If you place a small circle on the page area, it will be expanded to a circle as wide as the sheet of paper. Likewise, if your drawing is larger than the page, it will be scaled smaller to fit the page.

▲ Tile. Sometimes you will create a drawing larger than the page. If Tile is not selected, the portions that are off the page won't print at all. If Tile is selected, the portions that run off the page will be printed on additional pages.

▲ Scale. The Scale option allows you to adjust the size of the printout by percentage.

▲ Fountain Stripes. Later in the book you will learn about a special kind of fill called a *fountain*, which is a gradual change from one color to another. There is no way to avoid visible stripes when printing with a laser printer because the resolution is simply too low to allow for a truly smooth change over an area. A low value in this box will speed your printout. A setting of 30 will print rapidly on a laser printer and will be virtually indistinguishable from a setting of 128. If you are printing to a 1270 dpi typesetter, you should use the 128 setting. If you are printing to a 2540 dpi typesetter, run this value up to 200. On a typesetter, your fountains will be perfectly smooth.

▲ Print As Separations. You can create color separations with *CorelDRAW!*. A color separation will provide a page each for cyan, magenta, yellow, and black. These pages should be printed to a typesetting machine from which negatives can be created that can be turned into plates for an offset press. A laser printer doesn't have the necessary resolution for this kind of printing, and you will be disapppointed if you try to go from laser printed sheets to offset press. More about this follows in the next section, "Preparing Files for a Typesetter."

▲ Crop Marks & Crosshairs. If you select Print As Separations, this option will also be selected. Crop marks indicate the size of the page, if it is smaller than the sheet you are printing on, and the corners where the page should be cut, or "cropped," to make it the right size. Crosshairs are used to make sure the different colors are printing properly on the paper. If the crosshairs line up perfectly in the printout, the colors are aligned. If not, you will probably have some narrow margin of acceptable error; if the crosshairs go beyond this limit, the printout won't be acceptable.

▲ Film Negative. If you select Print As Separations, this option will also be selected. It simply prints black-for-white, like the negative of a black and white picture.

▲ Include File Info. This option will automatically be selected if you click on Print as Separations. This will print the name of the file being printed, the time, and the date on the extreme edge of the printed sheet of paper, outside the crop marks of a page that is smaller than the paper you are printing on. Unfortunately, you are usually printing a page that is exactly the size of the paper you are printing on. Therefore, you should click on Within Page if you want this information printed. Generally, you should save this option for printouts routed through a Linotype or other typesetter to help keep track of your printing jobs.

▲ All Fonts Resident. This is a very advanced feature for people who have purchased Adobe fonts for use with their PostScript device. It indicates that instead of using *CorelDRAW!*'s fonts, your printer should substitute downloaded fonts.

Now let's take a look at the options on the right side of the Print dialog box.

▲ Copies. This setting is fairly self-explanatory. You can either drag the mouse pointer through the text box and type in the number of copies you want to make or you can click on the up arrow until the number you want appears.

▲ Print to File. This powerful option will send all the instructions that would normally be sent to the printer to a disk file instead. If you take this option, you will be prompted for a filename. The extension should be PRN to indicate a printer file. If you don't have a PostScript laser printer (or a PCL printer, for that matter), you can print your drawing to a file, save the file on a floppy disk, and take (or mail) the disk to someone who has a PostScript device (or a PCL printer, if the PRN file was created while a PCL printer was selected). That person can simply use the COPY command to send the information to the printer exactly as if *CorelDRAW!* was sending it directly to the printer. For example, if your file was OORT.PRN, you can print it with the command

COPY OORT.PRN PRN

because DOS recognizes that PRN refers to the printer attached to the computer. This enables you to send a color-separated PostScript file on disk or over the telephone lines to a printing company that owns a typesetter and have the printer do the typesetting, then print a four-color version of your creation. When Print to File is selected, For Mac becomes available. This creates a PostScript file that a Macintosh will understand (they're slightly different from PC PostScript files).

▲ Print Setup. Selecting the Print Setup button calls up the dialog box shown in Figure 3.7.

This option allows you to select a different printer that uses the same basic driver. If you have an Apple LaserWriter selected but you want to create a file to be printed on a PostScript typesetter, you can select a typesetter in this box and create a PostScript file for it. It's simpler to use this option than to use the Control Panel.

▲ Flatness. This sets the amount of jaggedness permissible in a curve. It might surprise you to know that even in PostScript a curve is made up of a large number of very short straight lines. A setting of 1 means that a straight line making up a curve may only be one dot long.

▼ *Figure 3.7. The Print Setup Dialog Box.*

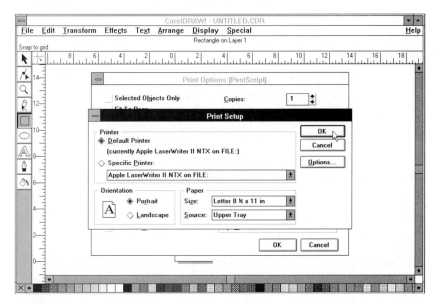

TIP

A flatness setting of 1—or a lower setting—may confound your printer or typesetter. PostScript is limited in the amount of complexity it can tolerate; therefore, if your printer "chokes" on a drawing, one of the things you can do to make it print is to increase its flatness. An increase to 2 may be sufficient and probably won't be noticeable on the printout. When the flatness increases beyond 3 or 4, it becomes increasingly obvious that curves are being broken up into short lines. The trade-off is not only the ability to print extremely complex graphics, but also a much faster printout. If you are not preparing a final "camera-ready" graphic, raise the flatness to 10 or so to ensure that everything is printing the way it should before investing the time to create a final image at a flatness of 1 or 2.

▲ Screen Frequency. A screen is the layout of dots on the page. Although the laser printer prints 300 dpi, it is only capable of producing a screen of around 60 lines. The reason for this is that in a screen, larger, more closely spaced dots are used to indicate a black or dark gray area and smaller, more spread-out dots are used for light gray or white areas. Because these dots are of variable size, they must be larger than the smallest possible dot. To indicate varying degrees of grayness between black and white, these screen dots must be made up of clumps of printer dots and these clumps must be laid out at regular intervals. A screen of 60 lines means that each screen dot can be made up of from 0 to 25 dots, providing 25 shades of gray. You can use this default setting or click on Custom and change the number of lines. Unfortunately, increasing the number of lines won't improve the performance of a laser printer. You can decrease the number of lines below 60 to get some interesting effects, however.

Let's try some exercises to see what a couple of printing features do. We'll print out a fountain fill at 60 lines and then at ten, so you will be able to see the difference. These exercises assume that you have a PostScript printer at your disposal. If you don't, you might want to insert an additional step and print to a file.

1. Start up *CorelDRAW!* or select New from the File menu to obtain a blank page area.
2. Pull down the File menu and select Page Setup.
3. In the Page Setup dialog box, click on **Custom**. Note that the Horizontal and Vertical boxes turn black so that you can enter some custom measurements.
4. Enter 4 as the horizontal measurement and enter 5 as the vertical measurement (or you can place the mouse pointer on the downward-pointing arrows at the right end of these text boxes and click until the value you want appears in the box). Click on **OK** to return to the page.
5. Make sure the rulers appear along the top and left edge of the screen as shown in Figure 3.6. If the rulers aren't visible, pull down the Display menu and select **Show Rulers**.

Note that the ruler shows the size of the page area. Although you will be printing on standard letter paper, the page area on that sheet of paper will be four inches by five inches. This is the difference between the paper setting in the printer setup and the page setup.

Now we will draw a circle on the page and fill it with a fountain fill (you'll learn all about fills in Chapter 7).

1. Click on the **ellipse** tool and press the **Ctrl** key. Drag diagonally on the page area, creating a circle about two inches in diameter.
2. Click on the **fill** tool in the toolbox (the tool at the bottom). The fill tool menu appears.

   Note that the second-to-last item in the top row of the menu looks like it's fading from white to black (it's between the double-headed diagonal arrow and the item marked "PS"). This is the gradient or fountain fill button.
3. Click on the **fountain fill** button. You will see the dialog box shown in Figure 3.8.
4. We'll cover this dialog box in detail in Chapter 7, but for now, click on the button at the top marked **Radial** and click on the button at the bottom marked **OK**.

When you return to the page area, note that the square at the right end of the status line shows a radial fountain fill that is light at the center and dark at the edges. When you print out the image, your circle will be gently shaded from light gray or white at the center to black at the edge.

▼ *Figure 3.8. The Fountain Fill Dialog Box.*

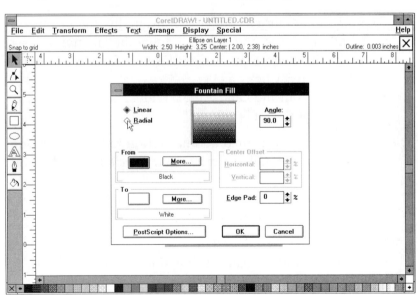

TIP

You will probably notice that there are bands in the printout. If you reproduce the drawing with a photocopier, the banding will be even more noticeable. The problem is unavoidable with a 300 dpi laser printer. The banding will disappear and the fountains will be perfectly smooth if you print the drawing with a typesetter.

Now we will turn to printing the image. We'll print it several times to illustrate the effect of changing the settings.

1. Pull down the File menu and select **Print**.
2. Click on the box marked **Crop Marks & Crosshairs**. This will delineate the page within the sheet of paper. You don't need to set screen lines for this example, but recall that your screen frequency is 60 lines. If you don't have a PostScript printer and you will be printing this on someone else's machine, to click on **Print to File**.
3. Click on **OK**.

CHECK YOURSELF

1. Four orientation terms you have heard in this chapter are *portrait*, *landscape*, *wide*, and *tall*. Pull down the File menu, select **Letter** in the Page Size area and select **Landscape** in the Orientation area. Click on **OK**.
    ▲ Portrait = Tall and Landscape = Wide. The page should appear wider than it is tall.

2. In this section, you learned another action to take when your PostScript printer fails to print your *CorelDRAW!* drawing. What was it?
    ▲ Increase the flatness value in the Print dialog box to reduce the complexity of curves.

When the printout appears, it should look like Figure 3.9.

1. Pull down the File menu and select **Print**.
2. Click on **Custom** in the Default Screen Frequency. The value 60 appears in the Per Inch text box. Click on the downward-pointing arrow at the right end of this text box until the value in the box is 10.

▼ *Figure 3.9. The Printout at 60 Lines with Crop Marks and Crosshairs.*

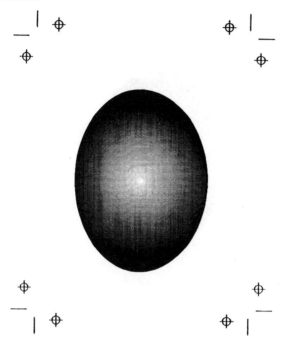

3. Click on **OK**.

   When the printout appears, it should look like Figure 3.10. Finally, we'll change the number of fountain stripes.

1. Pull down the File menu and select **Print**.
2. In the Default Screen Lines box, click on **Devices**, which will set the screen lines for the optimum for your printer.
3. Reduce the number of Fountain Stripes to 4.
4. Click on **OK**.

   When the printout appears, it should look like Figure 3.11.

Preparing Files for a Typesetter

Typesetters and large printing companies can accept files on disk or over the telephone lines. These files need to be color separated. From these files, the printer will create photographic negatives

▼ *Figure 3.10. The Printout at 10 Lines.*

▼ *Figure 3.11. The Printout with Reduced Fountain Stripes.*

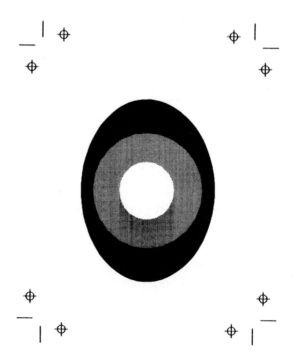

from which plates can be created for an offset press. There are two different methods for printing colors: spot and process. Using spot colors, you would indicate an area on the page and specify a color to place in that area, which is useful if you are printing one or only a few colors on a page. Process colors are best when the graphics might contain any color. Using this process, you would print the entire graphic three or four times with different colors that mix to create all the colors. The standard process colors are cyan, magenta, yellow, and black (known as CMYK). By varying the position of dots of these colors on the page, you can create any color.

How does process color work? It lays down a pattern of dots. You may not be able to see the dots in a magazine cover, but they are there. The screen fequency is so high that the dots are too small to see. Note the difference in screen frequency between Figures 3.9 and 3.10. The slight graininess in Figure 3.9 would be almost completely undetectable in a typeset graphic.

The first thing to do when preparing files for typesetting is to call the person who owns the typesetting equipment and ask questions about what format to use. PostScript is the most common, but some may prefer a different format. You may also find typesetters who are unable to handle PC output and who have to use Macintosh files. In that case, you should consider creating the Macintosh files (remember, that's one of the settings in the Print dialog box) and sending them to the typesetter by modem. Find out how many dots per inch and screen lines the typesetting equipment can handle. You should also call the printer and make sure the equipment needs photographic negatives with crop marks.

We will assume that your printer can handle four-color separated files in PC PostScript format.

To set up your file for color printing:

1. Open the file.
2. Pull down the File menu and select Print.
3. In the Print dialog box, click on the box marked "Print As Separations." The boxes marked "Crop Marks & Crosshairs," "Film Negative," "Include File Info" will automatically be selected.
4. Click on **Print to File**.
5. Make sure the screen frequency matches the maximum the typesetting machine can handle.

Preparing Files for a Typesetter

6. If the typesetter is a 1270 dpi machine, set the fountain stripes at 128. If it is a 2540 dpi machine, set the fountain stripes at 200.
7. Click on **OK**. You will see the dialog box shown in Figure 3.12.

TIP

Don't make any adjustments in this box. The settings are industry standards. However, note that you can change the number of screen lines. Reducing the number of screen lines can result in a very unusual printout.

8. Click on **OK**. You will see a printer setup box, which double-checks to make sure you have the proper settings.
9. When all the settings are correct, click on OK and *CorelDRAW!* will print your graphic to a file.

Your typesetter may prefer EPS (Encapsulated PostScript) files. These would be much more general than PRN files, which may contain information that applies only to a specific printer. In that case, you should not *print* the file but *export* it.

Exporting files will be covered in full at a later time, but we'll walk through exporting an EPS file now. It's a very simple procedure.

▼ **Figure 3.12. The Color Separations Dialog Box.**

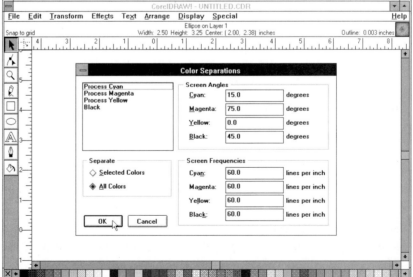

To export your EPS file:

1. Pull down the File menu and select **Export**. You will see the dialog box shown in Figure 3.13.
2. Don't change any of the settings. Click on **OK**. You'll see the Export PostScript dialog box. It has settings to make all fonts resident, convert color to gray scale, and export the image header (the little bitmap rendering that goes with some EPS files) in high, medium, or low resolution, or to leave off the image header entirely.
3. Enter a name in the File text box and click on **OK** to export the file in EPS format.

When the file is created in the format your typesetter wants, save it to a disk and send it to the typesetter. Unfortunately, printer files and EPS files can grow to staggering sizes, sometimes well over a megabyte. If the file is under 1.44MB, you can save it on a high density 3½-inch disk. If it's larger, you have little recourse but to send the file over the telephone lines with a modem.

Merge Printing

Merge printing is a fun feature of *CorelDRAW!*. It allows you to set up a datafile containing text and use this text in printing out *CorelDRAW!*

▼ **Figure 3.13. The Export Dialog Box with EPS Highlighted.**

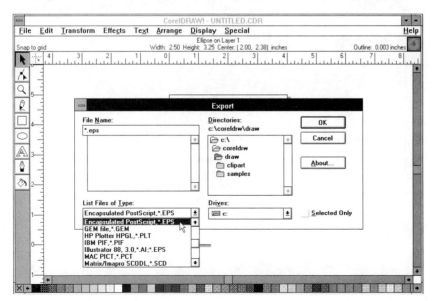

documents. You can create a certificate, for example, and leave the name on the certificate blank. Then, as the certificate is being printed, *CorelDRAW!* will automatically print the names you stored in the text file as it generates the certificates one by one.

1. Let's begin by creating a certificate of graduation from a truck driving school (See Figure 3.14).
2. Curving the text will be covered in a later chapter. For now, just enter the text and remember that you can cause it to curve.
3. As a separate piece of text, type the body text, leaving a large blank area where you see "Name" and "Instructor" in Figure 3.14 by pressing the **Enter** key three or four times. Click on **Center** as the alignment and make the text 24-point type before leaving the Text dialog box.
4. As two separate pieces of text, enter "Name" and "Instructor" in the positions shown in Figure 3.14. Make these 30-point type.
5. If your certificate isn't perfectly centered, click on the **pick** tool, pull down the Edit menu and click on **Select All**. Pull down the Arrange menu and select **Align**. Click on the option to center the objects vertically.

Note the words "Name" and "Instructor" on the certificate. These are called *primary text strings*. When we merge the file, these

▼ **Figure 3.14. The Truck Driving Institute Diploma.**

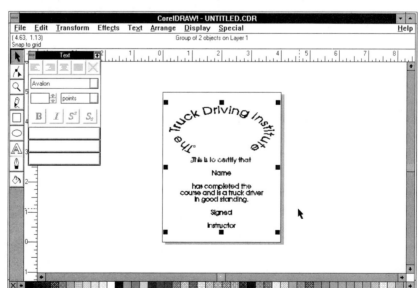

words will be replaced by information from the text file. The merged text will be in exactly the same typeface, style, size, and alignment as the type you see used for "Name" and "Instructor."

Next, you need to create a text file. This has to be a pure ASCII file with no special formatting and it should look like the file being created in Notepad in Figure 3.15. Notepad is the preferred source for your text file for two reasons: First, it generates plain ASCII files, and second, the files are automatically given the extension TXT when they are saved. These are two requirements for the text file for a *CorelDRAW!* merge print.

The file looks carefully formatted, and it is.

▲ On the first line, enter a number representing the number of text strings in the certificate. You can have as many text strings as you want, but each is unique. For example, on the first certificate, wherever the word "Name" appears in the certificate, it will be replaced with "Billie Wilder."

▲ On the second line, begin entering the primary text strings exactly as they appear in the certificate. At the beginning and end of each text string, you must enter a backslash. This is called a *delimiter*.

▲ After you have entered all the primary text strings, you must enter the *secondary text strings*—the strings that will appear in place of

▼ **Figure 3.15. The Text File Being Created.**

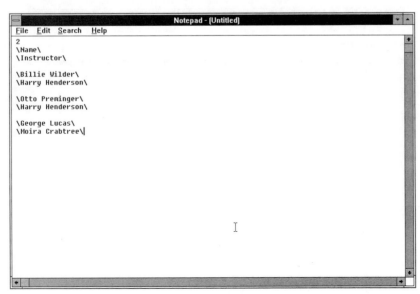

the primary text strings when the certificates are printed. These strings should be typed exactly as you want them to appear and should be delimited with backslashes before and after the secondary text string. These text strings should appear in the same order as the primary strings to which they correspond. The primary text strings appear with Name first and Instructor second. Likewise, in the secondary text strings, Billie Wilder will appear where Name is typed into the certificate and Harry Henderson will appear where Instructor is typed into the certificate.

Figure 3.16 shows an alternative arrangement of the text file. You can use either arrangement, but the setup in Figure 3.15 is preferable because it makes locating an individual piece of data easier.

1. Save the text file under the name MERGE.TXT by pulling down the File menu in Notepad and selecting **Save**.
2. Return to *CorelDRAW!* and select **Print Merge** from the File menu. You will see the dialog box shown in Figure 3.17.
3. Double-click on the filename of the file to merge: MERGE.TXT. The Print dialog box will appear. Make all the necessary settings in the Print dialog box and click on the button marked **OK** to commence printing.

▼ *Figure 3.16. An Alternative Text File for CorelDRAW! Merge.*

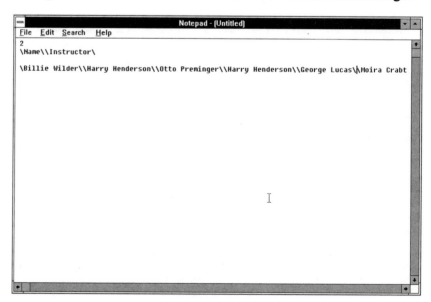

▼ *Figure 3.17.   The Print Merge Dialog Box.*

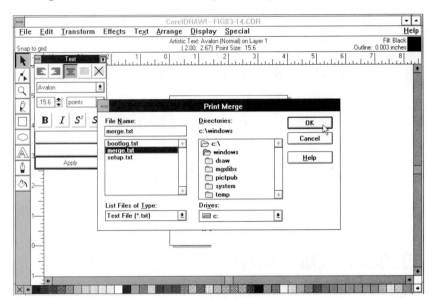

▼ *Figure 3.18.   The Merged Certificate.*

CHECK YOURSELF

1. Create a primary text string in Avalon bold, at 100 points and a secondary text string in 12-point Courier. Merge the files.
   - ▲ The secondary text will appear in bold Avalon at 100 points. The primary text string determines the appearance of the printed text.

2. Take out a delimiter in the secondary text and remerge the text.
   - ▲ The delimiter tells *CorelDRAW!* where one piece of secondary text ends and where the next begins. Without the delimiter, *CorelDRAW!* will become confused and place text in inappropriate places.

QUICK SUMMARY

Task	Procedure
Printing	Ctrl-P

PRACTICE WHAT YOU'VE LEARNED

This exercise assumes that you have *CorelDRAW!* running and a new, blank page area is visible. If you already have something on the screen, save it and select **New** from the File menu. This exercise also assumes that you are using a PostScript printer. The exercise will work the same no matter what kind of printer you are using, but the name of your type of printer will appear where "PostScript" appears in this exercise.

WHAT YOU DO

1. Draw a circle on the screen so you will have something to print. Pull down the File menu and select Control Panel.
2. Double-click on Printers.

WHAT YOU'LL SEE

1. The Control Panel will appear on your screen.

2. The Printers dialog box will open, giving you the option of adding a printer or configuring the current printer.

WHAT YOU DO

3. Click on the Connect button.

4. First, note the currently selected port. You will need to return to it in a moment. Scroll through the port selections until you arrive at FILE:. Click on **FILE:** and then click on **OK** in the Printers-Configure dialog box.

5. Click on **OK** in the Printers dialog box and double-click on the **close box** in the Control Panel.

6. Pull down the File menu and select **Print**. Click on **OK**.

7. Type PRINTERF as the name of the file you want to print to and click on **OK**.

8. Start up your printer, if it isn't already running. Exit from *CorelDRAW!* and open the Main window. Double-click on the DOS Prompt icon.

9. Type COPY PRINTERF PRN and press Enter.

10. Type EXIT to return to Windows. Start up *CorelDRAW!* again and repeat steps 1 through 5, but instead of selecting FILE: as the port, select the port that you had been using previously.

WHAT YOU'LL SEE

3. The Printers-Connect dialog box will open, giving you the options of selecting or removing a printer port or changing the setup.

4. The default printer selection will be PostScript Printer on FILE:.

5. You will be returned to *CorelDRAW!*.

6. You will see the Print to File dialog box.

7. The disk drive will spin for a moment while your graphic is printed to a file.

8. You will find yourself at the DOS command line.

9. Your graphic will be printed.

10. Your system will be returned to normal.

Managing
Files

The PC was provided with an extremely fast and reliable disk operating system. This book is written with the assumption that you are somewhat familiar with the disk operating system; thus, there is no chapter covering details like how to insert a floppy disk or how information is laid out on the disk. However, some points can only benefit from frequent reiteration, and some disk management tasks and techniques are unique to *CorelDRAW!*. In this chapter, you will learn about:

▲ Backups

▲ Importing and exporting art

▲ Using clip art

▲ Using Mosaic

Backups

As has been mentioned, it is important to back up your *Corel-DRAW!* installation disks and it is even more important that you save your drawings often while they are being prepared. You can save them under a single name on the hard disk, but this will cause DOS to destroy an old version of the file as it is creating a new version of the file.

Finally, once you have saved your file to disk, you must pause at the end of each day (or each week, or at some other regular interval) to save your work to floppies or on some other backup medium. You can accomplish this backup with DOS versions 3.3 and newer by using the command

    XCOPY *.* A: /M /S

This will locate all the files on the hard disk that have not been backed up and copy them selectively to the floppy disk in drive A. This will satisfy nearly all your backup needs. However, you should also consider setting up a real backup system, involving backup software like *Back It* or *FastBack* (there are more than a dozen major dedicated backup packages on the market). Another option is to use the backup module in *PC Tools Deluxe* or some other integrated package or utility.

Importing and Exporting Art

One of the most useful features of *CorelDRAW!* is its ability to pull in art created with other software packages (importing) and its ability to convert its art into other formats for use by other packages. As an example, we will import a graphic in TIFF (tagged image file) format and we will export it back to TIFF format.

Importing Art

Fortunately, Corel Systems has provided you with some pieces of graphic art to import. If you lack a scanner (TIFF is the standard output format for scanning equipment), you can use one of the sample graphics included with *CorelDRAW!*. Or you might want to import a BMP or PCX file or a file in one of the other graphic formats that *CorelDRAW!* supports.

To prepare to import your graphic:

1. Start up *CorelDRAW!* or clear the screen.
2. Pull down the File menu and select **Import** (it should be one of a very few selections available to you).
3. You will see the dialog box shown in Figure 4.1.
4. Use the Directories box to get to the WINDOWS subdirectory, if it isn't already the selected directory.
5. Locate the file in the Files list box and double-click on its name to import it (Figure 4.2).

You can rotate, flip, and perform other transformations on your imported bitmap, but some transformations will make it impossible for *CorelDRAW!* to show you the contents of the image. Therefore, if you are going to do any drawing based on the contents of the image, you should do those things before rotating or skewing the image (or do the rotating and skewing in your paint program before importing the image).

Importing and Exporting Art

▼ **Figure 4.1. The Import Dialog Box.**

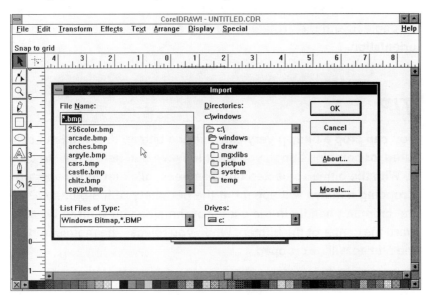

▼ *Figure 4.2. The Imported Bitmap.*

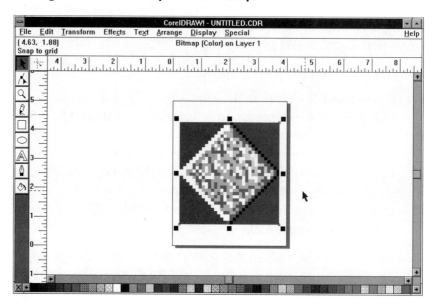

TIP

If you are going to rotate or skew a bitmap, do it with the Rotate & Skew command on the Transform menu. If you do it manually, you will have a hard time undoing it—rotating it or skewing it back to its original position so the bitmap is visible again. Because the Rotate & Skew dialog box works with exact values, you can rotate an object 90 degrees and then rotate it -90 degrees to return it to its original orientation.

TIP

You can crop a bitmap very easily. If the bitmap drawing isn't centered, or contains things you want to leave out, here's how to crop it. With the bitmap selected on the screen, click on the shape tool. Cropping handles will appear at the periphery of the bitmap. Drag the cropping handle in the center of the side you want to crop toward the center of the bitmap. When you release the mouse button, the bitmap will be cropped.

You can import art in any of the following formats: CDR (*CorelDRAW!*), EPS (*CorelTRACE!*), PCC or PCX (*CorelPHOTO-PAINT!*), WMF, GIF (CompuServe), PCX, PCC, TIF, BMP (Windows Paintbrush), EPS or AI *(Adobe Illustrator)*, GEM, CGM, PCT (a Macintosh draw format), PLT (HPGL the most commonly used plotter language), DXF *(AutoCAD)*, PIC *(Lotus 1-2-3)*, TGA, TXT (text), and PIF.

Importing and Exporting Art

TIP

It's important to note that *CorelDRAW!* is limited in the bitmap formats it will import. Although it will import the most popular formats, many other formats in existence will be completely foreign to *CorelDRAW!*. If you will be doing a lot of importing from different graphics packages, or different formats of clip art, you should invest in a graphics conversion program. A good one is *HiJaak* from Inset Systems. Another is *The Graphics Link*.

CHECK YOURSELF

1. Why would you want to use the import feature? Doesn't *CorelDRAW!* give you enough in a graphics package to make the rest of the programs irrelevant?
   ▲ Not really. You can't paint with *CorelDRAW!*, for example, and very little clip art is available in *CorelDRAW!*'s native CDR format.

2. What is the advantage of backing up your disks frequently?
   ▲ You will be less likely to lose a file because of a hard disk failure.

Exporting Art

For this task, we need to have a graphic on the page. Clear the page by selecting New from the File menu.

1. Click on the ellipse tool, hold down the **Ctrl** key, and drag a circle about an inch in diameter.

2. Click on the fill tool and select the fountain fill object (second from the right end). In the Fountain Fill dialog box, click on **Radial** (at the top) and **OK**.

That's the image we will export: a fountain-filled circle.

To export your graphic:

1. Pull down the File menu and select **Export**. You will see the dialog box shown in Figure 4.3.

We'll be exporting to TIFF format.

2. Pull down the List Files of Type list box by clicking on the downward-pointing arrow at the right end of the box. Scroll through the resulting dialog box until you locate TIFF 5.0 Bitmap *.TIF. Click on it.
3. Enter the name of the file in the File Name text box and click on **OK**. You will see the dialog box shown in Figure 4.4.
4. If you are using the drawing for any kind of presentation, pull down the Resolution list and select the 300 dpi setting, which will export the drawing at the maximum resolution of your laser printer (it also takes up the maximum disk space).

▼ *Figure 4.3. The Export Dialog Box.*

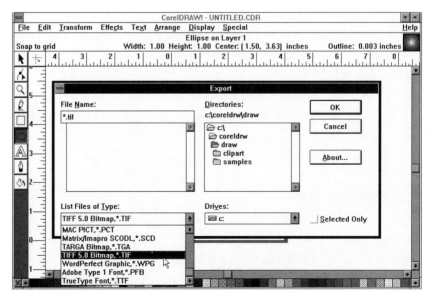

TIP

You can also opt to export the file in color or gray scale. If in color, you can select 16 colors, 256 colors, or 16 million colors. If you select 16 or 256 colors, the Dithered Colors option will become available. Your computer can approximate far more than the standard 256 or 16 colors by carefully mixing dots of different colors. You can also save some disk space by selecting Compressed.

You can export *CorelDRAW!* drawings to PCX, PCC, BMP, WMF, DXF, GIF, CGM, GEM, PLT, PIF, AI, PCT, SCD, TGA, TIF, WPG, PFB, and TTF.

Using Autotrace

Tracing is a method for creating a vector graphic from a bitmap graphic. Basically, a trace looks for the edge of a black area and plots a line along it. When the trace is finished, the line is converted into Bézier curves and straight lines with nodes that can then be edited with the node-editing shape tool. What is the value of a

▼ *Figure 4.4. The Bitmap Export Dialog Box.*

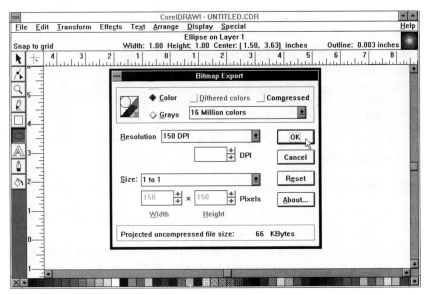

traced image? A traced image can be stretched and otherwise manipulated without the appearance of tell-tale jagged edges associated with bitmapped graphics that make the graphic look like a
computer graphic.

There are two different ways to trace a drawing. You can run
CorelTRACE! or use the autotrace option within *CorelDRAW!*.
CorelTRACE! is covered in full in Chapter 10. Here, we'll work
with autotrace.

Let's import a graphic. You can create an image and export it,
then import it for tracing. Create a shape, then export it as a TIFF file.

1. Import the graphic.
2. Make sure the bitmap is selected (you select a bitmap by clicking on the pick tool and then clicking on the rectangular outline that contains the bitmap). An imported file is automatically selected when the import function is finished. Click on the
   pencil tool in the toolbox. The mouse cursor turns into sort of
   a sideways dagger.
3. Place the long end of the mouse cursor (the right leg of the
   cross or the knife point of the dagger) on the line you want to
   trace. Trace each part of the drawing, including the shapes
   within the outline and the outside of the outline.

Experiment with the autotrace cursor. You'll discover that it
traces the line slightly to the left of the dagger point. In Figure 4.5,
the entire drawing was traced and dragged to a location away
from the bitmap (the bitmap is located above and to the left of the
traced image, which appears hollow). Note that you have to separately trace interiors of shapes. Holes aren't automatically traced
when you trace the exterior.

To complete the autotrace:

1. Get rid of the bitmap by clicking on the imported bitmap and
   pressing **Del**.

Now we will fill the shape.

2. Click on the pick tool and drag a selection rectangle including
   all the autotraced drawing.
3. Click on the black square in the palette at the bottom of the
   screen. The previewed text is shown in Figure 4.6.

▼ *Figure 4.5. The Autotraced Drawing.*

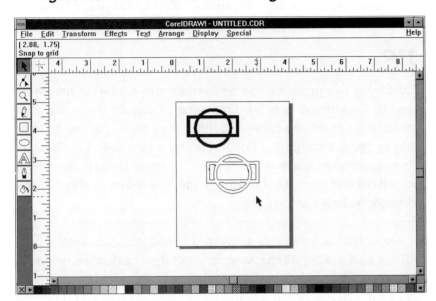

Note that the holes are hidden. In fact, they are filled with black just like the outlines of the figure. You could make the holes visible by selecting them, bringing them to the front with To Front from the Arrange menu, and filling them with white. But there is a better way.

▼ *Figure 4.6. The Filled Drawing.*

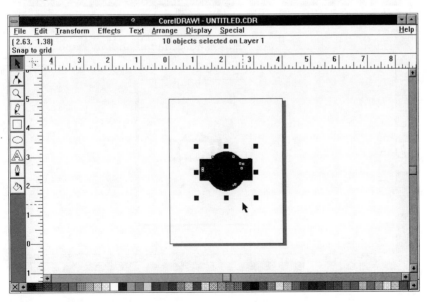

4. Drag a selection rectangle that completely encloses the shape.
5. Pull down the Arrange menu and select **Combine**. Your screen should look like Figure 4.7.

TIP

Combining two graphics can be used to "cut a hole" in one of the objects. Combining is better than simply coloring the holes white because if something appears behind the shape, you ought to be able to see it through the holes. Cutting a hole with the Combine command makes the hole transparent. To prove it, draw something, color it red and place it behind the shape. The red color should show through the holes in the shape.

Now that the shape is in vector format, you can use the node editing tool to alter its shape, shrink, bend, or perform any kind of transformation and discover on printout that the lines are smooth. In Figure 4.8, I have reimported the original drawing and printed it to show how jagged the TIFF file was (bottom) and how relatively smooth the vector graphic image is after tracing—and without any editing to make the outline smoother.

▼ *Figure 4.7. The Finished Drawing.*

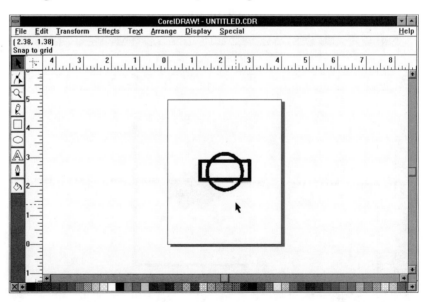

▼ *Figure 4.8. Bitmap Image (Top) and Traced Vector Image (Bottom).*

Importing and Exporting Art

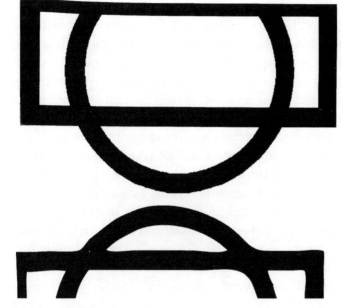

CHECK YOURSELF

1. Draw a circle and then a square that completely encloses the circle. Select them both and select Combine from the Arrange menu. With the circle and square still selected, click on a color in the palette.
   ▲ Combining objects causes them to cancel each other out where they overlap: Where one object existed before, the combined object can be filled, but where the objects both have solid areas, the combined object will show a hole. The object you just created should look like a square with a bullet hole through it. Combining more than two objects makes this coloration scheme unpredictable.

2. Open a *CorelDRAW!* drawing. Based on what you have seen, do you think you could trace a CDR drawing?
   ▲ A CDR drawing is already in vector format and tracing it would be pointless.

Using Clip Art

CorelDRAW! is shipped with a full complement of clip art and symbols. This collection is so complete that it's entirely possible to cultivate a reputation for yourself as a computer artist without ever drawing a thing. You may be perfectly happy with the collection provided by Corel Systems, but the clip art libraries are actually samples of far more extensive art libraries available from other manufacturers. *Symbol and Clipart Libraries* is one of the many documents provided with *CorelDRAW!*. Take a moment to open the book and flip through it. Look at the first page and note that each clip art image is accompanied by a description and a logo that will direct you to the origin of the image. If you like the style of a particular image, note its manufacturer and turn to the back of the book to the section marked "Sources." This section is full of advertisements for the companies that created the clip art in the book. Many of the advertisements offer special deals to purchasers of *CorelDRAW!*.

Let's import a piece of clip art.

To import clip art:

1. Begin by clearing the screen by selecting **New** or selection option **Select All** from the Edit menu and then pressing **Del**.
2. Select **Import** from the File menu.
3. Click on the button marked **Mosaic**. *CorelMOSAIC!* will start up. Mosaic makes it easy to deal with the massive number of drawings you will create in *CorelDRAW!*.
4. Pull down the File menu in Mosaic and select **Open Directory**.
5. Go to the CORELDRAW\DRAW\CLIPART subdirectory. A list of files will appear in the right side of the Mosaic dialog box containing things like AIRCRAFT, BIRD, and so on (MAMMAL is highlighted in Figure 4.9).

   This is not a drawing but a library of drawings.

6. Double-click on the MAMMAL entry in the right list box and the actual drawings located in that directory will appear.

▼ *Figure 4.9. The Mosaic Window.*

Using Clip Art

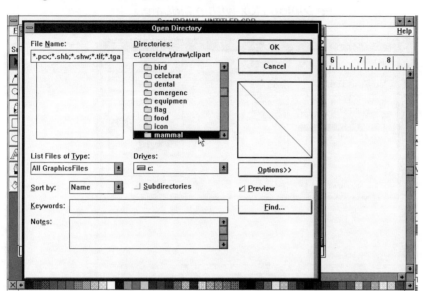

7. Click on SKUNK.CDR and you will see the preview of the skunk drawing in the example box at the right side of the Mosaic window (Figure 4.10).
8. Click on **OK**. A special screen providing thumbnail drawings of all the images in the library will open, as shown in Figure 4.11.
9. Click on the image of the skunk and click on Edit to pull down the Edit menu. Click on **Import into Draw**. The skunk will load into the main *CorelDRAW!* screen.

TIP

If you don't see any files in the Mosaic window, you are probably logged to the wrong directory or drive. Pull down the File menu within the Mosaic window and select a different drive and directory until you find the directory containing your files. If the files still don't appear, you may have the Library (CLB) button selected in the Mosaic Change Directory dialog box. Click on CDR to make your *CorelDRAW!* drawings appear in the window.

▼ *Figure 4.10. The Preview of the Skunk in the Open Directories Dialog Box within Mosaic.*

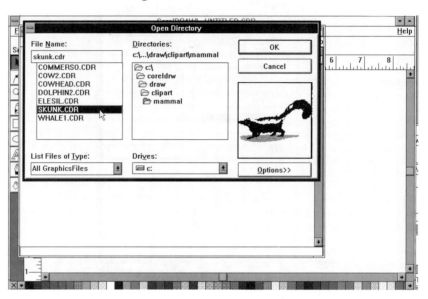

▼ *Figure 4.11. The Thumbnail Screen within Mosaic.*

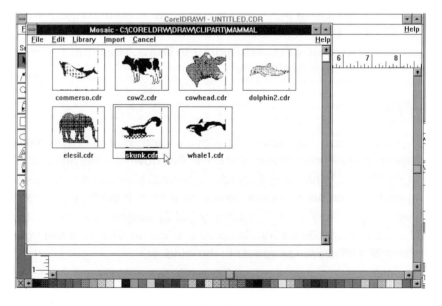

QUICK SUMMARY

Task	Procedure
Edit Wireframe	Shift-F9
Refresh Window	Ctrl-W

PRACTICE WHAT YOU'VE LEARNED

This exercise assumes that you have *CorelDRAW!* running and a new, blank page area is visible. If you already have something on the screen, save it and select New from the File menu.

WHAT YOU DO	WHAT YOU'LL SEE
1. Draw a circle on the screen. Fill it with black. Pull down the File menu and select Export.	1. The Export dialog box will appear.
2. Select TIFF as the file format for export and enter a filename in the File Name text box. Click on OK.	2. You will be prompted for a resolution and drawing size as the Export TIFF dialog box appears.
3. Click on OK.	3. Your hard disk will labor for a moment as the graphic is being changed into the new format and sent to a TIFF file.
4. Select New from the File menu and in the dialog box that prompts you to save your work, click on No. Pull down the File menu and select Import.	4. The Import dialog box will appear.
5. Click on TIFF as the file format to import. Click on CIRCLE.TIF as the file to import.	5. The TIFF file will be imported and will appear, grayed, on the *CorelDRAW!* screen.

WHAT YOU DO	**WHAT YOU'LL SEE**
6. Click on the pencil tool. You are now ready for tracing. Move the right end of the tracing cross to a position near the imported circle. Click.	6. *CorelDRAW!* will trace the circle in a moment. It will appear in the preview screen as an unfilled wireframe circle. Because of the coarseness of the exported image and the vagaries of programming, the circle may be more or less perfect.
7. Click on the imported circle to select it. Press Del to eliminate the imported circle.	7. The bitmap imported for tracing will disappear.
8. Import the circle again.	8. This time the imported circle will also appear on the preview screen. It should perfectly coincide with the traced circle, if you have followed directions to the letter.
9. With the imported bitmap selected, click on the shape tool. Place the mouse cursor on the lower left corner control handle of the bitmap selection rectangle. Depress the Ctrl key and move the mouse cursor to the center of the circle.	9. The image will be cropped, probably to a quarter section of the circle. The image in the preview screen will look like a pie graph.

Views

When you are working with your art, you will often want to take a closer look. Views give you additional control over your drawing. Grids and rulers are even more powerful. In this chapter, you will become familiar with using these powerful tools to your best advantage:

▲ **Magnification**

▲ **Grids and snap**

▲ **Guidelines and snap**

▲ **Rulers, status line, color palette**

Magnification

Magnification is the use of the zoom tool in the toolbox to allow you to take a more careful look at your drawing. You can examine it so closely that it is like looking at a picture through a jeweler's loupe or you can make *CorelDRAW!* take a step back so that you are looking at your graphic as if you were standing across the room from it. The close examination is most useful when doing detail work and the more distant, disinterested view is useful to make sure the design works well as a unit.

TIP

Many talented artists have no trouble creating a pleasing drawing but are unable to compose, which is another word for designing a graphic. They become too close to their work. Before printing a graphic, you should take the time to zoom back to the page view to make sure all the elements are working together, to make sure that the graphic isn't excessively balanced or lopsided, and (if you are going to do a separation or a color print) make sure the colors work together.

Let's draw something and examine it under each of the zoom levels.

Zoom In

To zoom in on a screen:

1. With the normal page view displayed, clear the screen or select **New** from the File menu. Make sure Snap to Grid doesn't appear in the status line. If it's there, pull down the Display menu and select Snap to Grid to turn off this feature.
2. Draw an ellipse and then draw a rectangle that completely encloses it. Try as hard as you can to make the top line of the rectangle *touch*, but not hide, the top of the ellipse.

    The purpose of this exercise is very realistic. When you think you have placed two lines next to each other, it's worth checking with the zoom tool to make sure that the relatively low resolution of the computer screen doesn't deceive you.

3. Click on the zoom tool. Take another look at the zoom tool menu (Figure 5.1).

    Note the slide bars that appear at the right edge and the bottom of the *CorelDRAW!* window.

4. Click on the first zoom tool—the zoom-in tool.

5. The mouse cursor turns into a little magnifying glass. With this glass, drag a selection rectangle about an inch on a side (refer to the ruler—if the ruler isn't visible, select **Show Rulers** from the Display menu) containing the area where the top of the rectangle and the top of the ellipse come together. Don't be surprised if you see something like Figure 5.2.

6. Repeat the zoom: Click on the zoom tool and select the zoom-in option on the zoom tool menu, then drag a selection rectangle that includes the area where the two lines are closest together. Do this again and again until *CorelDRAW!* won't zoom any more. You should see the equivalent of an area about $\frac{5}{8}$ inch square (Figure 5.3).

Note the tick marks on the ruler. Each represents $\frac{1}{16}$ inch. Note also how far apart the lines are in the zoomed screen. If you want to zoom in on another part of the page, you don't have to return to the

▼ *Figure 5.1. The Zoom Tool Menu.*

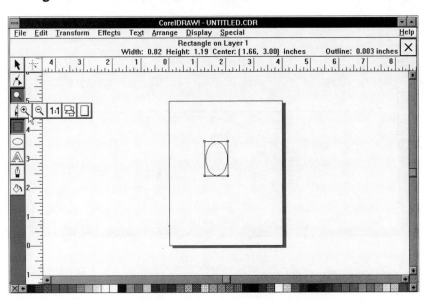

▼ *Figure 5.2. Two Lines Drawn Close Together.*

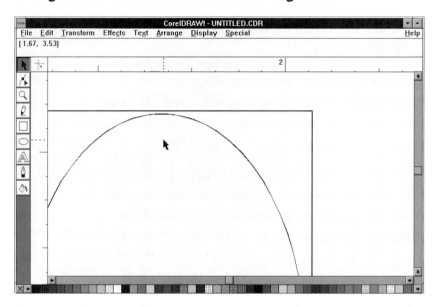

▼ *Figure 5.3. The Ultimate Zoom.*

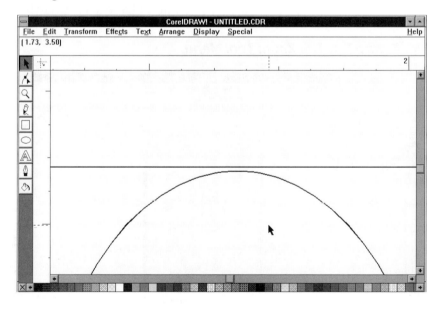

page view and then zoom in on that area. Rather, you can scroll the image on the screen so that the region of interest is visible.

TIP

Naturally, if the picture is very complex or has large empty fields, you may prefer to zoom out and zoom back in again so you don't become lost in the image.

You can also access the zoom-in option by pressing F2 on the keyboard.

Zoom Out

The zoom-out feature of *CorelDRAW!* is very interactive. *Corel DRAW!* remembers the steps you took zooming into the picture and it returns to previous levels of magnification.

To zoom out of a picture:

1. With the magnified image on the screen, click on the zoom tool and click on the second item on the zoom menu—the magnifying glass with a minus sign.
2. Repeat step 1 until you return to the page view. Note that you don't return directly but retrace the steps you took when you zoomed in. You can also access the zoom-out option by pressing **F3**.

Actual Size (1:1)

This item, the third on the zoom tool menu, allows you to see the image on the screen in approximately the same size as it will appear when you print it on paper. If you click on the zoom tool and select 1:1 (the third item on the zoom tool menu), you will see the view shown in Figure 5.4.

Because of their design, some monitors slightly distort the image that appears on the screen, so the actual size view may not be exactly what you will see on paper.

▼ *Figure 5.4. The 1:1 View.*

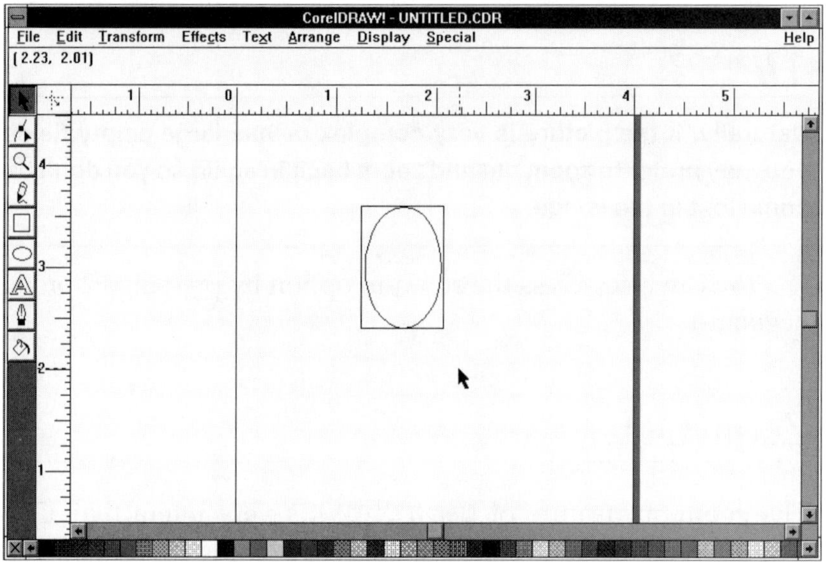

Fit in Window

Usually when you want to zoom into an object, you just want a good look at something small. If you are working on something that doesn't fill the page and you want to make it fill the *CorelDRAW!* window, click on the fourth item on the zoom tool menu—the fit-in-window option. You will see all the objects on the page magnified just enough to fill the *CorelDRAW!* window (Figure 5.5).

You can access the fit-in-window option from the keyboard by pressing **F4**.

Show Page

To return from any magnification to the page view, you can select the show page option, the last option at the right end of the zoom tool menu. You can access the show page option directly from the keyboard by pressing **Shift-F4**.

▼ *Figure 5.5. The Fit-in-Window Magnification.*

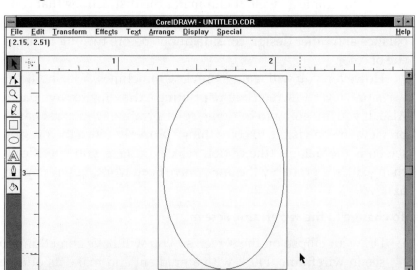

CHECK YOURSELF

1. Zoom in three times and then zoom out three times.
   ▲ You should see the screen that was visible before you zoomed in three times.

2. Zoom in on an object at the right side of the page area. Now move to an equally tight zoom in on an object at the left side of the screen.
   ▲ You could either zoom out from the initial object and then zoom back in on the second object, or you could just as easily use the scroll bars on the bottom and right side of the screen to scroll to a new position.

Previews

CorelDRAW! allows you to work with the wireframe alone or with preview. You will want to see the preview to get an idea of what the drawing will look like when printed. The wireframe alone allows you to work more quickly because it refreshes more rapidly (though in its latest version, the preview screen is probably fast enough for anyone's purposes). There are aesthetic reasons to prefer the wireframe as well. It eliminates the distractions that come with a complete preview screen, allowing a designer to focus on balance and other design considerations before turning to the issue of color.

However, you will want a preview sometimes. You should always preview the screen before printing a drawing to save paper. Also, if you are going to be doing color printing, you must have a preview screen visible to color things properly. Since the preview screen is the default (the option selected unless you specifically change it), it's probably the one you've been working with up until now.

To change to the wireframe screen:

1. Draw an ellipse on the screen so you will have something to see in wireframe. Fill it with a gradient and make its outline very thick (you should recall how to do these things using the fill and outline tools on the toolbox).
2. Pull down the Display menu and select **Edit Wireframe**. You'll see the image in Figure 5.6. Note that when the ellipse is selected, you can see the fill and outline at the left end of the status bar and a description of the selected object at the center of the status line.

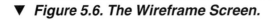

▼ *Figure 5.6. The Wireframe Screen.*

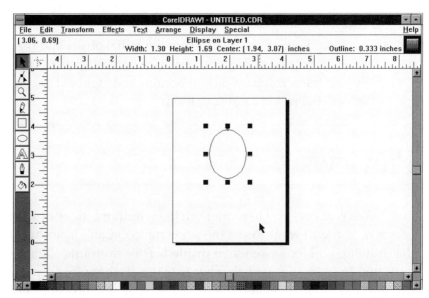

You can instantly toggle the wireframe screen on and off by pressing **Shift-F9**.

Although colors and fountains will appear on the preview screen, you will not be able to see PostScript texture fills (which are indicated by a fill with the letters *PS*).

Show Bitmaps and Refresh Wire Screen

Although these options don't specifically apply to the preview screen, they do relate to the appearance of the preview you enjoy on the page area.

If you import a bitmap, it will normally be displayed. This is because Show Bitmaps is normally turned on (if you pull down the Display menu, you will see a check mark next to the Show Bitmaps option in the menu, but unless there is a bitmap loaded, the options will be grayed). By clicking on this option, you will turn it off, preventing the bitmap from appearing. On the page area, the imported bitmap will appear as a rectangle that can be sized, skewed, or rotated.

TIP

With an imported bitmap selected on the screen, use the shape tool to crop it: You can move the individual sides of the bitmap, reducing the amount visible on the screen and limiting a bitmap to those areas that are interesting.

Refresh Window is an option that can be used when traces of a drawing are left behind on the page area as you make changes in the drawing. If you select this option, you will cause the page area to be refreshed, which means that it will be completely cleared and the wireframe will be completely redrawn. You can access Refresh Window from the keyboard by pressing Ctrl-W.

Grids and Snap

A grid controls the placement of objects on the screen. It's useful for two purposes: either placing objects at regular intervals or placing objects directly on top of one another. Let's create a series of rectangles and place them at ⅛-inch intervals. I arrived at this particular interval because the default grid is set at eight positions per inch (in a moment we'll see how to set this interval at any frequency you desire).

To illustrate snap to grid:

1. Pull down the Display menu and select **Snap to Grid** (or press **Ctrl-Y**).
2. Draw four rectangles. It doesn't matter where they are on the page area, but they ought to be far enough apart to make them easy to manipulate. As an alternative, you could draw one rectangle and select **Duplicate** from the Edit menu three times.
3. Drag the first rectangle by placing the mouse pointer on its upper left corner, pressing the left mouse button and moving the mouse. Note that as you move the rectangle, it seems to lurch ahead. This lurching is called *snap*. The rectangle is snapping to the grid. You can only move it in ⅛-inch intervals. Place it anywhere on the screen.
4. Place the mouse pointer on the upper left corner of the second rectangle and drag the rectangle so its upper left corner is superimposed on the upper left corner of the first rectangle. Then move it one snap down and one snap to the right.
5. Perform a similar action on the third and fourth rectangles so that the rectangles are placed as shown in Figure 5.7. Not only do the rectangles look as if they are placed at regular intervals, but you can be assured that they are exactly ⅛ inch apart.

Now let's adjust the grid and use our adjusted grid to place the lower right corners of the rectangles.

▲ Pull down the Display menu and select **Grid Setup**. You'll see the dialog box shown in Figure 5.8. Another way to obtain the Grid Parameters dialog box is to double-click on the ruler.

Using this box, you can set the position of the grid origin on the page using the grid origin. You may have noticed that the grid we used in the earlier example was exactly oriented to the page. The edges of the rectangles were placed at the ⅛-inch positions relative to the page edge. The horizontal ruler began with 0 at the left edge of the page and the vertical ruler began with 0 at the bottom edge

▼ *Figure 5.7. The Rectangles Snapped to a ⅛-inch Grid.*

Grids and Snap

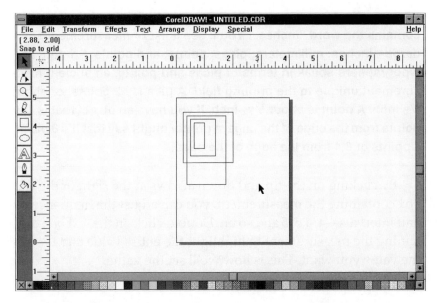

of the page. By changing the grid origin, you can shift the ruler relative to the page. You can adjust the grid frequency by changing the values in the text boxes in the lower half of the dialog box.

▼ *Figure 5.8. The Grid Parameters Dialog Box.*

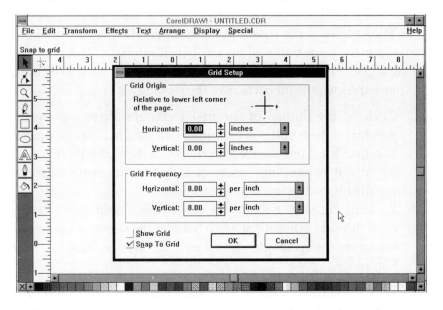

TIP

Click on the downward-pointing arrow to the right of the box that contains the word "inches." You'll see a list of measurement standards—inches; millimeters; picas, points; and points. Printers and typographers speak in terms of picas and points, an ancient measurement unique to the printing field. A pica is 12 points, or about ¹/6 inch. A point is about ¹/72 inch. If you have an object that is 100 points from the edge of the page, a printer might say that it's 8 picas, 4 points or 8,4 from the edge of the page.

By clicking on the up and down arrows at the right of the text box containing the measurement, you can adjust the frequency by half intervals—4, 4.5, 5 and so on. Double-click on the text box containing the measurement to highlight the entire value and type in the value you want. This is how we'll set the value.

To change the grid frequency:

1. Double-click on the **Horizontal** text box under Grid Frequency and type 3.
2. Double-click on the **Vertical** text box under Grid Frequency and type 3.
3. Click on **Show Grid**.
4. Click on **OK**.

Take a look at the rulers. What happened? The only evident change is the appearance of dots at 1-inch intervals. These are the visible grid, showing the unit of measurement. Now we're going to place the lower right corners of the rectangles:

1. Click on the outline of the first rectangle. Place the mouse pointer on the handle on the center of the right side and drag it to a new location. Notice that the snap is coarser than before because it's snapping less frequently. Do the same with the handle on the bottom of the rectangle.
2. Perform the same task on the other three rectangles, placing each side and bottom one snap beyond the side and bottom of the previous rectangle. You'll end up with a drawing like Figure 5.9.

Why not simply drag the handles in the lower right corners of the rectangles? The reason is that the rectangles are of irregular

▼ *Figure 5.9. Finished Drawing.*

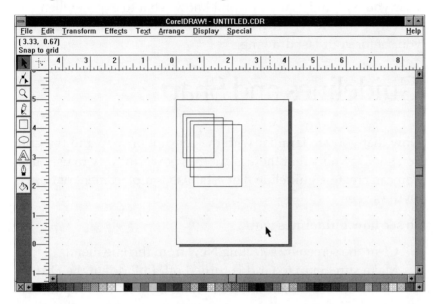

sizes. Dragging the lower right corner (or any corner handle) would adjust the size of the rectangle *proportionately*. Since it's unlikely that both the right and the bottom sides would end up snapping to the same grid mark, you could end up with irregular placements of the sides. Therefore, you have to adjust the sides independently.

To return the settings in the Grid Parameters dialog box to their previous settings:

1. Double-click on the ruler at the top of the screen. The Grid Parameters dialog box will appear.
2. Double-click on the **Grid Frequency Horizontal** text box and type 8.
3. Double-click on the **Grid Frequency Vertical** text box and type 8.
4. Click on the **Show Grid** box to uncheck it.
5. Click on **OK**.

The grid settings are saved with the drawing. If you save the drawing with the settings at 1/3-inch intervals, you will find the grid set at that interval whenever you load the picture. The grid settings are also saved when you exit *CorelDRAW!*, along with all the other dialog box settings you make. It's best to stick with the default settings unless you have some strong reason not to; otherwise you will find that you won't know what to expect when you start up *CorelDRAW!*. It will always reflect the requirements that you set for your last drawing.

Guidelines and Snap

Now that you are familiar with the concept of snap and the grid, you should know that there is another powerful way to use snap. You can create a guideline that establishes a placement of objects on the screen.

To see how guidelines work:

1. Clear the screen by selecting **New** from the File menu.
2. Make sure Snap to Grid is turned off. Pull down the Display menu and see if there is a check mark next to the **Snap to Grid** option. If there is, click on it. Selecting an option with a check mark turns it off.
3. Draw something on the screen. For this demonstration, we will create a series of irregular ellipses whose vertical diameter will be identical, so start with an ellipse.
4. Place the mouse pointer on the ruler at the top of the screen, press the left mouse button and drag the mouse downward. Note that a broken line follows your mouse downward. This is a guideline. Drag the guideline so it coincides with the top of the ellipse you just created.
5. Repeat step 4, only this time drag the guideline down until it coincides with the bottom of the ellipse. Your drawing should look something like Figure 5.10.
6. Now pull down the Display menu and select **Snap to Guidelines**. Now whenever you move something close to one of the guidelines (within about five pixels), it will snap to the guideline.
7. Draw a new ellipse. This time, before beginning to draw, place the mouse pointer close to the guideline. Drag the mouse as far horizontally as you please but vertically only as far as the other guideline. If you miss the guideline, the ellipse will still snap to it.
8. Pull two guidelines out of the ruler at the left edge of the screen. Draw ellipses that fit these guidelines as well. You can

▼ *Figure 5.10. The Ellipse and the Guidelines.*

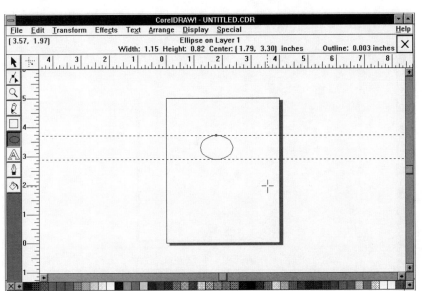

create as many guidelines as you please.

TIP

If you have Snap to Grid on, your guidelines will snap to the grid, so there isn't much point in using them. The guidelines are useful when you want to guide off of an object that is already on the screen.

To use the guidelines to align a letterhead:

1. Start fresh by selecting **New** from the File menu.
2. Pull down three guidelines. The first two will be about ¼ inch apart and the second and third should be about ¾ inch apart. Use the rulers to place the guidelines if you like, but as you have probably guessed, the exact placement doesn't matter very much. Your screen should look like Figure 5.11.
3. Click on the text tool and on the page area. Type "Bonzai and Dimbulb." Use the Avalon font. Click on the pick tool and size the text so it is about ¾ the width of the page area.
4. Drag the text until its baseline (the bottoms of the letters) is on the top guideline.

▼ *Figure 5.11. The Guidelines in Place for the Letterhead.*

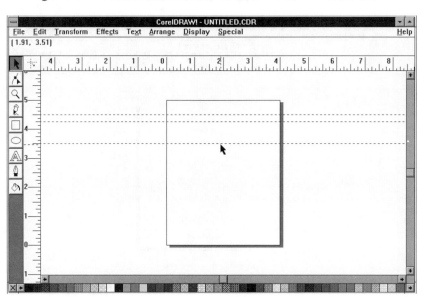

5. Click on the text tool and the page area again. Type "Attorneys at Law."

6. Drag the new text so its baseline is on the bottom guideline.

7. With the text tool still selected, press the **Shift** key and click on the page area. That will call up the Symbols dialog box. In the list box at the right, click on **Geographical Symbols** (you'll need to use the scroll bar to scroll through the options). In the symbols box, you will see a single symbol. Click on the lower right corner of this symbol to see a collection of symbols. Use the scroll bar to move horizontally through this collection of symbols. Select any symbol. I have selected a freighter. Note that you can also specify how large the symbol will appear. Click on **OK** and when you return to the page area, your symbol will appear.

8. Place the symbol at the left end of the middle guideline and use **Duplicate** from the Edit menu to make a copy. Place the copy on the opposite end of the top guideline.

9. Click on the page and type "Specializing in nautical law." Click on **OK** and use the pick tool to place this text on the middle line of the letterhead.

10. Now adjust the position of the guidelines to specify the position of the items on the page. Note that when you place the guidelines, you don't move the items that are on the guideline.

To make the items snap to the guideline again, you have to adjust them with the mouse. Figure 5.12 shows the final letterhead with the preview screen visible. The bottom guideline has been adjusted slightly and the text moved so it would snap to the guideline.

You may want to place guidelines at a particular position on the screen.

To set a guideline at a particular position on the screen:

1. Select **Guidelines Setup** or pull a guideline out of the ruler and double-click on it. You will see the dialog box in Figure 5.13.
2. Choose a vertical or horizontal guideline in the top section of the dialog box. Enter the exact position of the guideline in the text box at the bottom.

Rulers, Status Line, Palette

You have probably noticed that certain items are always on the screen—the rulers, status line, and the palette. The first two provide a wealth of information about the drawing and the third is a

▼ *Figure 5.12. The Finished Letterhead.*

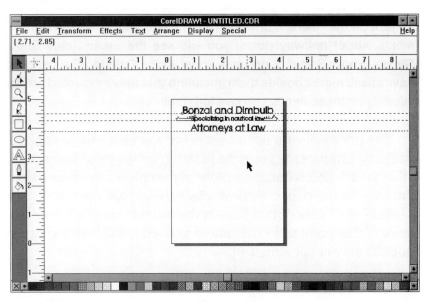

▼ *Figure 5.13. The Guidelines Dialog Box.*

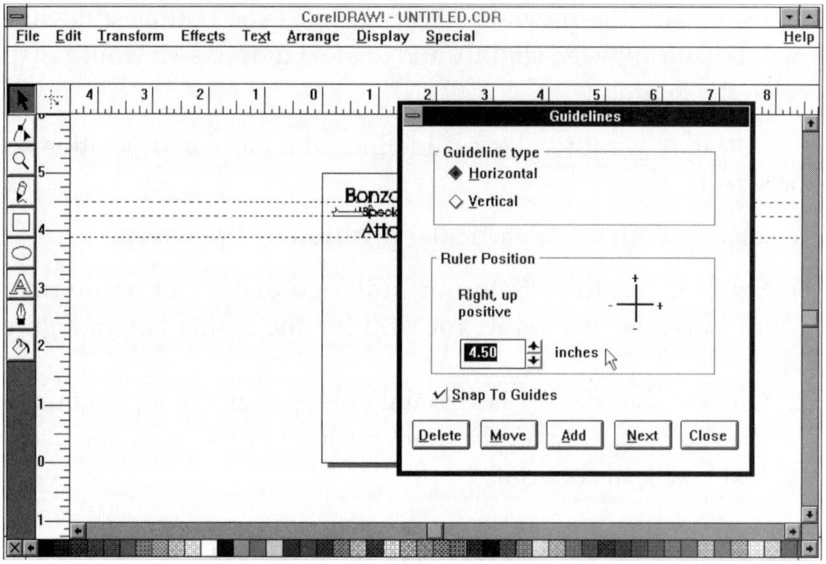

great convenience for coloring objects on the screen. But some people may not want them visible, either because they are working with wireframes alone, so the palette is useless to them, or because they restrict the screen somewhat. With all of these assists turned off, much more of the drawing can be seen on the screen.

TIP

To turn off the rulers, status line, and palette, pull down the Display menu. About halfway down, you will see the menu items Show Rulers, Show Status Line, and Show Color Palette. They should have check marks beside them, meaning that they are turned on. By clicking on these items, you can turn them off.

The ruler is useful because it helps you to see the size of the page and estimate the positions of things on the page, not just relative to each other, but in absolute terms reflecting distance from the edge of the paper. You can place the mouse pointer next to something and see dotted lines in the rulers that indicate the distance of that point from the bottom and the left side of the paper. But that may not be sufficient for you.

To use the rulers to measure distance from objects on the screen (instead of from the edges of the paper):

Rulers, Status Line, Palette

1. Draw two objects on the screen. We will measure how far apart these objects are, so make them at some distance from each other.
2. Place the mouse pointer on the place where the rulers come together at the upper left corner of the *CorelDRAW!* window.
3. Press the left mouse button and drag onto the screen. Crosshairs will follow the mouse pointer, which you can use to measure distances on the screen. Move the mouse pointer so it is next to an object on the screen.
4. Release the mouse button. Note what happened to the rulers. The 0 point on the rulers is placed where you released the mouse pointer. Now by moving your mouse pointer to another object on the screen you can use the indicators on the rulers to see how far apart the two objects are. Note that the values on the left end of the status line also reflect distances from the new 0 points on the rulers.

Now that you have the rulers in this position, how would you go about returning it to the previous orientation—with 0 at the left and bottom edges of the page?

To return the rulers to previous orientation:

1. Pull down the Display menu and select **Grid Setup** or double-click on the ruler.
2. In the top area of the resulting Grid Parameters dialog box, you will see your new settings in the Grid Origins section of the dialog box. Double-click on the text box corresponding to the **Horizontal** grid origin and type 0. Double-click on the text box corresponding to the **Vertical** grid origin and type 0.
3. Click on **OK**. The rulers should be back to normal.

CHECK YOURSELF

Turn on Snap to Grid and Snap to Guidelines. Call up Grid Setup and select Show Grid to make the grid visible. Pull a guideline out of the ruler and place it between grid marks (note that the guideline also snaps to the grid).

▲ You cannot place a guideline away from a grid mark. It will snap to the nearest grid no matter how careful you are or how far apart the gridlines are.

QUICK SUMMARY

Task	Procedure
Zoom in	F2
Zoom out	F3
Zoom to fit in frame	F4
Toggle Edit Wireframe on and off	Shift-F9
Toggle Snap to Grid	Ctrl-Y

PRACTICE WHAT YOU'VE LEARNED

This exercise assumes that you have *CorelDRAW!* running and a new, blank page area is visible. If you already have something on the screen, save it and select New from the File menu.

WHAT YOU DO

1. Pull down the Display menu and, if Snap to Grid is not turned on, turn it on now.

2. Pull down the Display menu again and click on Grid Setup. In the Grid Parameters dialog box, make sure the Show Grid check box is checked. Click on the button marked OK.

WHAT YOU'LL SEE

1. Snap to Grid will appear at the left end of the status line.

2. The grid will appear on the page area; in fact, it will fill the whole *CorelDRAW!* window.

WHAT YOU DO

3. If *CorelDRAW!* is set to Edit Wireframe, turn it off by selecting Edit Wireframe in the Display menu or by pressing Shift-F9. Click on the zoom tool in the toolbox. Select zoom in, the magnifying glass with the plus sign in it. Move the mouse pointer back to the page area.

4. Drag a rectangle about 1 inch on each side and release the mouse button.

5. Click on the rectangle tool in the toolbox and drag a rectangle $1/8$ inch on a side. Try to start and finish at a distance from the grid mark.

6. Click on the ellipse tool and create an ellipse with the point of origin at the first grid mark above and to the left of the rectangle and the terminating point at the first grid mark below and to the right of the rectangle.

WHAT YOU'LL SEE

3. The mouse pointer will now be a magnifying glass.

4. When you release the mouse button, you will see the page area fill with grid marks. If you haven't altered the defaults, these grid marks should be $1/8$ inch apart. If they are inconveniently far apart, pull down the Display menu and select Grid Setup and change the Grid Frequency settings to 8 per inch.

5. The rectangle will snap to the nearest grid mark, resulting in a perfect rectangle. The rectangle snaps to the correct grid mark. It should be exactly $1/8$ inch on a side.

6. A perfect circle will be formed. The rectangle will be centered in the circle.

WHAT YOU DO

7. Click on the pick tool and drag a selection rectangle that includes both the circle and the rectangle.
8. Click on the outline of one of the selected shapes.
9. Drag the top skew handle (the straight arrow in the center of the top of the selection rectangle) slightly to the right. Try to end with the corners of the skewed rectangle between grid marks.
10. Click on the zoom tool in the toolbox and select full-page view from the zoom menu.

WHAT YOU'LL SEE

7. Both objects will be selected, as indicated at the center of the status line (2 objects selected on Layer 1).
8. The rotate and skew handles will appear.
9. Note that you can rotate and skew without snapping to the grid.

10. Note how small the object is that you have been working on.

Node
Editing

As steady as my hands are and as powerful as my scanning equipment and tracing programs are, the art on the page never seems to be exactly the way I want it. I'm not a perfectionist, but I like to have control over the art I create. If the artist doesn't exercise some control, the "art" becomes simply another product of the machine. Nodes are the mechanisms by which computer artists exercise control over their drawings. In this chapter, you will learn about:

- ▲ Deleting nodes and adding nodes
- ▲ Control points and smoothing curves through nodes
- ▲ Breaking nodes
- ▲ Turning curves into lines and lines into curves
- ▲ Cusp and attaching nodes
- ▲ Making curves symmetrical
- ▲ More node-editing features

If your rulers aren't turned on, pull down the Display menu and select Show Rulers.

Let's start with some scanned art, which we will trace and then node edit. For the purposes of this trace, I will lend a common object, seen in Figure 6.1.

Ordinarily, it's difficult to scan three-dimensional objects, but the Chinon DS-3000 scanner is a flat-bed scanner that looks more like an overhead projector than a Xerox copier. Since its scanning hardware looks down on a flat plate rather than looking up through a piece of glass, this particular scanner makes it possible to scan three-dimensional assemblages. It's especially useful if you want to do something different with lighting.

If you don't have an image to scan, or if you don't have a scanner, use one of the TIF or PCX files in the SAMPLES subdirectory under your CORELDRW\DRAW directory.

To trace an object:

1. Start up *CorelDRAW!* or select **New** from the file menu to start with a clean slate.
2. Use the **Import** command on the file menu to import a PCX or TIF graphic. Figure 6.1 shows the imported bitmap graphic.

▼ *Figure 6.1. The Imported Bitmap Graphic.*

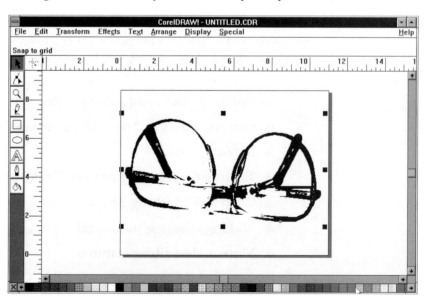

3. With the bitmap selected, click on the pencil tool. Trace the bitmap by placing the "point of the dagger" slightly to the right of the edge to be traced and clicking. If you accidentally trace the same edge a second time, remember to press Del immediately to eliminate the unnecessary object.
4. When all the edges have been traced, click on the rectangle that defines the bitmap and press **Del** to eliminate the bitmap. My trace resulted in the image shown in Figure 6.2.

Sometimes computer art can be extremely abstract and, because you know what the graphic is, it's difficult for you to tell when there are enough clues in the graphic to convey something to the viewer. To clarify the image just created, we will use node editing.

Delete Nodes

First, many of the nodes in this image are unnecessary. Begin by selecting Edit Wireframe from the Display menu:

1. Click on the zoom tool and select the zoom-in option.

▼ **Figure 6.2. The Trace.**

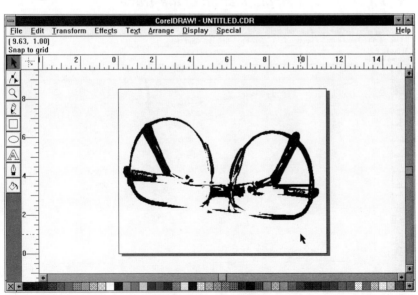

2. Select a section of the bitmap that appears somewhat irregular. You should end up with an image like Figure 6.3.

This trace appears jagged because the bitmap was very jagged. We'll begin by going around the image and deleting nodes, which has the effect of smoothing the image.

To delete nodes:

1. Click on the shape tool.
2. Click on the line whose nodes you want to edit.

The next step is to determine which nodes should stay and which should go. Generally, you will want to keep a node at the beginning, end, and middle of a curve. That means that in the large curve shown in Figure 6.4, you want to eliminate all but three of the nodes.

3. Drag a selection rectangle to select several nodes between one of the ends of the curve and the middle of the curve. Don't worry about selecting too many because you can always replace nodes.
4. Press **Del**. Don't worry if the curve looks weird—in fact, it almost certainly will (Figure 6.4).

▼ *Figure 6.3. A Magnification of the Trace.*

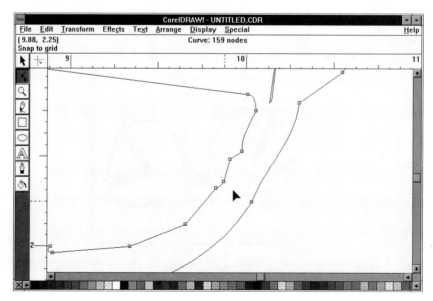

▼ *Figure 6.4. The Curve with Most of the Nodes Removed.*

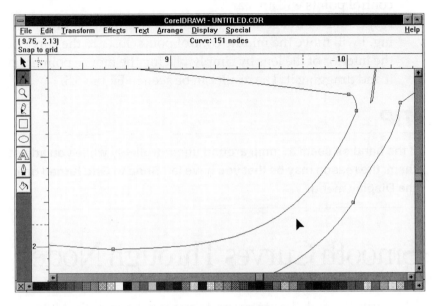

Now you have seen nodes deleted wholesale.

To delete a node individually:

1. Locate another unnecessary node, either in the curve or in some other part of the trace.
2. Double-click on the node. You will see the Node Editing dialog box.
3. Click on **Delete** or press **D**.

There is no advantage in one deletion scheme over the other. One stresses the mouse and the other stresses the keyboard. You can delete large numbers of nodes with the Node Editing dialog box. Simply drag a selection rectangle including a number of nodes and double-click on any of them. When you click on the **Delete** button, all the selected nodes will be eliminated.

Control Points

Now we'll make our curve look more like a curve by using control points:

1. Click on one of the nodes at the end of the irregular curve. Its control points will appear.
2. Adjust the control points so that the curve is more natural-looking. I will move the middle control point closer to the curve of the interior of the lens by simply placing the mouse pointer on it and dragging it. The result can be seen in Figure 6.5.

TIP

If the handles seem to jump around uncontrollably while you adjust them, the reason may be that you have left Snap to Grid turned on in the Display menu.

Smooth Curves Through Nodes

The curve through the central node ought to be smooth. Although the line curves away gently on either side of this node, it goes straight through the node itself. There is no cusp or hairpin turn here.

▼ *Figure 6.5. The Adjusted Curve.*

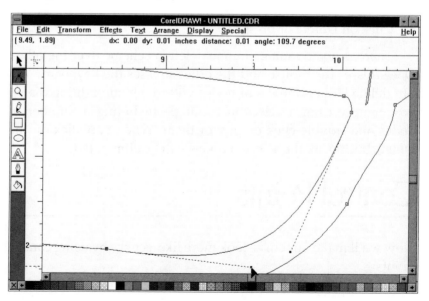

To smooth the curve through the node.

1. Double-click on the central node.
2. When the Node Edit dialog box appears, select **Smooth** or press **S**.

Break Nodes

You have probably noticed the temple. As a trace, the temple is of a piece with the lenses. This happened because the glasses were folded when the scan occurred. In fact, glasses with the temples attached to the lenses would be practically useless. It's one of the items in the graphic that will confuse a viewer. Therefore, it would be a good idea to separate the two images.

To break nodes:

1. Double-click on the node that marks the place where the lens holder and the temple come together.
2. When the Node Editing dialog box appears, select **Break**. Although the broken node looks much the same, it is actually two nodes. In Figure 6.6, I have moved one of the nodes slightly apart from the other.

▼ *Figure 6.6. The Broken Node.*

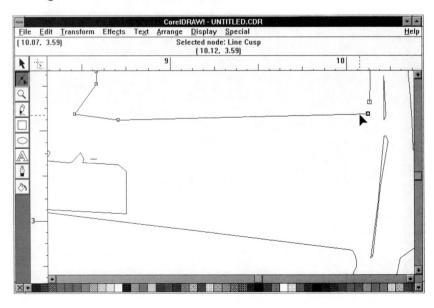

I will adjust the node so that it completely crosses the lens holder and break the node on the other side of the temple, as shown in Figure 6.7.

CHECK YOURSELF

Create a rectangle in a paint program and import it into *CorelDRAW!*. Trace it, then simplify the traced line.

▲ The fastest way is to select and delete nodes wholesale. Be careful to leave nodes in the middle of curves and at corners to retain the general shape. Then adjust the remaining nodes to make the shape correct again.

TIP

To reduce the number of nodes that appear when you autotrace, you can adjust the sensitivity of the trace. Pull down the Special menu and select Preferences. Click on the Curves button and note that in the resulting dialog box there is a setting for Autotrace Tracking. This can be set from 1 to 10. The lower the number, the higher the sensitivity of the trace and, consequently, the more nodes are generated.

▼ *Figure 6.7. The Second Broken Node.*

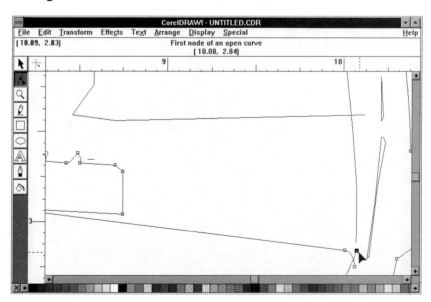

Attach Nodes

There are two ways to attach nodes. If two nodes are the end nodes of the same object, simply use the shape tool to drag a selection rectangle that selects the end nodes of an open object (or hold down the Shift key and click on both ends), then double-click on one of them. When the Node Edit dialog box appears, select Join. If two nodes are the end nodes of separate objects, you need to select both objects with the pick tool and select Combine from the Arrange menu.

To reconnect the ends of the open lens holder:

1. Hold down the **Shift** key and click on the two end nodes so that both are selected.
2. Double-click on one of the nodes.
3. In the resulting dialog box, select **Join**. You will see something like Figure 6.8.

Next, I adjusted the ends of the temple so they are in line with the temple that crosses the lens. Now I'll connect the ends with a line to make the temple object a closed object. This involves the use of the Combine command on the Arrange menu.

▼ *Figure 6.8. The Joined Ends.*

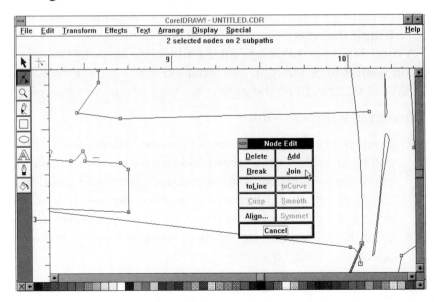

To add a line:

1. With the temple object selected, click on the pencil tool.
2. Place the pencil tool on one of the nodes of the temple and press the mouse button.
3. Drag the pencil tool to the other end of the temple object. When you release the mouse button, the line necessary to close the object will be in place.

TIP

You may discover that the Join option on the dialog box is grayed and not available. This could be because more than two nodes are selected or because only one node is selected. You might want to use the zoom-in option again to take an even closer look at the nodes you are connecting. It's very easy to end up with two nodes almost exactly on top of one another. In that case, use the delete command (or the delete key) in combination with the shape tool to eliminate any extraneous nodes. Also watch out for areas where three lines come together. You can't join more than two nodes.

Turn Curves into Lines

While editing another part of the drawing I discovered a section of the temple that was traced as a curve but should have been a line. A curve is a powerful thing, but it's difficult to keep straight when you want it to be straight, and what looks straight on the screen may not be straight on the page.

To convert a curve to a line:

1. Double-click on the end point of the line. Sometimes it's difficult to tell which is the correct node for the curve. If the wrong curve segment becomes highlighted, click on the **Cancel** button on the Node Editing dialog box and double-click on the node at the other end of the curve. Or you might prefer simply to double-click on the line or curve segment itself. That always selects the correct node.

2. When the Node Edit dialog box appears, click on the button marked **toLine** (or press **L**).

Cusp Nodes

In the same line, I ran into trouble with the next curve segment because it wouldn't bend. The control point wouldn't budge from a straight line with the line segment we just created. What does that mean? It means that during the trace operation, *CorelDRAW!*, in its infinite wisdom, made this a smoothed node. To get a smoothed node to bend independently, it's necessary to turn it into a cusp.

To change a node from smooth to cusp:

1. Double-click on the node again.
2. When the Node Edit dialog box appears, click on Cusp.

   This will give you complete control over the control point.

Add Nodes

In another part of the drawing, I became overly exuberant removing nodes and accidentally removed one that was important.

To add a node:

1. Double-click on the segment that needs an additional node.
2. Select **Add** from the Node Edit dialog box.

Turn Lines into Curves

This editing job did not require it, but frequently, you may have to turn lines into curves.

To change a line into a curve:

1. Double-click on the end node of the segment that should be turned into a node.
2. In the Node Edit dialog box, select **toCurve** or press **C**.

Make Nodes Symmetrical

A symmetrical node is one that not only has a smooth curve running through it but also has control points at equal distances from it.

To make a node symmetrical:

1. Double-click on the node.
2. When the Node Edit dialog box appears, select **Symmet** or press **Y**.

TIP

Symmetrical nodes are useful for regular, flowing curves. The nodes of a circle or an ellipse are symmetrical. If you make the "side" nodes of an ellipse unsymmetrical, you will create an oval.

More Node-Editing Features

One of the more interesting ways to edit nodes is to edit them in groups. To edit more than one node at a time, hold down the Shift key as you click on the nodes to be edited. There is no reason to select nodes in a single line or several nodes in a row (though you can do this by dragging a selection rectangle). Although you probably *will* edit nodes in groups only when they are close together, you can select any group of nodes. Then you can drag all the nodes by dragging one node, or make them all symmetrical, and so on.

Cropping Bitmaps

The same tool that you have been using for node editing can be used to crop bitmaps. Select the bitmap to be cropped and click on the shape tool in the toolbox. Special handles will appear around the edges of the bitmap. Simply drag the handles toward the center of the bitmap and the bitmap will be cropped, eliminating from view the portions you hid by moving the sides.

QUICK SUMMARY

Task	Procedure
Delete a node	Click on the node with the shape tool and press Del or double-click on the node and press D
Break a node	Double-click on the node and press B
Change a curve to a line	Double-click on the terminal node and press L
Change a smooth node to a cusp	Double-click on the node and press C
Align nodes	Double-click on the node and press I
Add a node	Double-click on the node and press A
Join two nodes that are part of the same object	Click on the shape tool, click on the two nodes to join while holding down the Shift key, double-click on one of the nodes, and press J
Join two nodes that are not part of the same object	Click on both objects holding the Shift key down, select Combine from the Arrange menu, click on the shape tool, click on the two nodes to join while holding down the Shift key, double-click on one of the nodes, and press J
Convert a line to a curve	Double-click on the terminal node and press T
Smooth a node	Double-click on the node and press S
Make a node symmetrical	Double-click on the node and press Y
Crop a bitmap	Click on the bitmap with the pick tool, then click on the shape tool and move the handles

PRACTICE WHAT YOU'VE LEARNED

This exercise assumes that you have *CorelDRAW!* running and a new, blank page area is visible. If you already have something on the screen, save it and select New from the File menu.

WHAT YOU DO

1. Pull down the File menu, select Import. In the Import dialog box, select TIFF as the format. In the Import Bitmap dialog box, go to the SAMPLES directory under your CORELDRW directory and locate a file called OUT_HOUS.TIF. Double-click on this filename.

2. Trace the house and the moon (don't bother with the bats). When the house and moon are traced, make sure the bitmap is selected and press Del.

3. Use the zoom tool to zoom in on the point where the top of the moon encounters the parapet. Click on the outline tool. Click on the node that appears where the moon meets the para-pet. Double-click on the same node.

4. Click on Break to break the node (and line) in two. Use the mouse pointer to drag the nodes slightly apart (that makes it easier to see what you're doing). Repeat this procedure with the other node that joins the moon to the parapet (this moon has an inside and an outside line). Use the same procedure to separate the moon from the lower part of the house.

WHAT YOU'LL SEE

1. The haunted house graphic will be loaded into *CorelDRAW!* for tracing.

2. The bitmap will be deleted.

3. The Node Edit dialog box appears, with all its buttons.

4. The moon is completely separated from the house. But the lines that make it up are still combined with the house lines.

WHAT YOU DO

5. Click on the pick tool. Click on the inside line of the moon (the one that's closer to the house) and pull down the Arrange menu and select Break Apart. Do the same thing with the line that makes up the outer part of the moon.

6. Click on the outer moon line. Hold down the Shift key and click on the inner moon line. Press Del.

7. Click on the house outside of the place where the moon once joined it, then hold down the Shift key and click on the part of the house that once lay between the two ends of the inner moon line.

8. Pull down the Arrange menu and select Combine.

9. Click on the outline tool and drag a rectangle that encloses the end nodes of both parts of the house where the moon was joined to it lower down on the roof. Double-click on one of the two selected nodes. In the resulting dialog box, select Join. Repeat this procedure with the two nodes where the moon met the parapet.

WHAT YOU'LL SEE

5. The moon and the house are now four completely separate lines.

6. The moon disappears.

7. Both parts of the house are now selected.

8. The house is now all one piece. But it isn't a closed object yet.

9. The house is now a closed object that may be colored as you please.

WHAT YOU DO	**WHAT YOU'LL SEE**
10. Use the control handles of the resulting joined nodes to make the roofs smooth again (or as smooth as a haunted house can be).	10. The outline of the house is now smooth and complete.

Lines
and
Fills

This chapter covers all the options on the fill menu, one of the most interesting and involved menus in *CorelDRAW!*. You will learn about:

▲ **Full-color and two-color patterns**

▲ **Fountain fills**

▲ **PostScript patterns**

▲ **Pen points**

▲ **Brush colors**

▲ **Color and shape blends**

▲ **Mixing colors**

Full-Color and Two-Color Fills

CorelDRAW! has a wide array of fill options, and we will cover all of them in some depth in this chapter. The vector and raster fills are the simplest, so we'll talk about them first.

TIP

A fill pattern in a draw program behaves differently than a fill pattern in a paint program. The pattern in a draw program always maintains its orientation regardless of the transformation of the outline of the drawing, whereas the fill and outline of a painted object will both be affected by transformations.

Full-Color Fills

The easiest way to see how full-color fills work is to use one.

To create an ellipse and fill it with a full-color pattern:

1. Click on the ellipse tool and drag the mouse on the page area. Make your ellipse narrower than it is tall.
2. Click on the fill tool. You will see the fill tool menu shown in Figure 7.1.

Along the bottom of the fill tool menu is a seven-gray-scale palette, a holdover from old versions of *CorelDRAW!* that didn't display the onscreen palette. Each of the items along the top of the fill tool menu refers to types of fills or methods for creating or choosing fills, some of which call up special dialog boxes so that you can set values. Clicking on the first item, color wheel, gives you access to a special Color Mixing dialog box that gives you access to literally millions of colors for filling objects. The second item calls up a versatile fill tool roll-up—a sort of freestanding dialog box that makes using fills simpler. The third item, which looks like an X, removes all fill from the selected object. Look at the right end of the Status line in Figure 7.1 (your screen probably looks the same). Note the rectangle with the X through it. That indicates that

▼ *Figure 7.1. The Fill Tool Menu.*

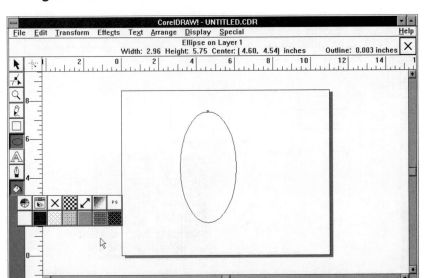

the selected object has no fill. A button with an X in it at the extreme left end of the onscreen color palette also removes all fill from the selected object onscreen.

The next item looks like a checkerboard. It's the two-color fill, which will be covered shortly. The item we'll discuss at this time is the full-color fill. It's the button with the two-headed arrow on it.

To use a full-color fill:

▲ Click on the fill tool menu item that has a two-headed arrow in it. This is the vector fill item. You will see the dialog box shown in Figure 7.2. Click on the example box to see the collection of available vector fills.

You have several different options from this dialog box. You can load a pattern by name by clicking on the button marked Load. A list of filenames will appear, each with the extension PAT. These are the patterns you can see in the figure, only identified by name instead of appearance. You can also click on the Import button to bring in a PCX drawing as a vector pattern. You can specify a large (1-inch), medium (½-inch), or small (¼-inch) tile. Click on the button marked Tiling to see the additional options shown in Figure 7.3.

Using these settings, you can specify a specific tile size, or create tiles that are not square. When you fill an object with tiles, the

▼ *Figure 7.2. The Full-Color Pattern Dialog Box.*

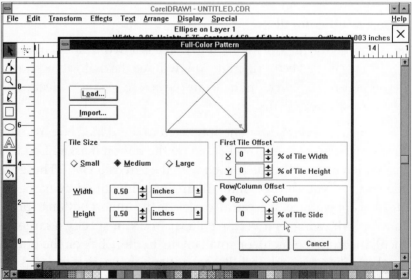

tiles start at the top left corner of the object. You can change this by altering the settings in the First Tile Offset and Row/Column Offset areas. If you click on Load and scroll to the item WEAVE2.PAT in

▼ *Figure 7.3. Additional Options for Full-Color Fills.*

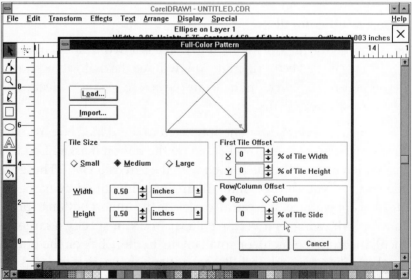

the list box and click on it and on OK in the Load Full-Color Pattern dialog box, the pattern will appear in the display box at the center of the Full-Color Pattern dialog box (top of Figure 7.4).

The patterns you see in the Full-Color Pattern dialog box are actually *CorelDRAW!* drawings. The only difference is that they have been given the extension PAT. Let's load a pattern and alter it. When we are through, we'll save the pattern as a new pattern.

To load a pattern into the page area:

1. Pull down the File menu. Select **Open**.
2. Make whatever adjustments are necessary to change directories to the directory containing your *CorelDRAW!* files.
3. In the File Name, type WEAVE2.PAT. Before you finish typing the name, the pattern you saw earlier in the Full-Color Pattern dialog box will appear in the example box.
4. Press **Enter** and the file will load, as shown in Figure 7.5.

This pattern is a grouped object, so to edit its elements, you will need to ungroup it.

5. If the pattern isn't selected, click on it.
6. Pull down the Arrange menu and select **Ungroup**.

▼ *Figure 7.4. The WEAVE2.PAT Pattern in the Dialog Box.*

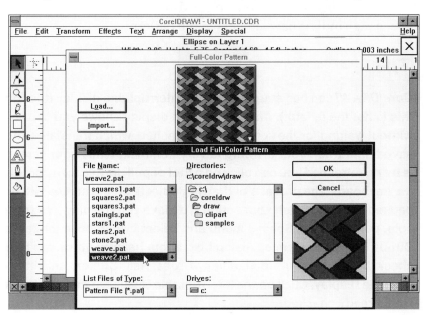

▼ *Figure 7.5. The Pattern Loaded into the Page Area.*

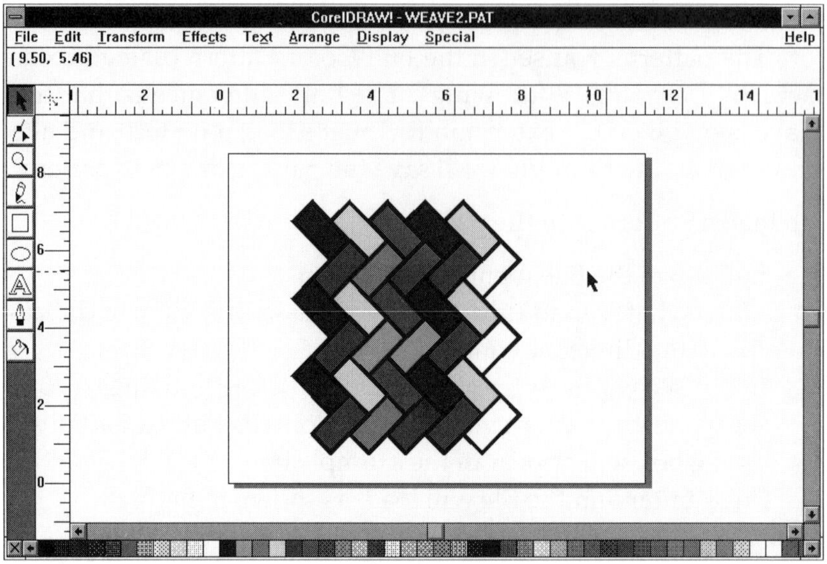

7. Make any changes you want in the individual elements of the pattern. For my pattern, I will simply change the fill of all the elements to white. If you want to do the same, you don't even need to ungroup the pattern, simply select it and click on the white color in the palette at the bottom of the *CorelDRAW!* screen (Figure 7.6). You do need to ungroup the pattern to change individual elements in the pattern.

TIP

CorelDRAW! can be set up to have an interruptable display (though this is not the default). An interruptable display allows you to draw without waiting for the screen to be refreshed, which translates into saved time when your drawing is very complex. While your screen is being refreshed you can click on a tool or pull down a menu or use the keyboard. The process of drawing objects on the screen will be paused until you finish your action. To make your display interruptable, pull down the Special menu and select Preferences (or press Ctrl-J). In the Preferences dialog box, about halfway down, are four check boxes titled Auto Panning, Cross Hair Cursor, and Interruptable Display. Click on the Interruptable Display, if the check box isn't already checked.

▼ *Figure 7.6. The Pattern, All Colored White.*

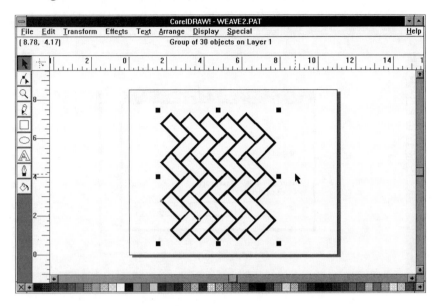

Now we need to save the pattern so it will be ours to use.

To save the pattern:

1. Click on the pick tool and drag a selection rectangle that includes the entire pattern. Pull down the Arrange menu and select **Group**.

2. Pull down the Special menu and select **Create Pattern**. You'll see the Create Pattern dialog box in Figure 7.7.

   You have the choice of saving the pattern as a two-color or a full-color pattern. If you save a two-color pattern, you can specify whether you want to save it as a low-, medium-, or high-resolution bitmap.

3. Click on the radio button marked **Full Color** and then click on **OK**. Your mouse pointer will turn into a crosshairs.

4. Drag a selection rectangle to include the part of the pattern you want to turn into a pattern used by *CorelDRAW!*. When you release the mouse button, you will see a small dialog box asking whether you want to create a pattern using the selected area. Click on **OK** if the selection rectangle contains the pattern you want to create.

5. The dialog box shown in Figure 7.8 will appear. Type the name of the new pattern in the **File:** text box.

▼ *Figure 7.7. The Create Pattern Dialog Box.*

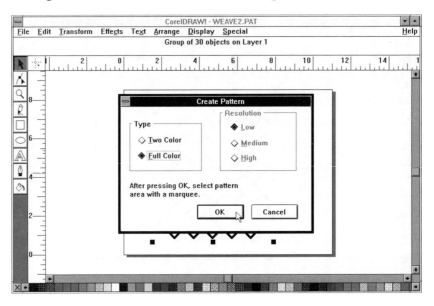

6. Click on **OK**.

All of the full-color fills discussed have been vector fills. You can also use raster full-color fills simply by selecting a color PCX file from the Full-Color Pattern dialog box.

▼ *Figure 7.8. The Save Full-Color Pattern Dialog Box.*

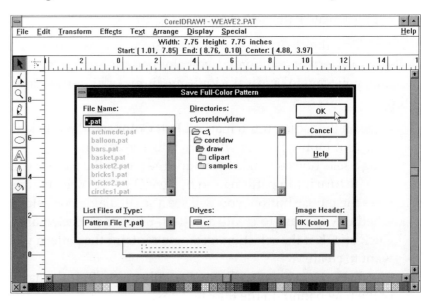

Two-Color Fills

Two-color fills can be as ornate and complex as full-color fills. They have the advantage of being easier to edit, and faster to print, and the disadvantage of coarser grain than the vector full-color fills.

To fill an object with a two-color fill.

1. If your page area isn't blank, select **New** from the file menu.
2. Draw an object to fill. I have drawn another oval, like the one that appears in Figure 7.1.
3. Click on the fill tool. Click on the checkerboard option on the fill tool menu. This is the two-color fill option. You will see the dialog box shown in Figure 7.9.

    This dialog box is significantly different from the dialog box you saw earlier. Click on the example box to see the patterns available.

4. Select a pattern by clicking on it. If you don't like any of the patterns shown, click on the arrow at the bottom of the scroll bar at the right end of the displayed patterns to scroll downward through the available patterns.

▼ *Figure 7.9. Two-Color Pattern Dialog Box.*

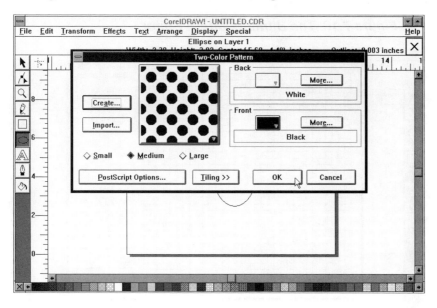

Several patterns are available, and a number of slots are unoccupied so that you can create and save your own pattern. Let's create our own pattern. If you read the section on full-color patterns, you saw that it was possible to create a pattern by saving it. You can also load any PCX or TIF file as a pattern. But there is another way, and I think it's more fun.

1. Click on **Create...** in the Two-Color Pattern dialog box. You will see the dialog box shown in Figure 7.10. It fills nearly the entire screen.
2. Click with the left mouse button on any square you want black (foreground color) and click with the right mouse button on any square you want to change from black to white (background color).

You can create a pattern as fine as 64 dots by 64 dots. The pen size setting can save you a lot of time by allowing you to fill an area quickly with a large (8x8) pen.

3. Click on **OK** when you are through.

To place the pattern in our object:

1. Click on the example box to see the palette of patterns available. Scroll to the end, where you will find the pattern you just created.

▼ **Figure 7.10. The Bitmap Pattern Editor.**

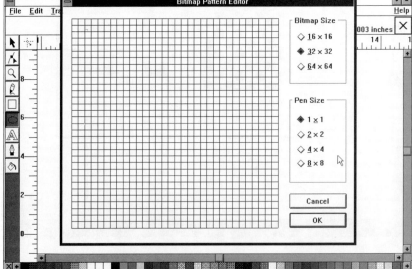

Whether you create a bitmap pattern or select one of the existing patterns or load a TIF or PCX graphic as a pattern, the next step is to select the foreground and background colors of the pattern.

2. Click on the **Back** example box (the box with the downward-pointing arrow in the lower right corner) to see a palette of colors. This is shown in Figure 7.11.
3. Use this box to change the color of the background (the areas that appeared in white in the Bitmap Pattern dialog box). Use the Front example box to see the color palette available for the foreground (the black areas in the Bitmap Pattern dialog box).
4. If you don't like any of the colors, click on the buttons marked **More...** to see a Color Mixing dialog box (Figure 7.12).

We'll discuss this dialog box in detail later on. Though simple to use, the range of options in the dialog box is so large that it deserves its own section. We will get into the differences between spot and process colors later in the chapter.

5. Click on **OK**.

When you return to the Two-Color Pattern dialog box and click on the button marked PostScript Options, you will see the

▼ **Figure 7.11. The Background Color Palette (Also Note Created Pattern in the Two-Color Pattern Dialog Box).**

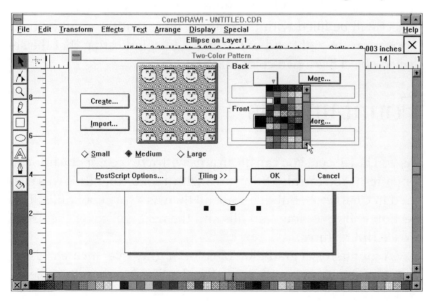

▼ *Figure 7.12. The Color Mixing Dialog Box.*

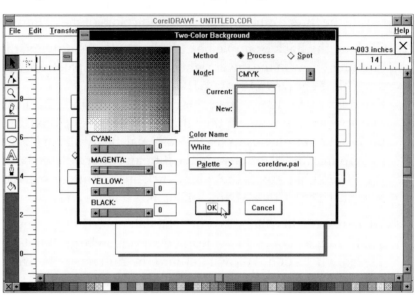

PostScript Options dialog box. This dialog box will be covered in detail later in the chapter, but it's important enough to take a glance at it now. Using this box, you can adjust how shades of gray are shown in the printout. The default is to use a dithering pattern. You can change this to dots, lines, or one of several different schemes. If you click on OK to escape the PostScript Controls dialog box and click on OK in the Bitmap Pattern Color dialog box, the object will be filled with the pattern. Note that the checkerboard appears at the right end of the status line, indicating that the selected object has a two-color fill.

Fountain Fills

As you have seen, you can fill an area with a two-color or a full-color pattern. You can also fill an area with a solid color (this was covered in Chapter 2). But that's not all there is to say about fills. This section will cover fountain fills and the next will cover the use of PostScript textures.

A fountain is a gradation of color or gray over an area. Using fountains, you can approximate the shading of a rounded object.

Let's try to make a circle look like a sphere. To see this function in action, begin by drawing a circle on the screen:

1. Clear the screen. Select **New** from the File menu.
2. Click on the ellipse tool in the toolbox at the left of the *CorelDRAW!* screen.
3. Place your mouse pointer in the drawing area. Press the left mouse button and hold it down while dragging the mouse diagonally. A circle will appear on the screen and will follow your pointer. (To create a true circle, rather than an ellipse, hold down the **Ctrl** key.) When the circle is large enough to suit you, release the mouse button and the circle will become solid. A single node will be visible at the top of the circle, indicating the the circle is currently selected. (This is visible in Figure 7.1).
4. Click on the fill icon at the bottom of the toolbox.
5. Click on the item next to the end of the menu. This is the fountain fill item. You will see the dialog box shown in Figure 7.13.

Here you have a broad range of options. The default option is to use a linear gradation between white and black at a 90-degree angle.

6. Click on **OK** to select the default gradient.

▼ *Figure 7.13. The Fountain Fill Dialog Box.*

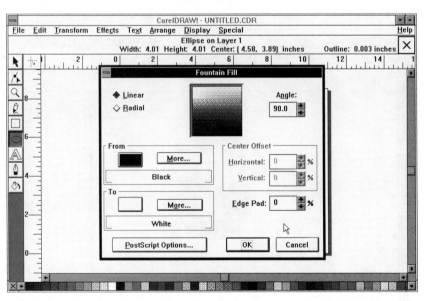

7. When you return to the main CorelDRAW! screen you will see the screen shown in Figure 7.14.

This sort of gradient would be fine for many purposes, but it doesn't make the circle look much like a sphere. If you return to the Fountain Fill dialog box, select the Radial fill option at the top of the dialog box, and click on OK, you will see the graphic in Figure 7.15.

Clearly it is closer to what we want. The highlight needs to be moved off center, to a top-right or top-left area, to make the shading look more realistic.

To draw the highlighting away from the center of the circle:

1. Return to the Fountain Fill dialog box.
2. In the **Center Offset** area, change the **Horizontal** setting to -20 and the **Vertical** setting to 20.
3. In the **Edge Pad** text box, change the value to 20. This will cause the black color to fill most of the object, as it would on a black ball with a highlight. The result is shown in Figure 7.16.

Let's talk a little about edge padding. Sometimes irregular objects have very large selection boxes, which causes much of the fountain fill to be distant from the actual object—which is to say

▼ *Figure 7.14. The 90-degree Linear Fountain from Black to White.*

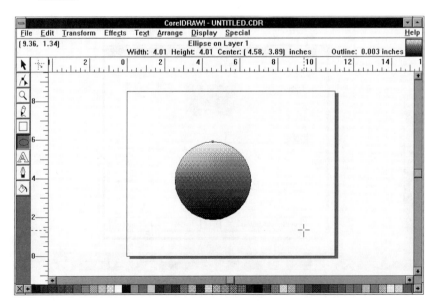

▼ *Figure 7.15. Closer to a Sphere.*

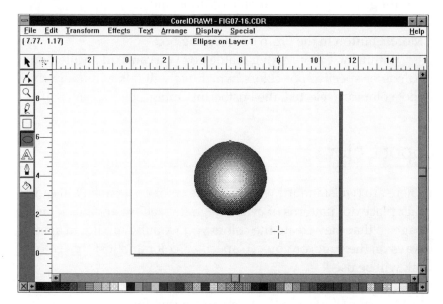

that it's invisible. By padding the edge, you can narrow the part of the selection rectangle that contains the actual fountain.

You can change your From and To colors by clicking on the rectangles in the From and To areas in the Fountain Fill dialog box.

▼ *Figure 7.16. The Offset, Padded Fountain Fill.*

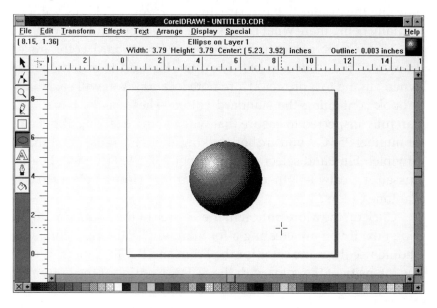

This will display a palette, from which you can choose a color by scrolling through the available options and clicking on the color you want to use. If you want to mix a custom color, click on the More... button in the From or To dialog box.

Within the Color Mixing dialog box you can load an alternative palette or specify spot colors, which we will talk about shortly. If spot colors are selected, the PostScript Options become available.

Spot Color

There are two standard ways to place color on a page. You can either place dot patterns of cyan, magenta, yellow, and black on the page so that they create the colors you want by mixing in specific ways on the page, or you can specify a color and just that color of ink will be used.

Call up the Fountain Fill dialog box and click on the From color More box (the box in the From area with More written in it). You will see a palette. If you haven't changed the default, you will be working with process colors (this will be the button selected at the top of the dialog box). Click on Spot and see how the spot colors are selected.

Click on a color. You will see that it is named. All of the spot colors are named so that you can specify a color on your end of the line and the printer will prepare this color; you will know without actually being there what color she or he will be printing with.

These color names represent specific standard color mixes known as the *Pantone colors*. They can be used to specify colors when talking to a printer at a remote location. You will each have a book containing the standard colors. These books have been carefully inspected to ensure that when you are talking about color number 257 CV, you are both talking about the same exact shade of violet. Find and select color number 257 CV. (This will be discussed at greater length under the headline "How and Why to Use Pantone Colors.")

Click on the More button in the To area of the Fountain Fill dialog box. If you are creating a fountain with Pantone colors, you should use the same color for the From and the To colors but vary the intensity of the color with the % TINT setting at the bottom of the dialog box. In the To spot color dialog box, set the % TINT to 0%, which is the same as white, though technically we are still printing 257 CV, no ink will actually be laid down.

You can specify the method used to display gradients if you are using spot color. The button is at the bottom of the Fountain Fill dialog box, marked PostScript Options. Click on this button and you will be taken to the PostScript Options dialog box (Figure 7.17).

Using the settings in this box, you can take complete control over how fine the dots or lines (or other screen) are that make up the fountain. Take a look at Figure 7.18.

Clockwise from the upper left circle, the circles are shaded with the Dot, Line, Diamond, and Dot2 screens. (In addition to these screens, you can select patterns known as Grid, Lines, Microwaves, Outcircleblk, Outcirclewhi, and Stars.)

TIP

If you intend to use color separations (if this term is unfamiliar to you, review Chapter 3) and you are working with spot colors, you should limit your fountains. They should only be between two tints of a single Pantone color.

▼ *Figure 7.17. The PostScript Controls Dialog Box.*

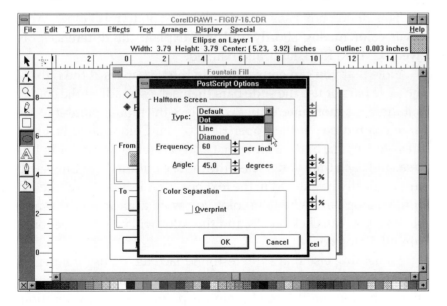

▼ *Figure 7.18. Four Fountain-Filled Circles.*

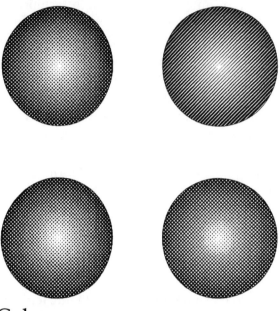

Process Color

If you want to mix your own colors, click on the radio button marked Process and then click on the button marked Other underneath the existing palette colors. You will see the dialog box shown in Figure 7.19.

This dialog box has several ways for you to mix colors. We'll cover color mixing shortly and will explain the differences between CMYK, RGB, HSB, and Named.

Note that you can enter values in the text boxes at the right of the slide bars or use the slide bars themselves to adjust the colors. But there is a more interesting way. Place the mouse pointer in the large colored box at the upper right of the Color dialog box and press the mouse button. Note that you can select any color in this area, and each time you release the mouse button the settings will automatically be entered in the text boxes and slide bars at the left of the dialog box. When the color you want appears in the example box, you can click on OK and the color will be set in the fountain fill dialog box.

Something else that's interesting: Place the mouse pointer on the tall, narrow box at the right of the color mixing box, press the mouse button, and drag the mouse pointer to a new location.

▼ *Figure 7.19. The Color Dialog Box.*

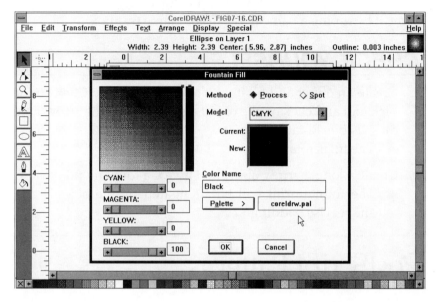

When you release the button, the colors in the large box will be changed. This bar adds a third dimension to the color mixing box.

Pull down the Model list box by clicking on the downward-pointing arrow at the right end. Click on RGB. The dialog box doesn't change much. The Cyan, Magenta, Yellow, and Black slide bars are replaced by Red, Green, and Blue slide bars. Its action is very similar to the CMYK box.

Use the Model list box to select the HSB option. You will see a color wheel on the screen. With this box you adjust the Hue, Saturation, and Brightness to specify a color—a slightly more abstract and less useful way to set colors.

The Palette model gives you access to the color palette currently selected, called CORELDRW.PAL. If you want to add a newly mixed color to the current palette, click on the Palette button and select Add Color to Palette.

If you want to change palettes, click on the Palette button and select Load New Palette. If you add enough new colors to a palette, you'll probably want to save that palette as a new palette so you can call it up to see your custom colors. In that case, click on Palette and select Save Palette As.

Finally, click on Model and select Named. You will be provided with a list box containing the names of dozens of colors available to you. As you click on the names, the color appears in a box at center bottom. When you mix a color that you like, you can name it by typing a name in the Color Name text box.

CHECK YOURSELF

1. Create an object and fill it with a linear fountain. Click on the pick tool and click on the object again to make the arrow handles visible. Rotate the object.
   - ▲ The fill is rotated, too.

2. Create a long, narrow object and give it a fountain fill.
   - ▲ The fountain fill will be attenuated by the object's odd shape. Use padding.

PostScript Patterns

The authors of *CorelDRAW!* provided an added option to users with PostScript printers. *CorelDRAW!* features a series of fills that can only be used in PostScript output (whether from a laser printer or a typesetter). These fill patterns include many eye-catching and beautiful options ranging from the simple geometrical patterns like Triangle, StarOfDavid, and StarShapes to the sinuous Spirals, Spokes, and DNA to the enigmatic Grass, Leaves, and Honeycomb.

In all, 49 different designs are available, each of which can be adjusted almost infinitely. Four favorites can be seen in their default states in Figure 7.20.

To use PostScript fills:

1. Create or select an object you want to fill. Its handles will appear at the four corners and sides.
2. Click on the fill tool. The fill tool menu will appear.
3. Click on the last item on the right end: the letters PS (which stand for PostScript). You will see the dialog box shown in Figure 7.21.

Reptiles was selected for the purposes of this figure. If you wanted to change the pattern, you could scroll through the options in the **Name:** list box and click on some other texture. Note that

▼ *Figure 7.20. Four Favorite PostScript Fill Patterns with
Default Settings: Grass, Honeycomb, Impact, and Reptiles.*

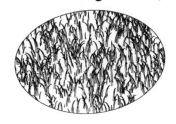

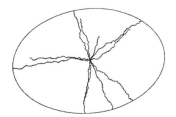

you can alter certain aspects of the drawing. You will see many different options as you click on different patterns. In the case of

▼ *Figure 7.21. The PostScript Texture Dialog Box with
Reptiles Selected.*

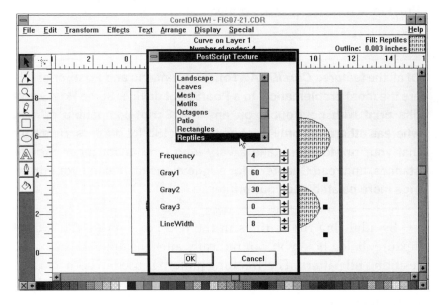

Reptiles, the options are Frequency, Gray1, Gray2, Gray3, and LineWidth. Let's change the pattern to TreeRings, another option.

4. Place the mouse pointer on the lower arrow of the scroll bar of the text box and click until TreeRings is visible.
5. Click on the word **TreeRings**. You will see the specifications in the PostScript Texture dialog change to MaxDistance, MinDistance, LineWidth, BackgroundGray, and RandomSeed.

These options determine the distribution of rings in the fill (MinDistance and MaxDistance), the width of the lines (Line-Width), the level of gray in the background (BackgroundGray, where 0 represents white and 100 represents black), and Random-Seed. RandomSeed affects the series of random numbers generated to create the fill. If you use the same random seed, you will always generate the same series of random numbers. That sounds self-contradictory, but it's true.

6. Adjust the values in the boxes either by dragging through them and typing new values or by clicking on the arrows at the right to increase or decrease the value.
7. Click on **OK**.

When you click on OK, the new fill will be applied. You won't be able to see it either on the normal *CorelDRAW!* screen or the Preview screen. It will only appear on the PostScript printout.

TIP

Of all the features *CorelDRAW!* offers, fountains and PostScript fills are the most problematical to a PostScript device. Some PostScript fills print with no trouble on any PostScript-compatible printer, whereas others will only print on true PostScript printers. Be aware that your printout will take a very long time under most circumstances, and read Chapter 3 for suggestions on making your drawings more palatable to your printer.

By adjusting the settings in the text boxes in the PostScript Texture dialog box, you can radically alter the appearance of the resulting fill pattern. The TreeRing pattern is used in both text sets in the lower part of Figure 7.22, but different values were specified in the dialog box.

▼ *Figure 7.22. Two Versions of TreeRings: Default (Right) and Changed (Left).*

Post Script Patterns

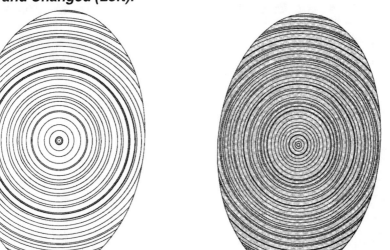

Pen Points

Like Rapidograph, *CorelDRAW!* provides a number of pen widths for your use, but unlike Rapidograph, Corel Systems doesn't charge extra for the points. They come free with the basic package.

A range of pen points is important because you will use them for a range of applications. If all you want to do is pick a thicker point, selecting pen points is as simple as selecting a fill. If you click on the outline tool (the pen nib) in the toolbox, the pen point menu opens (Figure 7.23).

The top part of the menu is pen thicknesses; the options are outline pen (which calls up a dialog box we'll discuss in a moment), outline pen roll-up, none (X), hairline (the default), and four additional thicknesses, each slightly thicker than the last. In the lower half of the menu, you are given the brush options, which are simply shades of gray for the pen. The options from left to right are color mixing, white, black, and then five shades of gray from light to dark, each slightly darker than its neighbor to the left.

▼ *Figure 7.23. The Outline Tool Menu.*

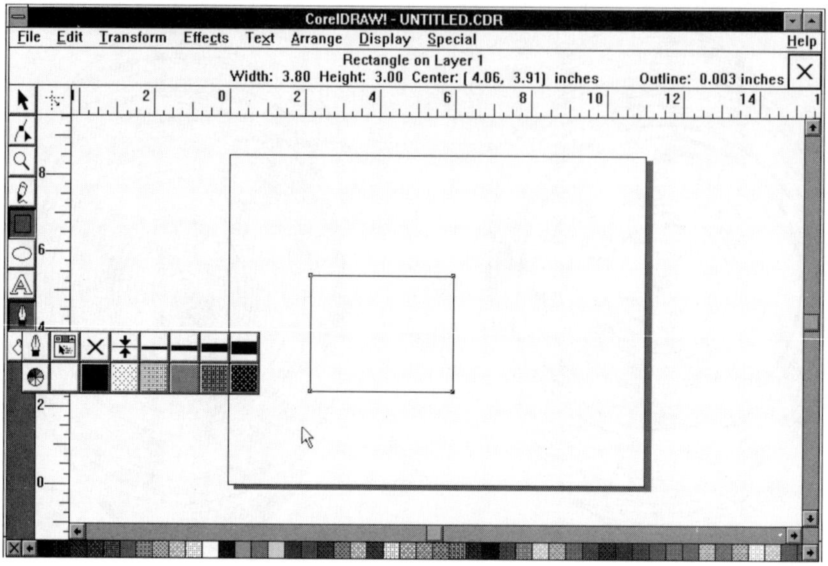

But that isn't all there is to a pen point, and shades of gray aren't the only colors available. To take the next step, you will need to have something drawn on the screen:

1. Select the pencil tool and draw a squiggle, or write a name.
2. Click on the pen nib in the toolbox. The pen point menu will open. Click on the pen nib in the menu. You will see the dialog box shown in Figure 7.24.

The contents of this dialog box are all related to the appearance of the pen. Starting from the top:

▲ **Color.** Calls up a palette of colors. More calls up the familiar Color Mixing dialog box with settings for spot and process colors as well as PostScript Options.
▲ **Width.** The width of the pen line. Using the measurement option, you can specify the pen width in any of four commonly used measures.
▲ **Corners.** You have three options, well illustrated, for cusps and corners on your drawings: pointed, rounded, and beveled.
▲ **Line Caps.** This refers to the ends of lines. The caps are square-at-end, round, and square-beyond-end.

▼ *Figure 7.24. The Outline Pen Dialog Box.*

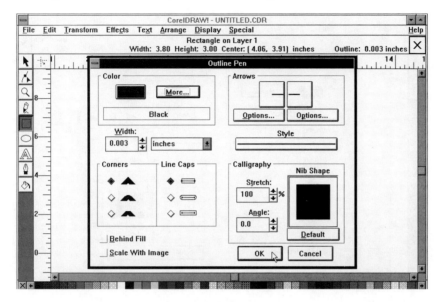

▲ **Behind Fill.** You can opt to have the line Behind Fill, which means that the pattern that makes up the inside of a closed object will cover half of the pen line. If you are drawing a thick line that occasionally loops very close to itself, this might be your best choice to prevent parts of the shape from looking as if they were pinched off.

▲ **Scale With Image.** Not so much when you are drawing but frequently when you are composing (putting drawings together into a page), you may find yourself continually changing the size of images. If you don't select Scale With Image, the lines will remain at the thickness you have set for them, possibly resulting in grossly thick lines on tiny images or very thin lines on larger images. This setting allows you to retain a proportional relationship between the thickness of the line and the size of the object.

▲ **Arrows.** When you click on the Arrows button, you'll see the dialog box shown in Figure 7.25.

The selection of arrowheads is quite extensive. To place an arrowhead at the start of the line, click on the left Arrows box. To place an arrowhead on the terminal end of the line, click the

▼ *Figure 7.25. The Arrowhead Dialog Box.*

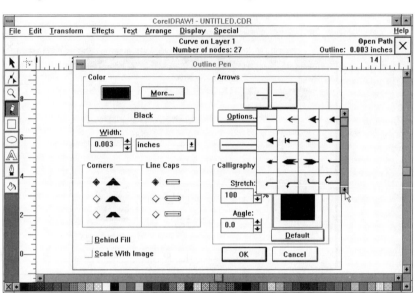

right Arrows box. Of course, not all the selections are actually arrowheads. Some are circles, squares, and the feather-end of the arrow. To see the complete selection, use the scroll bar at the right end of the selection box.

▲ **Style.** The pen type represents the kind of line drawn by the pen. You can opt to have no line (None), a solid line, a dashed line, or a dotted line. (Click on the line under Style to call up a list box filled with line styles.)

▲ **Calligraphy.** Most of this section of the box is related to calligraphy. Briefly, you can custom set the width of the pen or adjust the shape of the pen. Angle refers to degrees from the vertical and Stretch refers to the proportion between height and width. Try adjusting these. A stretch of 150 is very wide and a stretch of 50 is narrow. By adjusting the stretch to some value remote from 100 percent and clicking on the up and down arrow next to the Angle text box, you can see the pen nib rotate in the Nib Shape box at right. To return to the default pen shape and angle, click on the button marked Reset.

One of the interesting things you can do with pens is superimpose one line on another, which we will do now.

To superimpose lines:

1. Adjust the pen width to .5 inches by double-clicking in the Width text box and typing .5.
2. Click on **OK** and you will return to the *CorelDRAW!* screen. The current line is shown in Figure 7.26.
3. Duplicate the line. With the line selected, pull down the Edit menu and select **Duplicate**. A second image of the line will appear on the screen.
4. Click on the pick tool (the top tool in the toolbox) and drag a selection rectangle that includes both lines. Then pull down the Arrange menu and select **Align**. Select center vertically and center horizontally and click on **OK**.
5. Click away from the lines to deselect them, then click on the line again, which should select the line that is on top.

TIP

Once you have selected the top object in a pile of objects, you can select objects lower down by pressing the Tab key.

▼ *Figure 7.26. The .5-inch Line.*

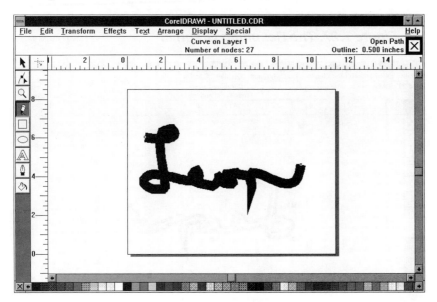

6. Click on the outline tool in the toolbox and click on the white box in the lower half of the menu to change the current line to white. If the lines aren't perfectly aligned (which isn't crucial for this project), you may see an interesting three-dimensional representation of your line.

7. Once again click on the outline tool in the toolbox. This time click on the pen nib in the menu that appears. In the resulting Outline Pen dialog box, adjust the pen width to about .1 inch either by clicking on the downward-pointing arrow next to the Width text box until the value 0.10 appears in the box or by dragging the mouse pointer through the box and typing .1 as the pen width. If you are in a mood to experiment, adjust the stretch and angle of the pen. Click on **OK**. You will see the preview shown in Figure 7.27.

CHECK YOURSELF

1. Fill an object with a PostScript pattern. Print it on a PCL printer.
   ▲ The object will have no fill at all. These patterns will only print on PostScript printers.

▼ *Figure 7.27. The Resulting Graphic.*

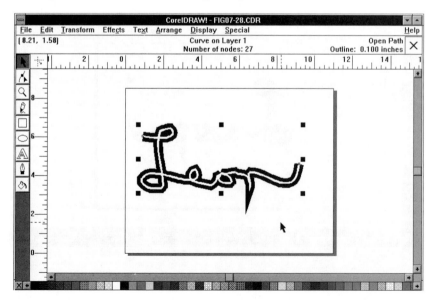

2. Draw a line on the screen and click on the outline tool in the toolbox. Click on the pen point; in the dialog box that appears, click on Arrows. Place an arrowhead on both ends of the line.

▲ Select the arrowhead for the origin of the line with the left arrowhead button and the arrowhead for the end of the line with the right arrowhead button.

Putting Fills to Work

Let's create a bowl of fruit. We'll use a variety of fills and line styles and create a pear and an orange.

1. Clear the screen by selecting **New**. Create a circle by selecting the ellipse tool on the toolbox and holding down the **Ctrl** key while dragging.
2. Give the circle a .25-inch thick line and select **Behind Fill** and **Scale With Image**.
3. Fill the circle with a **Radial** fill. Select **Spot** color. Click on the same orange color for both the From and To selections. Make the From selection 100 percent and the To selection 50 percent tint.
4. Adjust the horizontal offset to -20, the vertical offset to 20, and the Edge Pad to 20. The result can be seen in Figure 7.28.

▼ *Figure 7.28. The Orange for Our Still Life.*

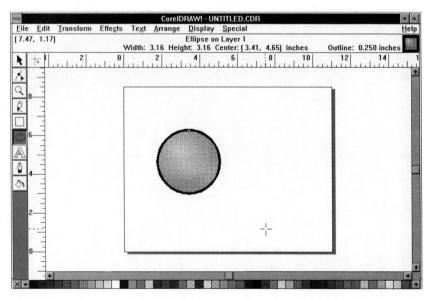

5. Create another ellipse. This time it doesn't matter whether it is perfectly circular.

6. Change it into a free-form object by pulling down the Arrange menu and selecting **Convert to Curves**. At this point, your ellipse should have four nodes.

7. Use the node-editing skills you gained in Chapter 2 to alter the ellipse into a pear shape (see the next few steps).

8. Click on the shape tool (second from the top in the toolbox). Click on the node at the left side of the ellipse. You will see the control points.

9. Drag the top control point of the left node slightly to the right.

10. Perform a similar action on the node at the right of the ellipse, dragging the top control point slightly to the left. The pearlike shape can be seen in Figure 7.29.

11. Use the pen point tools to give this drawing a .33-inch thick line. Once again, select **Scale With Image** and **Behind Fill**. Call up the Fountain Fill dialog box and select **Spot** color and **Radial** and select the same greenish tint for both palettes. Enter 100 percent for the From % TINT box and 0 percent for the To % TINT box. Because of the odd shape of the pear, there is no need to take special pains to move the highlight off center; however, elevate it slightly by selecting a vertical offset of 30. The pear can be seen in Figure 7.30.

▼ *Figure 7.29. The Pear Shape.*

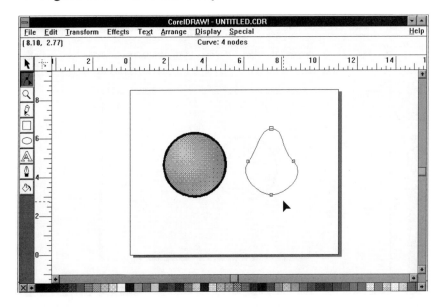

▼ *Figure 7.30. The Orange and the Finished Pear.*

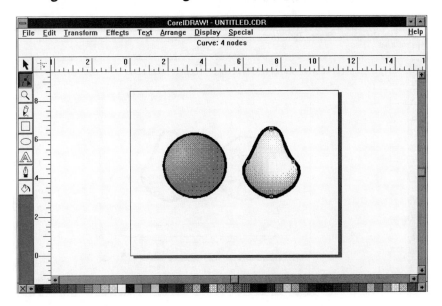

12. Finally, we will create a bowl to contain this fruit. Draw a very wide ellipse.

13. Duplicate the ellipse and position the duplicate on top of the original. Select just the new ellipse by clicking away from both of them, then clicking on them again. The top ellipse should be selected.

14. Pull down the Arrange menu and select **Convert to Curves**. Click on the node-editing tool (second from the top in the toolbox).

15. Double-click on the node at the left side of the new ellipse. This is advanced node editing, which was covered in Chapter 6. You will see the Node Edit menu. Click on **Cusp**.

16. Move the top control handle of the left node until it lies at about a 45-degree angle to the right of the bottom control handle.

17. Perform a similar adjustment on the node at the right side of the bowl. Then drag the top node downward so that it is a short distance from the bottom node. This will create the shape of a wide, shallow bowl (Figure 7.31).

18. Click on the pick tool and drag a selection rectangle around both parts of the bowl so that they'll both be selected.

▼ *Figure 7.31. The Bowl.*

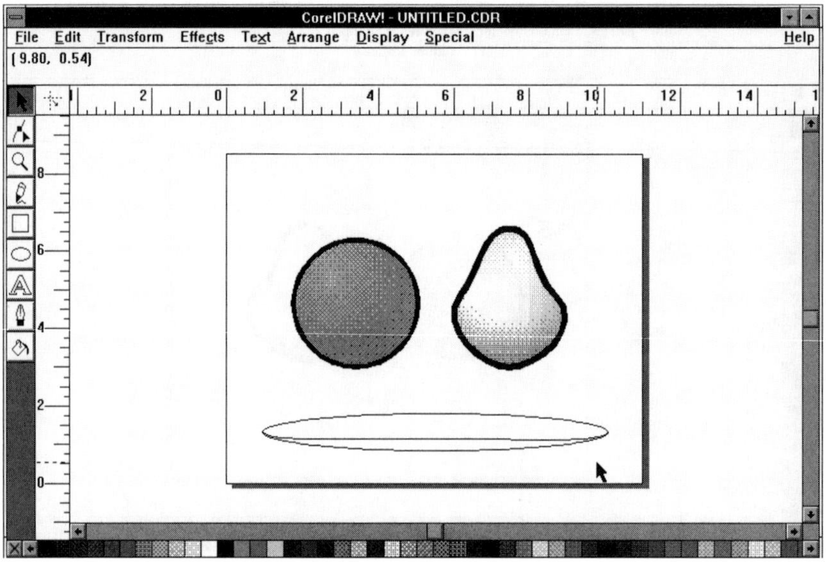

19. Call up the Outline Tool dialog box and make the line .1 inch thick and click on **Behind Fill** and **Scale With Image**.

To make the bowl terra-cotta:

1. Use the Fountain Fill dialog box to give the outside of the bowl (the part we adjusted) a 180-degree linear fill. Select a brownish Pantone color for both palettes. Make the From % TINT 100 percent and the To % TINT 50 percent.
2. Use the **Duplicate** command on the Edit menu to create several fruits of different sizes. Double-click on a couple of the pears and drag a corner handle to tip the pears slightly. Arrange the fruits in the bowl. What happened? Because we drew the fruits first, they have a lower precedence than the bowl, so they appear to be behind the bowl. It's all right for the front of the bowl to be in front of the fruit, but the back of the bowl (or the interior) should appear behind it. Here's how to solve the problem.
3. Click on the original ellipse you drew to make the fruit bowl. Pull down the Arrange menu and select **To Back**. This will automatically give the bowl's interior the lowest precedence in the drawing, so all the fruit and the front of the bowl will appear in front of it, which is what you want.

4. Pull down the File menu and save your work. As an added challenge, you might want to create a few bananas and grapes to balance the creation, as well as stems for the pears.

Putting Fills to Work

The completed still life study can be seen in Figure 7.32. The drawing is dark because the colors can only be represented as gray in black-and-white printouts.

Brush Color

As mentioned in the section on pen points, you can change more than just the shape and thickness of the pen point. You can also adjust the color. The color adjustments will be familiar to you if you have read the section on fountain fills or the section in Chapter 2 on solid fills. In fact, virtually the same dialog box is used.

TIP

You can establish a new default pen thickness or color or a new default fill simply by making sure that nothing is selected before click-

▼ *Figure 7.32. The Still Life Study.*

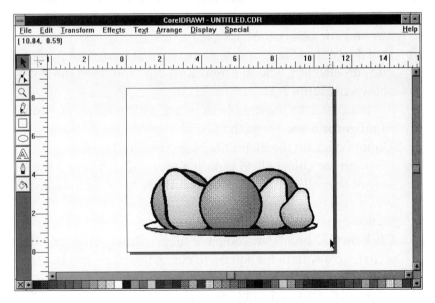

ing on the outline or fill tool in the toolbox. You will be shown a dialog box asking you to confirm the kind of default you are establishing. Then, when you have chosen the pen thickness or color or fill, each object drawn thereafter will have that attribute.

Color will be covered in full in the upcoming sections "Mixing Colors" and "How and Why to Use Pantone Colors." If you would prefer to select colors from a palette rather than mix the colors, click on the button marked Palette.

The PostScript button calls up the PostScript Controls dialog box. By providing an object with different PostScript halftone for the interior and the outline, you can create some very striking drawings.

Color and Shape Blends

One of the most exciting aspects of the new *CorelDRAW!* is its ability to create blends. The best way to explain a blend is to create one.

To create a blend:

1. Create two shapes on the *CorelDRAW!* page area: a circle and a square.
2. Click on the pick tool and drag a selection rectangle that contains both shapes (alternately, you could hold down the **Shift** key and click on both shapes).
3. Pull down the Effects menu—a real treasure trove of powerful and fun effects. Click on **Blend Roll-Up**. You'll see the roll-up shown in Figure 7.33.

   It's easier to see the blend in action if you select a lower number for Blend Steps than 20.
4. Double-click on the Blend **Steps** text box and type 4.
5. Click on the color wheel button about halfway down the left side of the roll up and click on **Rainbow** to select it. Note that when you do so, you can select a rainbow going in either direction around the color wheel.
6. Click on **OK**. Note that you have shapes slowly changing from a circle to a square (or square to circle, if you prefer) but there is no change in color. That's because we didn't put color or any other sort of fill in the objects to begin with.

▼ *Figure 7.33. The Blend Roll-Up.*

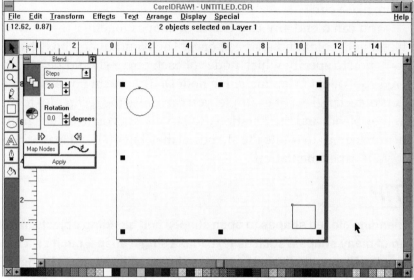

7. Click on the circle and color it red with the onscreen palette. Click on the square and color it blue with the onscreen palette. You'll get something like what is shown in Figure 7.34.

▼ *Figure 7.34. The Square Blended into a Circle.*

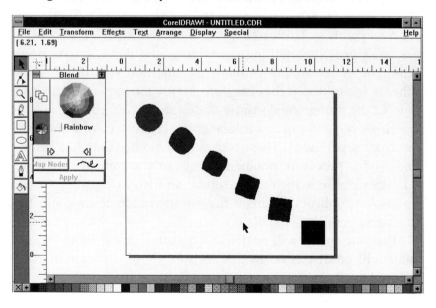

Note how each of the four intermediate shapes moving from the square to the circle is slightly less like a square and slightly more like a circle.

You can blend any two colors or shapes together this way, or blend both color and shape at once. The Blend dialog box also allows you to specify which nodes of each object should be considered equivalent (Map matching nodes). By selecting opposite corners of rectangles, for example, you can cause the rectangles to flip as they blend, and the Rotation text box allows you to enter a number of degrees to rotate the shapes as they blend. I will leave these to your experimentation.

TIP

Blending closed shapes to open shapes and blending objects made up of many shapes, such as text, into a single shape, such as a rectangle, will result in some or all of the intermediate shapes being left open. This can result in some interesting effects.

Mixing Colors

Most people won't use color in their printouts. There is a very limited amount of rather expensive technology available at this time for color printing. The least expensive ink-jet and dot-matrix printers don't provide anything resembling commercial-grade printouts. The better-quality printers, like thermal wax printers and other new desktop technology, are simply too expensive for anyone but the professional printer or designer to afford.

However, you can mix colors (or use Pantone colors) and print out color separations. These separations can be taken to a printer and used as proofs for photoengraving, or you can "print to disk" a PostScript file, which a typesetter can turn into real separated proofs for publication. This is the real intent for desktop illustration packages like *CorelDRAW!*.

Pantone colors will be discussed in the next section. Process color will be discussed in this section. Color separations were covered in Chapter 3.

Process colors are a bit of a risk. If you are creating something professionally, you would be wiser to stick with the Pantone colors, because it's difficult to estimate the real printed color from the color that appears on the screen. If you have ever read a review of computer monitors that shows the displays of several monitors on the same page, you have probably been struck by the wide variation in the appearance of the screens. Some seem to have a green cast, some blue. Even manufacturers of so-called paper-white monitors seem to take this seemingly absolute standard liberally. However, if you want complete control of your printout, you will want to use process color. There are hundreds of spot colors in the standard—enough for most applications—but there are millions of process colors.

Mixing Colors

The process color universe has four primary colors: Cyan, Magenta, Yellow, and Black. The Color Mixing dialog boxes of *CorelDRAW!* provide a potential of 104,060,401 different colors: percentages of saturation from 0 to 100 of the four primaries. Naturally, the difference between two colors one percentage apart is invisible to the human eye and could not be displayed on even the best personal computer monitor, though this is approximated by dithering, which ends up close to the color, but will never match it exactly. (Actually, the number of potential colors is even higher than 104 million because the text boxes allow you to enter decimal values.)

You will want to mix your own colors, so we won't provide a long list of percentages to achieve colors here. However, it might be useful for you to know the following color mixtures:

Blue = 100% Magenta + 100% Cyan
Green = 100% Cyan + 100% Yellow
Red = 100% Magenta + 100% Yellow
Black = 100% Black + anything
Black = 100% Magenta + 100% Cyan + 100% Yellow
Gray = equal proportions Cyan, Magenta, and Yellow

How and Why to Use Pantone Colors

Colors appear in ranges, some of which will complement other colors, and some of which will not. If you specify red and blue and the printout comes back reddish orange and a blue bordering on chartreuse, you will probably be disappointed in the appearance of the product.

With the emergence of color as an important medium of design and communication, the printing industry needed a standard that could be used to communicate color information exactly from one place (usually the publisher or design house) to another (the printer) so that unpleasant surprises wouldn't happen.

There are a trade-offs, though, for the power of spot color: You can only use a few colors; you can't create fountains from one spot color to another, if you are planning to do color separation; and spot colors are anything but flexible. Therefore, the decision to use spot colors should be based on the number of colors in the art (you can use multiple tints of the same Pantone color without penalty, however), the importance that the colors be exact, and whether there are fountains in the artwork.

Roll-Ups

Both the outline tool and the fill tool menu feature special roll-ups for you to use. These roll-ups are like complex dialog boxes that remain on the screen as long as you need them (Figure 7.35).

The Pen Roll-Up

Click on the up and down arrows at the right of the top section of the pen to select a width of pen from invisible and hairline to very thick.

The line ends beneath the first section are used for assigning arrowheads. Click on the right line end to provide a line end for the line terminus and click on the left line end to provide a line end for the origin of a line.

The solid bar beneath the line ends section allows you to select a line style (solid or broken). The thick colored bar is your access to a color palette for the line.

Click on Update From to pick up a style and color from another object. Click on this part of the roll-up and click on the object you want to copy the line style from. The roll-up will take on the at-

▼ *Figure 7.35. The Pen (bottom) and Fill (top) Roll-Ups.*

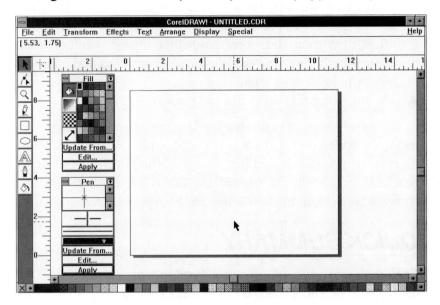

tribute you selected. All you have to do to assign these to the currently selected object is to click on the Apply button.

Clicking on the Edit button gives you access to the Outline Pen dialog box. None of the changes you set in the roll-up will take effect until you click on the Apply button.

The Fill Roll-Up

The Fill-roll up (which appears on top in Figure 7.35) offers four buttons down the left side of the roll-up:

▲ The fill color with palette (shown).

▲ The fountain fill with buttons to select radial or linear fill and From and To colors. By clicking in the example box, you can set the direction of the fountain. A line will appear between the center and the location of the mouse pointer, which will determine the direction of the linear fill.

▲ The two-color fill. Clicking on the example box gives you access to all available two-color fills. By clicking on the color boxes, you can select or create colors for the foreground (normally black) and the background (normally white). Clicking on Tile makes two tiles appear on the object to be filled. One tile is fixed in place, but you can drag the other off center to create an offset, or you can drag a rectangle that appears where the tiles come together to drag the tiles large or small to make the pattern appear large or small.

▲ The full-color fill works like the two-color fill.

Update From works like the Update From command in the Pen roll-up. Clicking on Edit calls up the dialog box associated with the fill type currently selected (for example, the Fountain Fill dialog box, if the fountain fill part of the Fill roll-up is selected). No changes take effect until you click on the Apply button.

QUICK SUMMARY

Task
Call up the Preferences dialog box

Procedure
Press Ctrl-J

PRACTICE WHAT YOU'VE LEARNED

This exercise assumes that you have *CorelDRAW!* running and new, blank page area is visible. If you already have something on the screen, save it and select New from the File menu. We're simply going to try different kinds of fills.

WHAT YOU DO

1. Draw a series of six rectangles on the screen. Or draw one rectangle and duplicate it five times. Click on the first rectangle and click on a red color in the palette in the bottom of the screen. If a red color isn't available, scroll through the palette until one appears.

WHAT YOU'LL SEE

1. The rectangle in the preview screen will be colored red.

WHAT YOU DO

2. Click on the second rectangle. Click on the fill tool and click on the color wheel.

3. Click on the Palette button.

4. Select Load New Palette.

5. Click on DITHERED.PAL and click on the OK button (the default palette is the CORELDRW.PAL, so you can return to it when you're through with this exercise).

6. Click on the Model button and select Palette.

7. Click on a dark violet color and click on OK to return to the *CorelDRAW!* screen.

8. Click on the third rectangle. Hold down the Shift key and click on the fourth so both are selected. Click on the Fill tool and select the fountain fill option. Select a radial fill, process color, from red to green, and click on OK.

WHAT YOU'LL SEE

2. You are at the main Uniform Fill palette. It has more capabilities than the palette at the bottom of the screen. From here, you can mix colors or load a different palette, or use the PostScript button to specify a special screen, as was done earlier in the chapter for fountain fills.

3. The Palette dialog menu lists a series of commands related to palettes.

4. The Open Palette dialog box appears.

5. The new palette will appear in the Uniform Fill dialog box.

6. The dithered palette will appear.

7. You will return to the screen, and the selected rectangle will be colored purple.

8. Each will fill in turn, with one color at its center and the other color at its periphery.

WHAT YOU DO

9. Now pull down the Arrange menu and select Combine.

10. Click on the fifth rectangle. Click on the fill tool and select full-color fill from the fill tool menu (it's the one with the double-headed arrow in it).

11. Select CUBES.PAT as your pattern. Select Small. Click on OK.

12. Click on the sixth box. Click on the fill tool in the toolbox and click on the two-color fill option (it looks like a checkerboard). In the resulting Two-Color Pattern dialog box, click on a brick pattern.

13. Select a dark red color for the background and gray for the foreground. Click on OK.

WHAT YOU'LL SEE

9. The rectangles will be re-drawn and refilled. This time, the color at the center of the radial fill will be halfway between the two rectangles and the other color will appear at the edges of the rectangles that are farthest apart.

10. The Load Full-Color Pattern dialog box appears.

11. The box will fill with a tiny cube pattern.

12. Still in the Two-Color Pattern dialog box, select a foreground and a background color.

13. Your last box should be filled with a fairly realistic brick pattern.

Text

We talked about text to some degree earlier in this book. It was necessary to provide a foundation in the use of text in *CorelDRAW!* early so you could learn to use the other tools. However, I have waited until now to go into text in detail. Text is a powerful design feature. Not only does it communicate immediately ("text" is just another word for "words," after all), but the typeface itself tells you something important about the information being conveyed. *CorelDRAW!* is shipped with a generous collection of fonts that range from the whimsical to the formal. In this chapter, you will learn about:

▲ **Creating and displaying text**

▲ **Fitting text to path**

▲ **Interactive kerning**

▲ **Editing character outlines**

Creating and Displaying Text

You've already seen text created in *CorelDRAW!*, but to recap, there are two basic methods. You can:

1. Click on the text tool in the toolbox.
2. Click on the page area.
3. Enter the text.

   Or you can:

1. Click on the text tool in the toolbox.
2. Drag a rectangle to contain the text on the page area.
3. Enter the text.

You can also paste text into *CorelDRAW!* from the Clipboard, thus allowing you to enter the text with a tool more suited to text entry (a word processor or text editor), cut or copy it to the Clipboard, switch to *CorelDRAW!*, and paste it into the Text dialog box.

A related procedure would be to create text with the Notepad utility provided with *Windows* and import it.

Windows and *CorelDRAW!* now support OLE, so you can Paste Special text from a word processor document and have that text changed automatically in the *CorelDRAW!* drawing whenever it is changed in the text file.

Getting text to appear on the *CorelDRAW!* screen is not a problem. The creators of *CorelDRAW!* recognize the design value of text and they have made it as easy as possible to use it. Since you are already familiar with the rudiments of text, we can plunge directly into altering text to make it more interesting and pleasing to the eye.

Fitting Text to Path

There are several terms that you should know when dealing with text. However, because we can cover only a handful of them here, if you are interested in type and type design, you can obtain books on the topic in your library.

The important terms for you to know now are baseline, ascender, descender, and x-height. If these terms are already familiar to you, just skip ahead to the end of this section.

▲ **Baseline:** The baseline is the bottom of letters like b, c, d, and all uppercase letters. The baseline is the line on which the type appears to rest.

▲ **x-Height:** The x-height is exactly what it sounds like—the height of the lowercase letter x of a given font. Note that this height is almost always also the height of lowercase letters a, c, e, i (without the dot), m, n, o, r, s, u, v, w, and z. Since this height represents another invisible line in a line of type, it's an important way to describe type.

▲ **Ascender:** An ascender is any part of a letter that pokes up above the x-height. Generally, the ascender is approximately the same height as the cap-height of a font—the height of the capital letters. The term "ascender" refers to the aerial parts of lowercase letters b, d, f, h, k, l, and t.

▲ **Descender:** A descender is the part of the letter that falls below the baseline. Most descenders are of approximately the same depth. Letters with descenders are g, j, p, q, and y.

For a graphical representation of these terms, refer to Figure 8.1.

▼ *Figure 8.1. Elemental Type.*

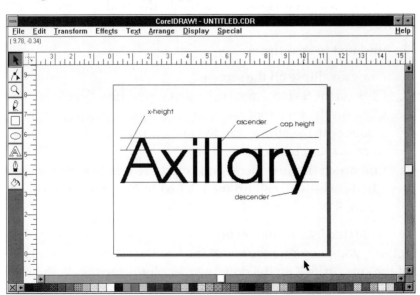

TIP

This short list of terms is only a spare introduction to type. There are many excellent books on type and desktop publishing, which you should consult for the complete story on text. Generally, the advice they provide boils down to keeping your text simple, avoiding elaborate fonts for long stretches of text, using only one or two fonts in a given page, and choosing those fonts with an eye to harmony. Remember that fonts too similar (for example, Bangkok and Brooklyn) can clash as disturbingly as fonts too different (for example, Paradise and Homeward_Bound). Use fancy faces for accents and major heads. Don't be afraid of being too plain; a conservative look is usually preferable to an overly flamboyant one.

Altering the Baseline

Sometimes design requires that you alter the baseline. You can do this in many ways, but the most interesting involves making a curving baseline. If you wanted to work with a curving text baseline, you could break up the text and use the pick tool to manually reposition text (you often may prefer this method). But *CorelDRAW!* comes equipped with an automatic routine that binds text to any baseline. You can't do this with paragraph text, however.

To bind text to an ellipse:

1. Draw an ellipse on the screen.
2. Click on the text tool and click on the page area. Type some text.
3. Click on the pick tool and drag a selection rectangle that includes both the ellipse and the text (or use one of the other options to select both).
4. Pull down the Text menu and select **Fit Text to Path** (or press **Ctrl-F**). This will call up the Fit Text to Path roll-up shown in Figure 8.2.

Note that by clicking on one of the wedges at the center of the roll-up, you can center the text at the top, the bottom, or either side of the curve. Click on the downward-pointing arrows at the right end of the top two list boxes to see the styles of text wrap (top list)

▼ *Figure 8.2. Text Bound to an Ellipse.*

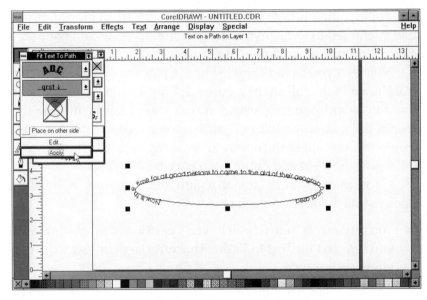

or position of text relative to the curve (bottom list). Checking the Place on Other Side check box allows you to fit text to the bottom of the curve (the default places text on top of the curve.)

5. Make no changes to the roll-up defaults and click on **Apply**. The results of binding text to a path can be seen in Figure 8.2.

Letting *CorelDRAW!* handle the details results in the placement of each letter in its proper position. But, just as many drummers dislike drum machines because they eliminate the human feeling from the beat, many graphic artists prefer to place letters themselves. We'll talk about this a little later.

With an ellipse, it would be very simple to make the text "bite its own tail" by sizing the ellipse smaller before the Fit Text to Path operation.

TIP

Watch out for concave curves. You may have to take great pains to keep letters from being placed atop one another at a bend in the line. In the next section, "Interactive Kerning," you will learn how to move individual letters closer together and farther apart to make text look more attractive when it is fitted to a path.

The text was centered on the top of the ellipse because the top quadrant of the ellipse was selected in the Fit Text to Path roll-up. The roll-up shown in Figure 8.2 was specific to an ellipse. If you had attempted to wrap text to an open curve, you would have seen a different roll-up, as shown in Figure 8.3.

Note that you have a third list box in place of the quadrant control shown in the roll-up in Figure 8.2. This list box, if you click on the downward-pointing arrow, allows you to left-justify the text (begin the text at the left end of the open curve), center the text (center the text along the open curve), or right-justify the text (end the text at the right end of the open curve).

If you want to "unfit" text to a path, there are three options are open to you, in order of preference:

▲ You can select Undo (if you haven't performed any action since you selected Fit Text to Path). This returns your text to its previous appearance.

▲ You can select Separate from the Arrange menu, select the text alone, then select Straighten from the Text menu. This returns text to its straight baseline.

▲ You can select Align to Baseline. This has an almost humorous effect, literally dropping all your text to the lowest common

▼ *Figure 8.3. The Roll-Up for Fitting Text to an Open Curve.*

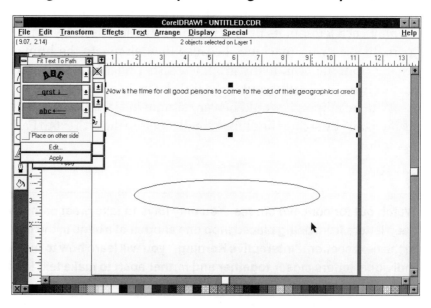

baseline, with all rotation and spacing still in effect. The letters sometimes look as if they were dumped out of a sack.

CHECK YOURSELF

1. Enter some text on the screen—several words. Draw a very short curve, shorter than the text. Select both and click on the option Fit Text to Path in the Arrange menu.
   ▲ The text will appear on the curve, continuing to the end and then bunching up at the end of the curve.

2. Remove the path once the text has been fitted to it.
   ▲ Select the text and select Separate from the Arrange menu. Click away from the text to unselect it, then click on the curve that served as the path for the text. If nodes appear on the line, you've selected it. Otherwise try again. Then drag the line away.

Interactive Kerning

Interactive kerning is a powerful capability, because it puts you in charge of the complete appearance of the text on the page. You can manipulate the individual letters with the mouse pointer and the shape tool, or use a special capability known as *nudge* that employs the cursor keys to make fine, even adjustments in spacing and positioning. Let's start by placing some text on the *CorelDRAW!* screen:

1. Click on the text tool in the toolbox and click on the page area.
2. Type "AVIONIX."
3. Select the text with the pick tool.
4. Pull down the Edit menu and select **Edit Text**. You will see the Artistic Text dialog box shown in Figure 8.4.
5. Enter 100 in the **Size:** text box so changes in the text will be easy to see.
6. Click on the **Spacing** button in the Artistic Text dialog box.
7. Click on **OK** and the text will appear on your screen as shown in Figure 8.5.

Note that each letter has a tiny box associated with it (the lower left corner of the space the character occupies). The box is like a

▼ *Figure 8.4. The Artistic Text Dialog Box.*

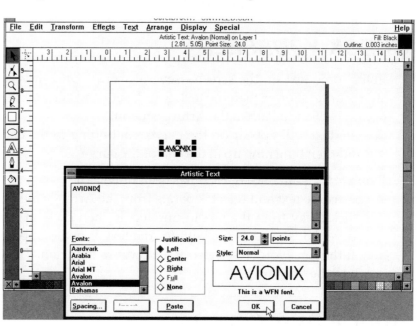

little handle that will allow you to use the shape tool to grasp the letter and move it around on the screen.

▼ *Figure 8.5. The Starting Text.*

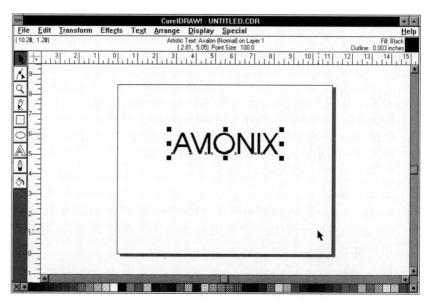

To move letters around:

1. Click on the shape tool. Your page area should look something like Figure 8.6.

    Note that you have two additional tools on the screen. They appear at the lower right-hand and lower left-hand corners of the text and look like little springs. These are called the *spacing control handles.*

2. Click on the box to the lower left of the first I. The box will turn black, indicating that it is selected. You now have complete control over the I. You can move it to any position on the screen simply by placing the mouse pointer on its handle and dragging. To return it to its proper position, select Straighten from the Text menu. Unfortunately, this has the effect of straightening all the letters, undoing all your interactive kerning.

A few paragraphs ago, I spoke of nudging text. Each time you press the cursor key, the letter will move the same set distance in the direction of the arrow on the cursor key.

To change the distance moved by a letter:

1. Pull down the Special menu.

▼ *Figure 8.6. The Text Selected with The Shape Tool.*

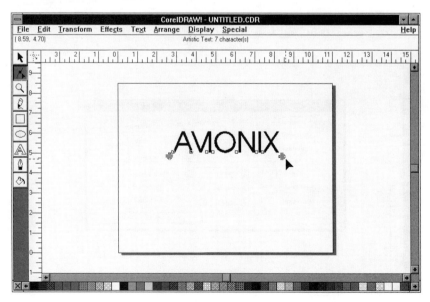

Interactive Kerning

2. Select **Preferences**. You will see the dialog box shown in Figure 8.7.

Note that in the **Nudge:** text box, the value entered is .10 inches. As with all measurements in *CorelDRAW!*, you can change inches to millimeters; picas, points; or points.

To change the amount of nudge for each press of the cursor key:

▲ Enter a different value in the text box and click on **OK**.

Now let's take a look at the spacing control handles.

The vertical spacing control handle, which appears under the lower left corner of a block or line of text, affects the interline spacing of multiline text. If you move a letter beneath the baseline of a single line of text with the nudge or the mouse pointer, the vertical spacing control handle will follow the letter down so that it defines the lower extent of the text. If you have multiple lines of text on the screen and you drag this handle downward, the text will "open up," increasing the leading or the spacing between baselines.

The horizontal spacing control handle appears under the lower right corner of the text and is used to affect the intercharacter or interword spacing of text. You should now clear the screen by se-

▼ *Figure 8.7. The Preferences Dialog Box.*

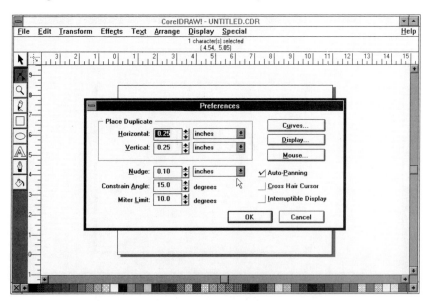

lecting New from the File menu, and use the text tool to enter the following text on the page area:

CorelDRAW!
Self-Teaching Guide

You can break text into two lines simply by pressing Enter after finishing the first line. This text should be centered and in large enough type to be easily seen without overrunning the limits of the page area. A 60-point size should be adequate (use the Edit Text command on the Edit menu to make these settings). If you then click on the shape tool and place the mouse pointer on the horizontal spacing control handle at the lower right corner of the text, you can drag this handle to the right. When you release the mouse button, the spaces between the letters should be increased. The text will remain centered, however, in accordance with its alignment, as set in the Artistic Text dialog box (Figure 8.8).

To change the interword spacing of the text:

1. Return the horizontal spacing control handle to approximately its previous position.

▼ **Figure 8.8. The Text with Intercharacter Spacing Increased.**

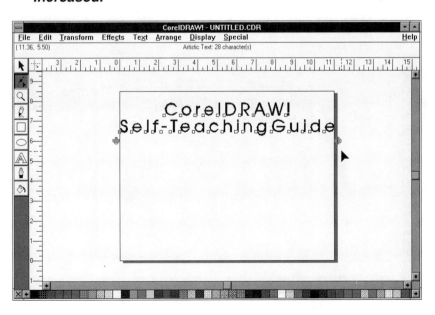

2. Hold down the **Ctrl** key and drag the horizontal spacing control handle. When you release the mouse button, the text should look like Figure 8.9.

To change the interline spacing:

1. Press the **Ctrl** key and return the horizontal spacing control handle to its previous position. This will return the interword spacing to its previous setting.
2. Drag the vertical spacing control handle downward an inch or two. When you release the mouse button, you will see the text as shown in Figure 8.10.

Interactive Kerning with Multiple Characters

You may recall that you can use the shape tool to select multiple handles by dragging a selection rectangle containing more than one control handle or by holding down the Shift key and clicking on multiple handles. This is also true when interactively kerning text. You can use either of these techniques to select several letters at once for manual alteration.

▼ **Figure 8.9. Interword Spacing Increased.**

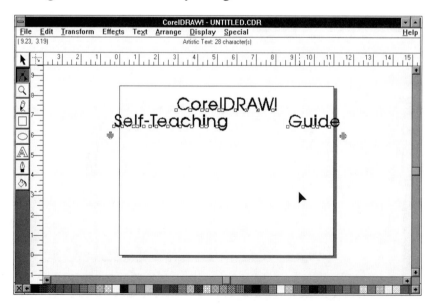

▼ *Figure 8.10. Interline Spacing Increased.*

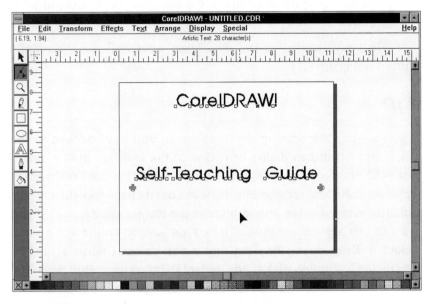

Changing the Character Attributes

The interactive kerning mode is closely related to the many settings in the Text roll-up. Let's use it with the *CorelDRAW! Self-Teaching Guide* text to make it more interesting.

You can't type text in different fonts and sizes using the tools in the Text roll-up—it has a global effect. But you can use the Text roll-up to alter text once it is entered. Let's reduce the size of the first word of *CorelDRAW! Self-Teaching Guide*. To affect the appearance of individual characters, you might want to use the Text roll-up option.

To use Text roll-up:

1. Pull down the Text menu and select **Text Roll-Up**.
2. Select the text, then click on the shape tool.
3. Drag a selection rectangle that selects all the handles in the first line. If you want to select individual characters instead, hold down the **Shift** key and click on the handles next to the letters.
4. Click on the downward-pointing arrow next to the character size (should still be 60.0) in the Text roll-up until the value is 30.1. Click on the **Apply** button in the Text roll-up. Note that by using the individual settings in this box, you can adjust the

size, face, and style of the individual characters, as well as their relationship to the baseline. We'll leave other settings to your experimentation.

When you return to the page area, you will see the results shown in Figure 8.11.

TIP

If you select Character in the Text menu, you have access to the Character Attributes dialog box. One of the settings in this dialog box is Character Angle. Adjusting the angle of text does not make it italic. An italic font is generally distinct from its base font (this is particularly evident in the appearance of the lowercase *e* and *a*). If you want to see a good example of this, type *eaeaea* on the screen and select it. Drag down the Text menu and select Character. In the Character Attributes dialog box, select PalmSprings. Pull down the Style list box and select Italic. Note the change in the appearance of the letters in the example box at the bottom right of the Character Attributes dialog box.

▼ *Figure 8.11. The Results of Editing the Character Attributes.*

CHECK YOURSELF

1. Place some text on the screen with center alignment. Click on the shape tool and click on one of the letters to select it. Use the nudge feature to move the letter far beyond the right end of the text.
   ▲ As you nudge the letter, the text slowly creeps to the left to maintain the centered alignment. Similar effects can be caused with left and right alignment.

2. Enter a trademarked name (like *Kleenex*) and type *TM* after the text. Make this text small and elevated above the baseline.
   ▲ Use the tools in the Text roll-up.

Editing Character Outlines

Editing the position of text is only the beginning. You can use the shape tool to affect the overall shape of the letters. One of the interesting things about text is that it is composed of individual graphics; that is, each letter is a graphic. Generally, these tiny, elemental graphics are not amenable to shape editing, but you can make them so, and edit them as shapes in exciting ways. Let's write the name of a famous guitar player on the screen and alter the letters in his name to look the way they might have looked on a poster in the 1960s:

1. Begin by clicking on the text tool and the page area and typing JIMI in the Text dialog box.
2. Click on the pick tool and drag the control handles until the text is large enough to fill the page from left to right.

   Now it's time to alter the text, to change it from text into something else—shapes for editing.

3. Pull down the Arrange menu and select **Convert to Curves** (or press **Ctrl-V**).

   After converting the text to curves, you will be unable to convert it back to text again. You are stuck with the text as graphic from that point on.

TIP

Whenever any shape is converted to curves, including ellipses and rectangles, it cannot be converted back again.

Although the text is now converted to curves, it is still combined, which means that although the letters look separate and discrete to *us*, *CorelDRAW!* considers them to be parts of a single object.

4. Click on the shape tool and drag a selection rectangle that encompasses all the control points in the lower half of the text.
5. Place the mouse pointer on one of the selected handles and drag them all down and to the left (Figure 8.12).

   This makes the text look slightly like italic text.

6. Click away from the text to deselect all handles. Now click on the right handle of all handle pairs at the bottoms of the letters as shown in Figure 8.13 (it's difficult to see, so if you want to be sure, select **Edit Wireframe** to make the fill of the letters invisible).

▼ *Figure 8.12. The Slightly Distorted Text.*

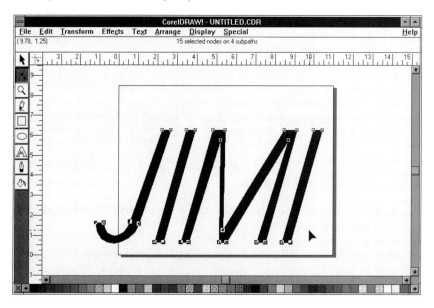

▼ *Figure 8.13. Preparing for Additional Distortion.*

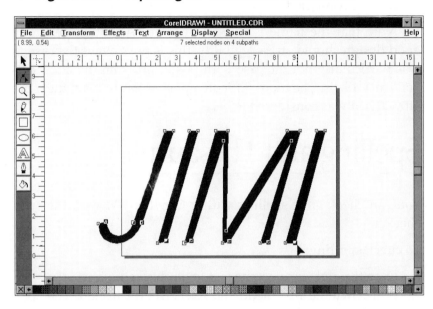

7. Now drag one of these handles to the right. They will all follow, resulting in the graphic shown in Figure 8.14. The alter-

▼ *Figure 8.14. The Resulting Text.*

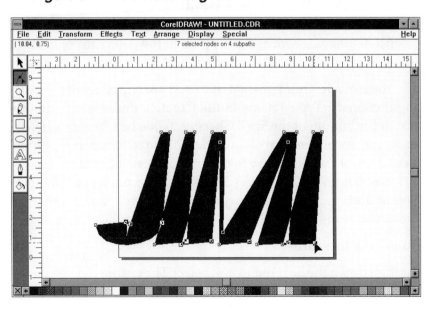

nating black and white areas occur because the objects in the text are combined.

Note that the name is difficult to read. Although generally good design should stress legibility, this is not always the case. It was particularly not the case with poster art from the late 1960s and early 1970s. The more difficult a poster was to read, the more attractive it was considered to be.

Spelling and Thesaurus

You can check your spelling within *CorelDRAW!* with the spell checker.

To check spelling:

1. Drag through or select the text to be checked.
2. Pull down the Text menu and select **Spell Checker**. The Spell Checker dialog box will appear.
3. Click on **Check Text**. Any questionable words will appear in the Word to Check box (you can also type a word in this box to check a word without first entering it on the *CorelDRAW!* screen, then click on **Check Word**).
4. If you would like to see alternate spellings, click on **Suggest**. A list of alternate words will appear in the Alternatives list box, with the most probable word in the Alternatives box.

You can add your personal dictionary to supplement the existing dictionary. Type a name in the **Create a Personal Dictionary** box at the bottom of the Spell Checker dialog box. You can, in fact, have a series of personal dictionaries intended for special purposes and select the dictionary to use in this particular case.

CorelDRAW! also features a thesaurus—a reference that helps you to find exactly the right word, if you have some idea of what word you want to use.

To use the thesaurus:

1. Pull down the Text menu and select **Thesaurus**.
2. Enter the word you want to find a synonym for in the Synonyms For text box and click on the **LookUp** button. The

definition for the word will appear in the definitions box and a possible synonym will appear in the Synonyms box.

3. If there are multiple meanings for the word, click on the meaning that most closely matches your purposes and the synonyms that match that meaning will appear.

QUICK SUMMARY

Task	Procedure
Fit text to path	Ctrl-F
Convert to curves	Ctrl-V
Align to baseline	Ctrl-Z
Access Text roll-up	Ctrl-2

PRACTICE WHAT YOU'VE LEARNED

This exercise assumes that you have *CorelDRAW!* running and a new, blank page area is visible. If you already have something on the screen, save it and select New from the File menu.

WHAT YOU DO

1. Click on the text tool in the toolbox and click the mouse pointer about halfway across the page area. Type NATIONAL in all uppercase letters. Call up the Text roll-up and select Left as alignment, Fujiyama as the font, and 100 as the point size; then click on Apply.

2. Click on the pencil tool. Draw a curvy line along the bottom of the word. Hold down the Shift key and click on the word. Then pull down the Arrange menu and select Fit Text to Path.

WHAT YOU'LL SEE

1. NATIONAL will appear on the *CorelDRAW!* page area. It should be legible. Use the pick tool to size the text until it fills the page area left to right.

2. The word will be fitted to the path. Depending on how curvy the line is, it may not even be legible anymore.

WHAT YOU DO	WHAT YOU'LL SEE
3. Pull down the Arrange menu and select Separate. Click away from the text so nothing is selected, then click on the text again. Pull down the Text menu and select Straighten.	3. The text will return to its original appearance.
4. Click on the curving line and press Del to delete it. Click on the shape tool and drag the node at the lower left of the letter I until it is centered on the O. Drag a selection rectangle with the shape tool that encompasses all the nodes of the first three letters of the word. Drag the node of the T until the T is next to the O.	4. All three of the first three letters move at the same time to close up the word.
5. Click away from the text and then double-click on the node of the N.	5. The Character Attributes dialog box appears.
6. Increase the size of the N by about 20 points and select Fujiyama_ExtraBold as the font. Click on OK.	6. The N appears larger and "fatter" than the other letters.
7. Click on the text tool again and this time hold down the Shift key when clicking on the page area.	7. The Symbols dialog box appears.
8. Select Household as the symbol library and click on the track light with three lights on it. Click on OK.	8. The track lights appear in the page area, very tiny.

WHAT YOU DO

9. Click on the pick tool and size the track lights so they are about half the size of the text. Move the track lights so they are tight against the underside of the text. Size it further so that it runs from the right leg of the left A to the left leg of the right A.

10. Make sure the track lights are selected and click on black in the palette at the bottom of your *CorelDRAW!* window.

WHAT YOU'LL SEE

9. The result should look a little like a business logo.

10. Note what parts of the lights are colored and what parts are not colored.

Advanced
Topics

In this chapter we will explore some of the powerful options that really make *CorelDRAW!* stand out from the competition. You will learn about:

▲ Blends

▲ Manipulating envelopes

▲ Perspective

▲ Extruding

▲ Programming the right mouse button

▲ Repeat

Blends

We discussed blends briefly in Chapter 7. Here are some more ideas about how to use this feature. What if you want to make several copies of an object in a row? How would you accomplish that? For me, this most often comes up when I want to provide lines to fill in on a sign-up sheet or graphlike setup. Here's how to accomplish it.

To repeat a series of objects:

1. Click on the pencil tool.
2. Click on the page area where the left and top margins would come together. Move the pencil tool to the right side of the page area (hold down the **Ctrl** key to make sure your line is perfectly horizontal) and click where the right margin should be.
3. Click on the pick tool and select the line, if it isn't already selected.
4. Pull down the Edit menu and select **Duplicate**. Drag the duplicate line so it is at the bottom end of the area you want filled with lines.
5. Select both lines and pull down the Arrange menu and align the lines either at their centers or their right or left ends. Since the lines are of identical lengths, their alignment doesn't matter.
6. Pull down the Effects menu and select **Blend Roll-Up**, or press **Ctrl-B**. You will see the roll-up shown in Figure 9.1.
7. Double-click in the Blend **Steps** text box (it shows 20 in Figure 9.1) and enter the number of lines you want *between* the two you have just created. Click on **Apply** and *CorelDRAW!* will place the intervening lines for you almost instantly. Figure 9.2 shows the result.

You're probably thinking that blends are pretty simple. You're right and you're wrong. Blends *are* simple, but you haven't seen many of the possibilities yet. Blends can be created that change one shape to another. Let's change a guitar into a circle.

To blend one shape into another:

1. Click on the text tool, hold down the **Shift** key and click on the page area. Open the **Musical** library and scroll through the images until you find an electric guitar. Click on a guitar and click

▼ *Figure 9.1. The Blend Dialog Box.*

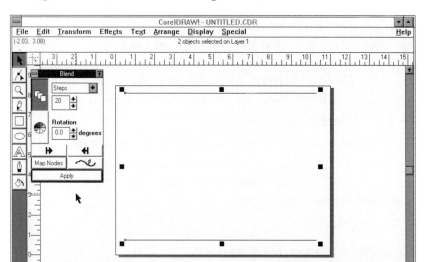

on the **OK** button. Enlarge it so that it's large enough to see easily, and rotate it so it's standing upright. With the guitar still selected, pull down the Arrange menu and select **Break Apart**.

▼ *Figure 9.2. The Completed Blend.*

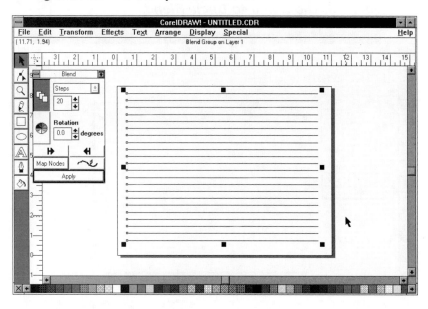

2. Click on the Ellipse tool and hold down the **Ctrl** key and drag a perfect circle next to the guitar. Click on the pick tool and then click away from the circle to deselect it.

3. Hold down the **Shift** key and click on the ellipse and the outline of the guitar.

4. If the Blend roll-up isn't visible, pull down the Effects menu and select **Blend Roll-Up**. Reduce blend steps to 2.

5. Click on **Apply**.

What you are left with is a guitar, two shapes that look increasingly like a circle, and then the circle (Figure 9.3).

If either of the objects you are blending contain spot color, they must both contain spot color.

To blend colors:

1. Create an ellipse. Fill it with red.

2. Duplicate the ellipse and fill the duplicate with white. Place the circles at opposite corners of the page area, select both, and blend them, making any number of blend steps between them. The result is shown in Figure 9.4.

You can perform similar blends on the color and thickness of the outline of an object. Try blending other shapes—circles to rec-

▼ *Figure 9.3. The Guitar-to-Circle Blend.*

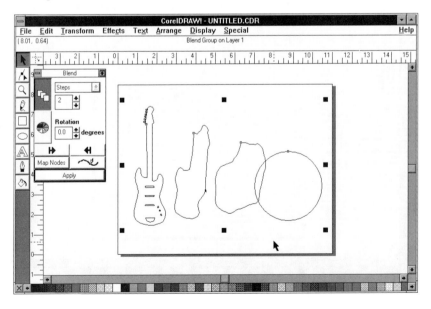

▼ *Figure 9.4. Blended Colors.*

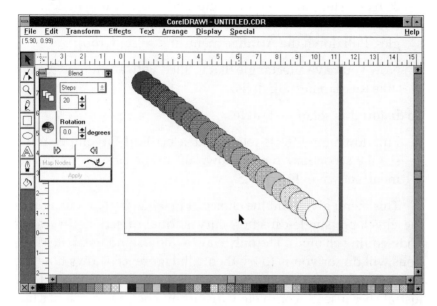

tangles, letters to shapes, and so on. You can even blend from an open object to a closed object.

The other options in the Blend dialog box are interesting. You can specify a rotation, which causes the blend steps to rotate. You can also specify which nodes in the two objects should match. That means that the node you specify in the first object will be the same node as the node you specify in the second object.

Manipulating Envelopes

An envelope is approximately the same as a selection rectangle, but it's much more flexible. Let's create a blend from a large rectangle to a small rectangle so the distortions imposed on it by manipulating the envelope will be obvious.

To blend a large rectangle to a small rectangle:

1. Create a rectangle. Duplicate it and size it using one of the corner handles. Select both rectangles and use **Align** on the Arrange menu to center the rectangles both horizontally and vertically.

2. Pull down the Effects menu and select **Blend Roll-Up**. Make 20 blend steps, no rotation angle, and no matching nodes.

3. Drag a selection rectangle that encompasses all of the rectangles. Pull down the Arrange menu and select **Group**.

Now you have a rectangle that is filled with additional rectangles like Russian nesting dolls.

To distort this set of rectangles:

▲ Pull down the Effects menu and select **Edit Envelope**. You'll see the secondary menu shown off to the side of the Effects menu shown in Figure 9.5.

This menu gives you the choice of making angular changes in the envelope, single-direction curves, dual-direction curves, or node-editing changes. The only way to understand what these options will do for you is to try them all. Figure 9.6 shows how the first three options operate. Node editing would be difficult to illustrate because it's completely free-form. The envelope looks like a selection rectangle. You manipulate it by dragging its handles. In node-editing mode, you are also provided with control points with which you can change the curvature of the envelope.

▼ *Figure 9.5. The Edit Envelope Menu.*

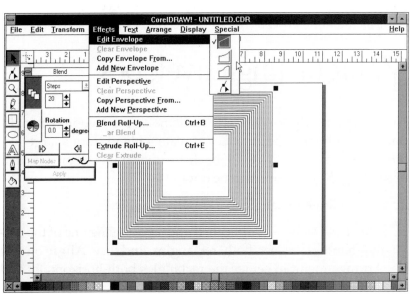

▼ *Figure 9.6. Examples of Envelope Editing Options.*

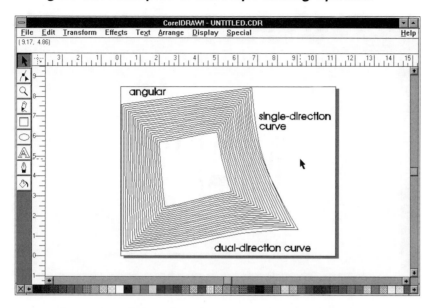

To use the node-editing, free-form option to fit the text in a circle:

1. Draw a circle (hold down the **Ctrl** key while dragging an ellipse).
2. Place the name MARY on the screen in the font of your choice. Place the text inside the circle and enlarge the text so it fills the circle as nearly as possible.
3. With the text selected, pull down the Effects menu and select **Edit Envelope**. Select node editing. Place the handles of the envelope on the perimeter of the circle and adjust the control points associated with the handles until the envelope is as close to a circle as possible.
4. Click on the circle and press **Del** to eliminate it.

   You'll see the screen shown in Figure 9.7.
   The Edit Envelope command has three interesting constraint features, if you are using one of the constrained editing options (angular, single-, or double-curve). Holding the Shift key down while dragging one of the envelope handles will cause the handle on the opposite side to move in the opposite direction. Holding the Ctrl key down will cause the handle on the opposite side of the envelope to move in the same direction as the one you are moving. Holding both the Shift and Ctrl keys down and dragging a corner node will cause all the corner nodes to mirror each other. Dragging

▼ *Figure 9.7. The Resulting Text.*

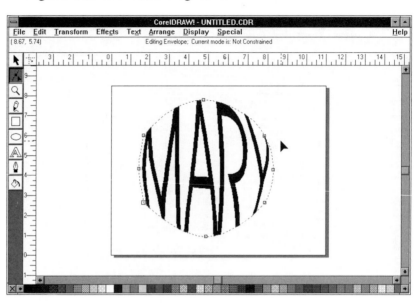

a side node with the Shift and Ctrl keys held down will cause all four side nodes to mirror each other.

Clear Envelope, the second option on the Effects menu, clears the last change you made to the envelope.

TIP

If you are editing the envelope of an object that has been converted to curves, and then you want to edit its nodes with the shape tool, you will discover that the shape tool returns you to envelope editing. You must select Convert to Curves again from the Arrange menu to edit the nodes of the object.

Copy Envelope From is another interesting option we'll take a closer look at now.

1. Place the name BOB on the screen next to MARY.
2. With BOB selected, pull down the Effects menu and select **Copy Envelope From**.
3. Click the mouse cursor on MARY. BOB will instantly change to resemble MARY's shape (Figure 9.8).

▼ *Figure 9.8. BOB's Envelope Copied from MARY's.*

If you have edited a shape's envelope and you want to start with a fresh, rectangular envelope, select **Add New Envelope**. This does not undo the distortions you have imposed on the drawing. It just starts you with a fresh, rectangular envelope.

CHECK YOURSELF

1. Draw a line on the page area with the pencil tool and duplicate it. Place the two lines next to each other. Pull down the Effects menu and select Blend. Enter 100 for the blend steps and 360 for the rotation. When you click on OK, the blend starts.
    ▲ The blend should look a little like a spoked cartwheel.

Perspective

CorelDRAW! now allows you to create images as if they were on a plane and then change the position of that plane relative to the apparent plane of the screen. Let's use MARY again to see how this works.

To create perspective:

1. Enter the text MARY on the screen.
2. Pull down the Effects menu and select **Edit Perspective**. A rectangle will appear around the text very similar to the envelope edited in the previous section, except this envelope only has four handles situated at the corners of the envelope.
3. Place the mouse pointer on the handle in the upper left-hand corner and drag it upward. Note that you are able to move the handle horizontally as well as vertically. To constrain the horizontal movement of the handle, press the **Ctrl** key. Note the tiny X that appears at the right of the text. This is the vanishing point. The result is shown in Figure 9.9.

This form of perspective is called one-point perspective because it only has one vanishing point. To add some complexity to the drawing, you can do two-point perspective.

To create two-point perspective:

▲ Drag the lower left corner to the right until a second tiny X appears on the screen. This is the second vanishing point. The X's need not appear on the screen. If you use perspective, the X

▼ *Figure 9.9. One-Point Perspective.*

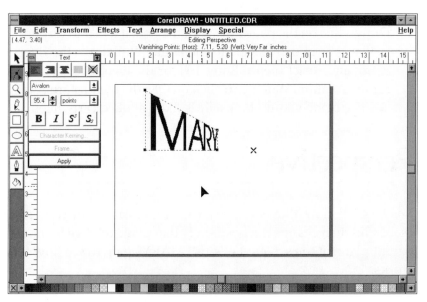

may not be visible, but there is always a vanishing point. You can reposition the vanishing point by dragging it, if it's visible.

TIP

Moving a control handle toward the center of a drawing causes the drawing to appear to move away from you. Moving a control handle away from the center makes the drawing appear to be coming closer to you.

You can constrain the drawing to a single vanishing point by holding down the Ctrl key when you move the control handles. If you hold down the Shift and Ctrl keys, moving the control handle up on one side will cause the control handle on the other end of that side to move downward a proportional amount.

If you have done everything you feel you can with the existing perspective, you can start again by adding a new perspective. This treats the drawing as if it were flat on the screen again, giving you a new, rectangular perspective box, though the drawing retains its distorted appearance. To accomplish this, select Add New Perspective from the Effects menu.

To get rid of all the changes made since the most recent perspective was added, select Clear Perspective from the Effect menu.

TIP

If you are editing the perspective of an object that has been converted to curves, and then you want to edit its nodes with the shape tool, you will discover that the shape tool returns you to perspective editing. You must select Convert to Curves again from the Arrange menu in order to edit the nodes of the object.

Let's say you have created some text in perspective and you want to add more text to it. You can use Copy Perspective From. In Figure 9.10, we have some text already in perspective and some new text added with no evident perspective.

To add text in perspective:

1. Select BOB.
2. Pull down the Effects menu.

▼ *Figure 9.10. The Problem: Add Perspective to BOB.*

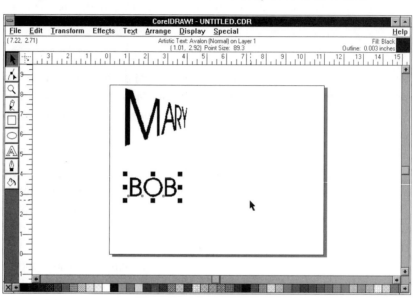

3. Select the option **Copy Perspective From**.
4. Click the mouse cursor on the object from which you want to copy the perspective (MARY). Instantly, BOB will take on MARY's perspective (Figure 9.11).

▼ *Figure 9.11. The Solution: Copy Perspective From.*

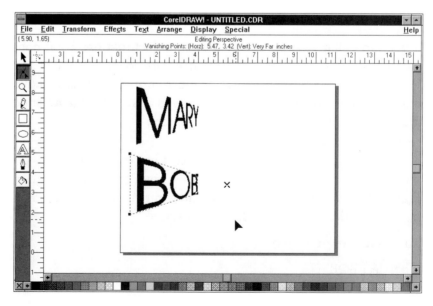

But, even now, they're not perfect. The names have the same perspective, but they look as if they belong in the same spot rather than next to each other. Why is that? It's because they each have the same vanishing points relative to themselves, but different vanishing points from each other. How are you going to resolve this problem?

To make the vanishing points coincide:

1. Begin by clicking on the object you want to leave alone. Pull down the Effects menu and select **Edit Perspective**. This will display the vanishing point (if it doesn't, try reducing the size of the entire drawing).
2. If the rulers aren't visible, select **Show Rulers** in the Display menu. Place the mouse pointer on the top ruler and drag downward. A guideline will come down with the mouse. Place the guideline on the visible vanishing point. If a second vanishing point is visible, pull out a second guideline for it.
3. Pull similar guidelines out of the left ruler, placing them on the vanishing points.
4. Click on the other object. If you're still in perspective-editing mode, the vanishing points of the second drawing should appear instantly.
5. Place the mouse pointer on the vanishing points of the currently selected object and drag them to the intersections of the guidelines. The result should look something like Figure 9.12.

Extruding

Not only can you do perspectives, blends, and envelope manipulation, but you can also take a two-dimensional object and push it—*extrude* it—into three dimensions.

Let's start with a simple example.

To turn a rectangle into a rectangular solid:

1. Use the rectangle tool to create a rectangle on the page area. Fill the rectangle with a white color.
2. Pull down the Effects menu and select **Extrude Roll-Up** (or press **Ctrl-E**). You will see the roll-up shown in Figure 9.13.

▼ *Figure 9.12. The Vanishing Points Aligned.*

There are four buttons along the top left of the roll-up. They control the vanishing point/extrusion offset, the rotation of the extruded object in three dimensions, the ray-path of light shining on the extruded object, and the color of the outside of the extruded object.

▼ *Figure 9.13. The Extrude Roll-Up.*

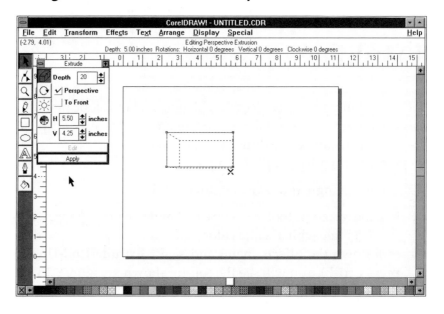

The Vanishing Point

The vanishing point (if Perspective is selected) or the extrusion off-set (if Perspective is not selected) establishes the direction the ex-trusion takes when it leaves the existing limits of the object. The vanishing point/extrusion offset can be seen onscreen as an X in Figure 9.13. Within the vanishing point/extrusion offset box, there are four important controls.

▲ The perspective box. With this checked, the extrusion will give the appearance of three-dimensionality.
▲ To front. With this box checked, the extrusion will appear in front of the existing shape. If it isn't checked, the extrusion will appear behind the existing shape.
▲ The H and V text boxes that allow you to enter the horizontal and vertical position of the extruded shape (only available if Perspective is not selected).
▲ The depth of the extrusion (only available if Perspective is selected).

Rotation

Click on the rotation button and the Extrude roll-up will look like Figure 9.14.

The X near the center of the sphere will return your extruded object to its original rotation. The arrows above and to the sides of this X rotate the object in the indicated direction. The arrows around the periphery of the sphere rotate the object in the third di-rection. This page of the Extrude roll-up is very powerful because it provides for complete spatial orientation of an extruded object. A rotated object can be seen in Figure 9.15.

Ray Path

Figure 9.15 shows the ray-path page of the Extrude roll-up. This page is used to specify from what direction the light is coming.

Click on 1 to turn on the light. A sphere appears in the cage-like cube in the ray-path indicator. By clicking at the intersecting lines of the cube, you can specify a light direction, which *CorelDRAW!*

▼ *Figure 9.14. The Rotation Page of the Extrude Roll-Up.*

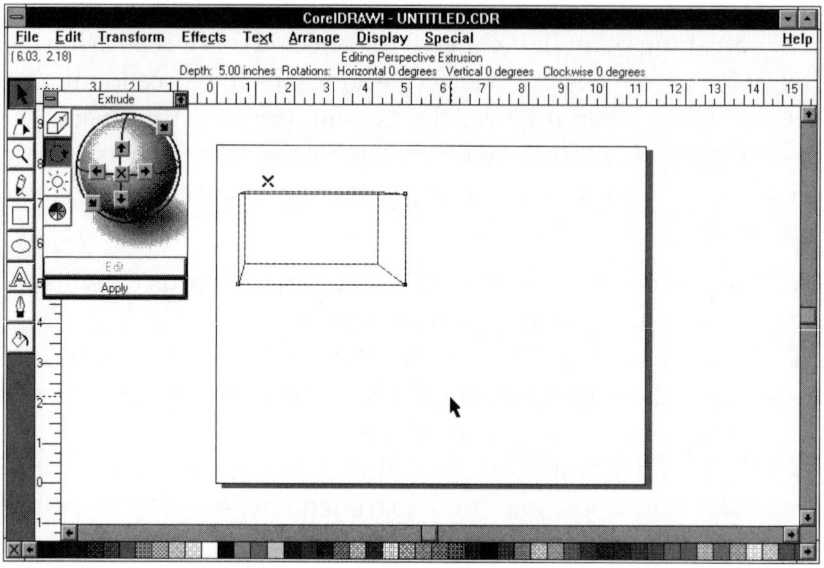

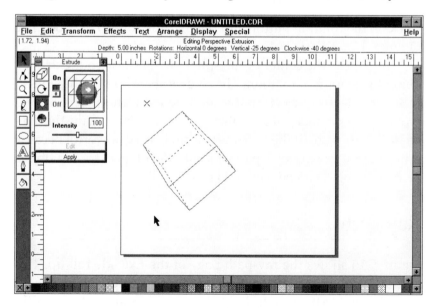

will interpret with different shades on the extruded object. This is not nearly so interesting in a rectangular solid as it is in a cylinder.

▼ *Figure 9.15. The Ray-Path Page of the Extrude Roll-Up.*

Figure 9.16 shows two cylinders lit from the lower right front corner of the screen. You can also adjust the intensity of the light.

Color

This page of the Extrude roll-up allows you to specify the colors of the fills in your extruded object (Figure 9.17).

▲ Use Object Fill fills the object with the color in the shape from which the object was extruded.

▲ Solid Fill provides a palette from which you can select a color for the extrusion different from that of the original object. Click on the color box to see the palette. Click on a color in the palette to select it.

▲ Shade allows you to specify different colors for the shade. Generally, the shade is from either the selected solid fill color or the object color (depending on which was selected) to black. Selecting this option allows you to specify different colors for the shading—red to green, for example. You select the From and To colors by clicking on the color example box, which calls up a palette. Select a color from the palette by clicking on it.

▼ *Figure 9.16. Two Cylinders.*

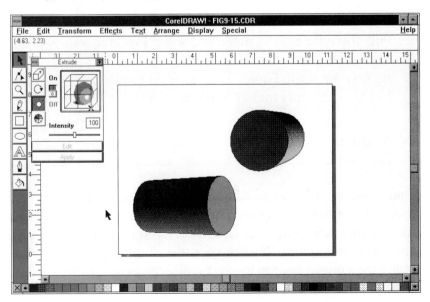

▼ *Figure 9.17. The Color Page of the Extrude Roll-Up.*

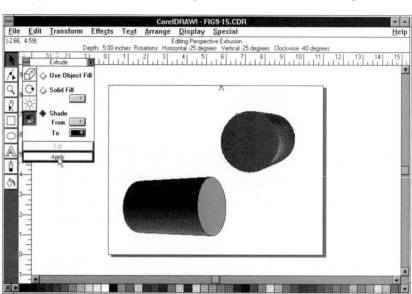

Programming the Right Mouse Button

The right button of the mouse can be programmed for a variety of functions:

1. Pull down the Special menu and select **Preferences**.
2. Click on the button marked Mouse.
3. As you can see in Figure 9.18, the right mouse button is set to Not Used. Simply make the alternate selection you prefer.

Repeat

One command that doesn't fit under any other heading, but is so useful that it deserves mention, is the Repeat command found on the Edit menu. Selecting this command has the effect of issuing the last command again. This can be a tremendous timesaver when doing the same operation to several objects on the screen.

▼ *Figure 9.18. The Mouse Dialog Box.*

Repeat

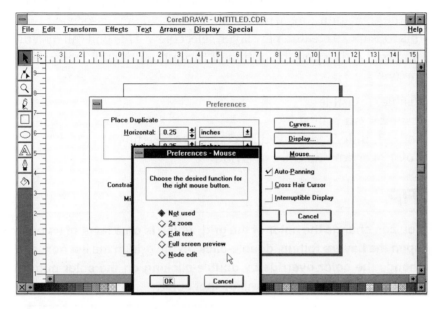

CHECK YOURSELF

1. Draw a rectangle and select Edit Perspective from the Effects menu. Hold down the Shift and Ctrl keys and drag the upper right handle up.

    ▲ The left handle should move down.

2. Continuing checkup 1, keep moving the upper right handle until the vanishing point appears on the screen. Note which side of the screen it's on.

    ▲ The vanishing point should appear on the right side of the object.

3. Draw a curving line on the screen, then select Extrude from the Effects menu. Make the offset 1 inch in both X and Y direction and set the Absolute Coordinates at 50.

    ▲ The curving line should look like a ribbon.

Layers

CorelDRAW! has a layer feature allowing you to, in effect, superimpose different drawing surfaces on top of one another, locking them, making the objects on them invisible, and so forth. To access the layers, press Alt-A,L. This will call up the Layers roll-up. Click on the right-pointing arrowhead to see the menu associated with this roll-up. To create a new layer, select New. This will call up a dialog box giving you the option of turning on the following parameters:

Visible/invisible
Printable/unprintable
Locked/unlocked (locked layers cannot be edited)
Color override/no color override

TIP

You can change the color of the grid, which is on a layer of its own. Open the Layers roll-up, double-click on the grid in the list box, and change the color override by double-clicking on the color button. Select a color and the grid will be that color.

Using the Delete option on the menu associated with the Layers roll-up, you can delete a whole layer, including everything on it.

QUICK SUMMARY

Task	Procedure
Call up the Blend roll-up	Ctrl-B
Make opposite nodes move proportionally in perspective editing	Ctrl-drag node
Call up the Extrude roll-up	Ctrl-E

PRACTICE WHAT YOU'VE LEARNED

This exercise assumes that you have *CorelDRAW!* running and a new, blank page area is visible. If you already have something on the screen, save it and select New from the File menu.

WHAT YOU DO

1. Enter the text IMP in capital letters in Avalon text. Draw a rectangle around it that is about twice as tall and four times as wide as the text. The text should be roughly centered in the rectangle. If they are not aligned pretty closely, select both and use the Align command on the Arrange menu to center them vertically and horizontally. Click on the pick tool and drag a selection rectangle around both the text and the rectangle.

2. Pull down the Effects menu and select Blend. In the Blend dialog box, enter 10 as the number of blend steps. Click on OK.

3. Make sure the pick tool is selected. Drag the blend an inch to the right.

4. With the blend steps still selected, pull down the Arrange menu and select Separate.

5. Pull down the Arrange menu and select Break Apart.

WHAT YOU'LL SEE

1. Both the text and the rectangle will be selected.

2. Note that most of the blend steps are broken.

3. The blend steps will move along with the original rectangle and text.

4. Selecting Separate has the effect of separating the original objects—the text and the rectangle—from the blend steps.

5. The individual parts of the blend will be grouped, but the blend as a whole is no longer a group.

WHAT YOU DO

6. Click away from the blend so that nothing is selected, and then click on any individual part of the blend. Pull down the Arrange menu again.

7. Select all of the blend steps and press Del to eliminate them. Click on the original text. Pull down the Effects menu and select Edit Envelope. In the resulting menu, select the second from the bottom entry. Hold down the Shift and Ctrl keys and drag the node in the middle of the bottom of the envelope downward.

8. Pull down the Edit menu and select Undo.

9. Hold down the Shift key and drag the top left corner of the envelope up to the corner of the rectangle.

WHAT YOU'LL SEE

6. Break Apart is still available because each stage of the blend is still a grouped object. Selecting Break Apart again will break up this step. If you want everything ungrouped, you will have to click on each step of the blend and select Break Apart from the Arrange menu.

7. The text will expand to a diamond shape as all four side handles move outward in concert.

8. The text will return to its original appearance, but it will still be available for envelope editing.

9. Both left corners will move the same distance in opposite directions. The envelope will look a little like a ketchup bottle lying on its

CorelTRACE!

What is *CorelTRACE!*? It's an extremely advanced way to turn raster graphics into vector graphics. It intelligently traces TIF or PCX images while you watch. Why would you need such a tool when *CorelDRAW!* has an autotrace built right into it?

Imagine this scenario. Your boss hands you a sheaf of papers about fifty pages thick, with orders to scan them and trace them so the images on the papers can be used in *CorelDRAW!*. Wait! Don't quit your job. There is a better way to trace bitmap images than to trace by hand! In this chapter you'll learn about:

▲ Starting *CorelTRACE!*

▲ **Creating color and gray scale tracings**

▲ **The Batch feature**

I first saw *CorelTRACE!* in action in the Summer PC Expo in New York City in 1990 and it took my breath away. The demonstrators had loaded a very complex drawing, and *CorelTRACE!* was quickly and efficiently tracing it from top to bottom, turning it into a vector graphic that could be converted for use with *CorelDRAW!*. That's right—it doesn't trace directly into CDR format. It traces into EPS format, a format you could convert for use with another vector graphics program.

To use this chapter, you will need a ready source of traceable art. Fortunately, *CorelDRAW!* provides a supply in the SAMPLE subdirectory that should be underneath the CORELDRW\ DRAW directory. Use these or any clip art you have available, or for the sake of an exercise, you could do a *CorelDRAW!* drawing and export it as a PCX or TIF file for tracing (of course, you would never do this in real life).

Starting *CorelTRACE!*

The installation program you ran to set up *CorelDRAW!* should have created a program group known as Corel Graphics. To get to this program, follow these steps.

To access Corel Graphics:

1. Start Windows.
2. Pull down the Window menu in the Program Manager window and select **Corel Graphics**.
3. When the Corel Graphics program group opens, the *CorelTRACE!* icon will look like a lightbulb with a sheet of paper above it and a pencil above that. Double-click on this icon and you will see the window shown in Figure 10.1.

First you must use the various controls in the window to locate your raster image file. That shouldn't be difficult, if you know where your CORELDRW\DRAW directory is and you are going to use the files in the SAMPLES directory. Let's load up a file and trace it.

To find a file:

▲ Click on **Open** in the *CorelTRACE!* window. You will see the dialog box shown in Figure 10.2.

▼ *Figure 10.1. The CorelTRACE! Window.*

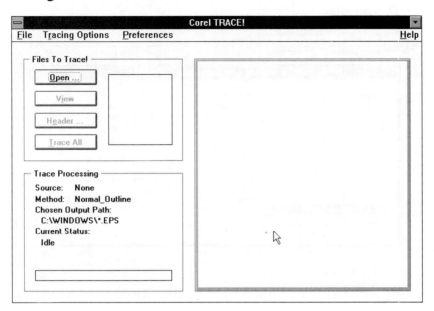

By now you should be fairly comfortable with this dialog box, which is similar to the Open and Import dialog boxes in *CorelDRAW!*.

When you locate the directory with your traceable files in it, the filenames should appear in the list box at the left of the dialog box. Here, you can click on a filename. If you would like to see the contents of the file, click on View or Auto View. And you can click on OK to return to *CorelTRACE!*.

To view the file you are about to trace:

1. The file you selected will be listed in the list box at the middle left of the dialog box. Click on it.
2. The View button should become available when you click on the filename. Click on the **View** button and your graphic file will appear in the preview screen at the right side of the *CorelTRACE!* window (Figure 10.3).

I have scanned in a computer disk for tracing. Many of the details in the disk are irrelevant. We will remove them in *CorelDRAW!*.

You could load several files of several types, one by one, and set them up to trace in a batch, but for now, we'll just trace this one.

▼ *Figure 10.2. The Open One or More Files to Trace Dialog Box.*

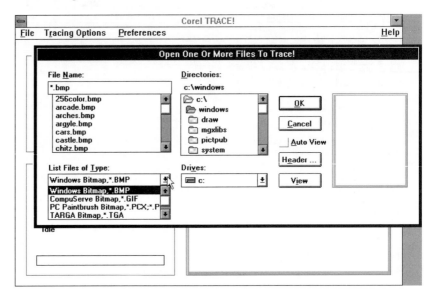

To trace a file:

▲ Click on the **Trace All** button at the left side of the *CorelTRACE!* window. When you click on the Trace All button, the image will

▼ *Figure 10.3. The File, Waiting to Be Traced.*

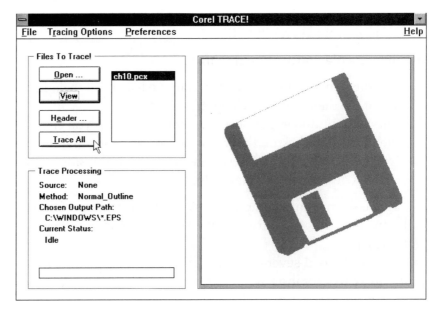

disappear from the preview screen and a bar will appear at the lower left corner to show you how far the trace has gone.

When the trace is completed, you will see the complete trace on the screen. This file has already been saved to disk when the trace appears in the window, as shown in Figure 10.4. It will retain the same filename as the bitmap file that served as its source, but it will have the extension EPS.

To load the trace into *CorelDRAW!*:

1. Click on the minimize box or double-click on the close box of the *CorelTRACE!* utility.
2. Start up *CorelDRAW!*.
3. Pull down the File menu in *CorelDRAW!* and select **Import**.
4. In the list box of the Import dialog box, you will see two different EPS formats: Adobe Illustrator and *CorelTRACE!*. Select ***CorelTRACE!* EPS.**
5. A list of EPS files will appear in the File Name list box. Double-click on the file you just traced—remember that it retains the same filename as the bitmap file.

In Figure 10.5, you can see the traced image. It's been sized to make it easier to see. By dragging a corner handle, it was scaled and retains the original proportions of the bitmap.

▼ *Figure 10.4. The Trace Completed.*

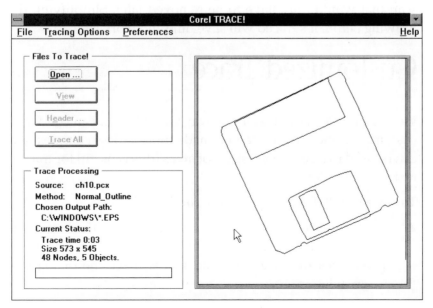

▼ *Figure 10.5. The Traced and Imported Graphic.*

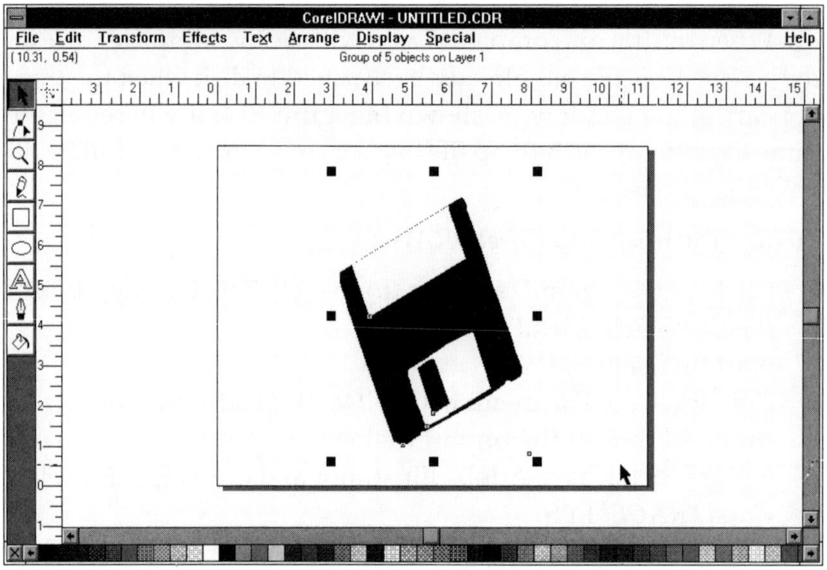

In all, there are five objects in the trace. I've traced objects that ended up with dozens of objects—a real challenge to trace by hand, but simple to trace with *CorelTRACE!*. In fact, this simple trace would have been much more complicated if I had not taken the time to simplify it considerably in a paint program before tracing it. I removed text and errant shadows that would have confused the tracing program or added unnecessary objects to the scan that would only have to be removed later. Simplifying the drawing before it's traced will save time and work later.

Customized Trace

We're going to take a look at the way *CorelTRACE!* can conduct a customized trace. Traces can be made more or less complex and can be used to trace lines instead of areas (this is useful for tracing text, for example).

To close *CorelDRAW!* and restart *CorelTRACE!*:

▲ Pull down the Tracing Options menu. The options are Edit Option, Normal Outline, Normal Centerline, and a series of ellipses. Click on an ellipsis and you will see the dialog box shown in Figure 10.6.

Use this box to specify how closely the tracing program should trace the bitmap file. You will want to experiment with the settings to get them the way you want, but the settings you see in Figure 10.6 are the settings used for the trace of the computer disk. Here are some settings that will make the trace less complex and more workable (or at least more printable):

▲ Select Lines in the Convert Long Lines box
▲ Select Very Loose in the Fit Curve box
▲ Enter 20 or more in the Remove Noise text box
▲ Select Smooth Points in the Outline Filtering box
▲ Select Coarse in the Sample Rate box

When you have the settings the way you want them, double-click on the text box in the Option Name dialog box and type a name, like COARSE. When you pull down the Tracing Options menu, this option will appear in the menu, so you can select it from the menu without having to make the settings each time. By setting up a series of personalized tracing schemes, you can have a special kind of trace ready to use for any task. If you ever want to edit the contents of your Tracing Options dialog box, click on its name in the Tracing Options menu and click on the Edit Options option.

Customized Trace

▼ *Figure 10.6. The Tracing Options Dialog Box.*

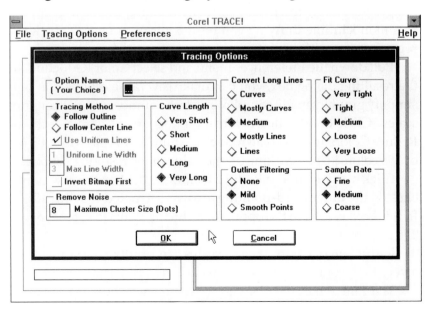

TIP

You probably noticed the selections Follow Outline and Follow Center Line in the Tracing Options menu and similar options in the upper left corner of the Tracing Options dialog box. For solid objects and gray scale objects, you should use Normal Outline, which traces the edges and fills the resulting trace to resemble the bitmap image. The Normal Centerline trace is intended for tracing text or other bitmaps that consist of thin lines that should be traced in the form of lines and not solid objects.

Create Color and Gray Scale Tracings

What you saw in the previous section was a trace of a monochrome PCX file into an EPS graphic. If you want to work with black and white images only, with no shades of gray, you need read no further. However, most real-world images are images with many colors and many shades of gray, not just areas of black and white.

Fortunately, *CorelTRACE!* makes tracing gray scale and color images very easy. You need to remember, though, that as complex as a monochrome drawing can be, a color or gray scale drawing represents a multiple of this complexity.

Pull down the Preferences menu and select Color Reduction. In the resulting dialog box, you can make several selections that will simplify graphics made complex by a large number of colors or gray scales. Click on the downward-pointing arrow at the right of Reduce Colors To.... You can reduce the number of colors to 8, 16, 64, or 256 colors just by clicking on the value in the resulting list box.

Click away from the Reduce Colors To list box to close it and click on the downward-pointing arrow next to Reduce Grays To.... In this box, you have the option of reducing grays to 4, 8, 16, 64, or 256 gray scales.

Reduction of colors or gray scales can result in a graphic with a very high contrast color scheme known as *posterization.*

The function of the Convert to Mono check box is obvious: It will reduce any drawing—color or gray scale—to black and white.

Also on the Preferences menu are selections that will allow you to Trace Partial Area (you are provided with a selection box within the tracing window). There are also three selections that change the onscreen information you see during the trace: Show Progress Rate, Show Tracing Info, and View Dithered Colors.

Create Color and Gray Scale Tracings

The Batch Feature

If you have a number of bitmaps to trace, simply load them all into the Files to Trace list box. Set them up to trace overnight and your computer will not only do the tracing work for you, but it will do the file-management work as well.

Partial Traces

You might want to trace only part of a picture. In that case, pull down the Preferences menu and select Partial Trace. When you click on the Trace All button, a selection rectangle will appear around the perimeter of the example box at the right end of the *CorelTRACE!* window. An OK button will also appear in the example box. Drag the handles at the centers of the sides of this selection rectangle until the area you want to trace is completely enclosed. Click on the OK button and the trace will proceed, but the trace will only occur within the area defined by the selection rectangle.

QUICK SUMMARY

Task	Procedure
Open a file to trace	Press Alt-F, O
Enter color reduction	Alt-P, C

PRACTICE WHAT YOU'VE LEARNED

This exercise assumes that you have *CorelTRACE!* running and a TIF or PCX file available for tracing. If you don't have a file to trace, start up Windows Paintbrush and create something, or create a drawing in *CorelDRAW!* and export it as a bitmap painting that *CorelTRACE!* can accept.

WHAT YOU DO

1. Click on the Open button.

2. Find the file you want to trace using the settings in the Open dialog box. Click on the filename and click on OK button.

3. Click on the filename in the list box to select it. Click on Trace All.

4. Go through the above steps again.

WHAT YOU'LL SEE

1. The Open dialog box will open, allowing you to add a bitmap graphic to the File to Trace list.

2. You will be returned to the *CorelTRACE!* window and the filename you specified will be in the Files to Trace list box.

3. The file will load and be traced. This is largely an automatic process, so there is nothing to do until your computer finishes its task.

4. This time when you click on Trace All, you should see a dialog box telling you that there is already a file on your disk with the specified name. *CorelTRACE!* simply appends the EPS extension on the filenames of files that are traced. Therefore, if you trace SOMETHING.PCX and then trace SOME-THING.TIF, you will over-write the first trace. *CorelTRACE!* makes it more difficult to make this mistake.

CorelPHOTO-PAINT!

*C*orelDRAW! just expanded. Previously it was only one of the best drawing and illustration products on the market. Now it contains one of the best paint programs, too: *CorelPHOTO-PAINT!* In this chapter, you'll learn about:

▲ **Elements of painting**

▲ **Darkroom software**

▲ **Viewing your photo**

▲ **Spray paint, fill, airbrush**

▲ **Cloning**

▲ **Using contrast and brightness**

▲ **Blending, smearing, and sharpening**

▲ **Using filters, transforming, and undoing**

Elements of Painting

This chapter will cover *CorelPHOTO-PAINT!* as concisely as possible. The program is rich with features, however, so you should feel free to experiment as you proceed through the chapter. This chapter presents the major aspects of working with a darkroom-style paint program. Along the way, you will glimpse other controls and commands that either will not be mentioned or will be mentioned only in passing. You should pause to familiarize yourself with these parts of the program.

The difference between a paint and a draw program was touched upon earlier. Paint programs are not object oriented and they only have one drawing plane. This is an advantage for the artist who wants to have parts of the program interact, change the outline of an object or the texture, or copy small parts of an object. These tasks would be difficult or impossible in a drawing program, but they're a simple matter in a paint program.

A paint program works with bitmap images exclusively. *CorelPHOTO-PAINT!* can work with BMP, GIF, Microsoft Paint MSP, Targa TGA, TIF, or PCX files. Figure 11.1 shows the *CorelPHOTO-PAINT!* window with a TIF image already loaded.

When you start up *CorelPHOTO-PAINT!*, you will have a blank screen and three toolboxes. The largest toolbox on the right side of the figure contains the lion's share of the tools, which we will discuss one by one. The Palette toolbox next to the Tool toolbox contains everything you need to select and mix colors for use in *CorelPHOTO-PAINT!*. The Width toolbox contains settings for pen or brush width and shape. If you want to turn off one or more of these toolboxes, you can do so with options on the Display menu or by double-clicking on the close box at the upper left corner of the toolbox. Let's go through the tools one by one.

Zoom

The zoom tool is used to magnify the image. Click on the area you want to see in close-up. To zoom out, right-click on the picture.

▼ *Figure 11.1. The CorelPHOTO-PAINT! Window.*

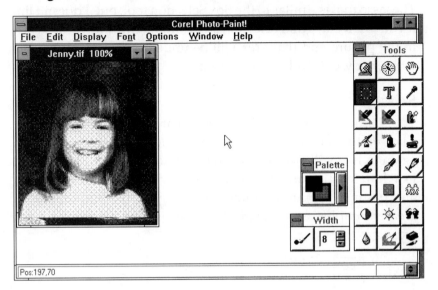

Locator

To display the same area in all open windows on the picture, click on the area with the locator tool.

Hand

If only part of a picture is visible in a window, drag the picture with the hand tool to reposition it relative to the window.

Box Selection

This tool allows you to define a rectangular area for cutting and pasting. Clicking on the folded corner of an icon like the Box Selection icon will call up an icon menu containing additional icons. If you click on the lower right corner of the Box Selection icon, you will have access to the following icons. Selecting one of these icons will cause it to replace the icon in the toolbox.

Magic Wand

Click on a color with the magic wand and the entire range of that color will be selected. You can delete the area that is that color, for example, or copy it and use it in another graphic.

Lasso

The lasso tool is similar to the Box Selection tool, but it doesn't limit you to a rectangular selection area. Simply draw any closed area in the picture and that area will be under your control. You can move, copy, cut, and paste the area.

Scissors

The scissors tool will select an irregular area in any polygon shape. Click on the picture, move the tool to another position, and click again. A line will appear between the two positions. Double-click in a third location and a triangular area will be selected for cutting and pasting. You aren't limited to triangles. You can scissors an area as complex as you want. The lines of your polygon can even cross.

Text

Clicking on this icon calls up the dialog box shown in Figure 11.2.

Enter the text you want to appear in your graphic. To alter the typeface, select Select in the Font menu. You'll see the dialog box in Figure 11.3. This dialog box provides all the controls necessary to select the typeface, size, style, and effects. The text rectangle can also be seen in the figure.

Drag the handles of this box to affect the way the text wraps in the graphic.

Eyedropper

By clicking on a colored area of the picture with the eyedropper, you select that color for drawing and painting. Click with the left button to set the outline color and with the right button to select the fill color. Watch the Palette toolbox. The color you click on will appear in the toolbox.

Eraser

Dragging this tool through a colored area of the drawing eliminates the color and returns the area dragged through to the color of the "canvas"—the screen color.

▼ *Figure 11.2. The Enter Text Dialog Box.*

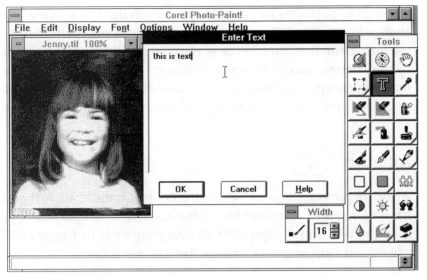

Color Replacer

The color replacer tool eliminates a colored area just like the eraser, but with this tool you can specify a color to erase (and only that color will be erased) and a color to replace it with (and only that color will appear where the original color was).

▼ *Figure 11.3. The Font Dialog Box.*

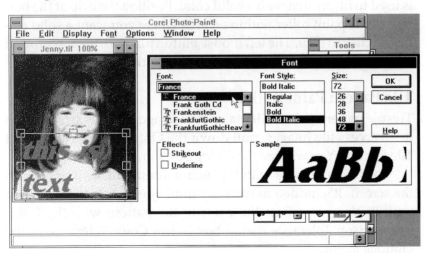

Local Undo

Local undo performs like a magic correction fluid. If you make a change in an area and you don't like it, you can select Undo from the Edit menu to eliminate the entire change. But if you like most of the change, except where it has covered up something you wanted to keep, select the local undo and drag the pointer over the area you want to return to its original appearance and it will come back.

Airbrush

Airbrush provides a gentle spray of color for subtle change. If you have a large area you want to tint freehand, use the spraycan, but if you have a photograph with an unsightly mole or baggy eyes, use the airbrush to gently remove these imperfections.

Spraycan

The spraycan should be used to cover areas with a color freehand. It isn't appropriate for subtle changes.

Paint Roller

Note that this icon has a folded corner. Clicking on the folded corner opens a new menu containing additional tools. The paint roller is used to fill an area with a solid color. Position the drip at the bottom of the paint roller within an area where you want a solid color and click to fill it. The left mouse button fills with the foreground color and the right mouse button fills with the background color.

Tile Pattern Paint Roller

The tile pattern paint roller takes any image and fills an area with it. To access tile images, pull down the Options menu and select Tile Pattern. You will see the dialog box shown in Figure 11.4.

Loading an image with this menu doesn't make it appear on the screen. It's hidden in memory until you decide to fill an area with it. You can adjust the color of the pattern with the Color Comparison Tolerance dialog box (select Color Tolerance in the Options menu).

▼ *Figure 11.4. The Load a Tile Pattern from Disk Dialog Box.*

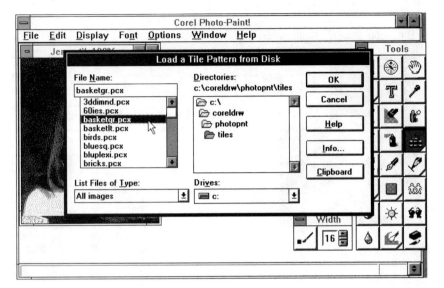

Gradient Paint Roller

You should be familiar with gradient fills if you have read earlier chapters. This is the gradient fill in the paint program. You set the gradient by using the options found in the Select Gradient Effect dialog box (called up by selecting Gradient from the Options menu).

Paintbrush

The paintbrush is used to paint on the screen. As you paint, moving the brush rapidly will result in a pale version of the color. Painting more slowly or going over an area more than once will make the color darker. Click on the brush icon in the Width toolbox to see a series of brush shapes, as shown in Figure 11.5.

Adjust the width of the paintbrush by selecting a value in the Width toolbox.

Fountain Pen

The fountain pen acts just like the paintbrush, but it doesn't fade colors in like the brush. Wherever the pen is when the mouse button is pressed, the foreground color is placed. You can set the shape

▼ *Figure 11.5. The Select a Brush Style Dialog Box.*

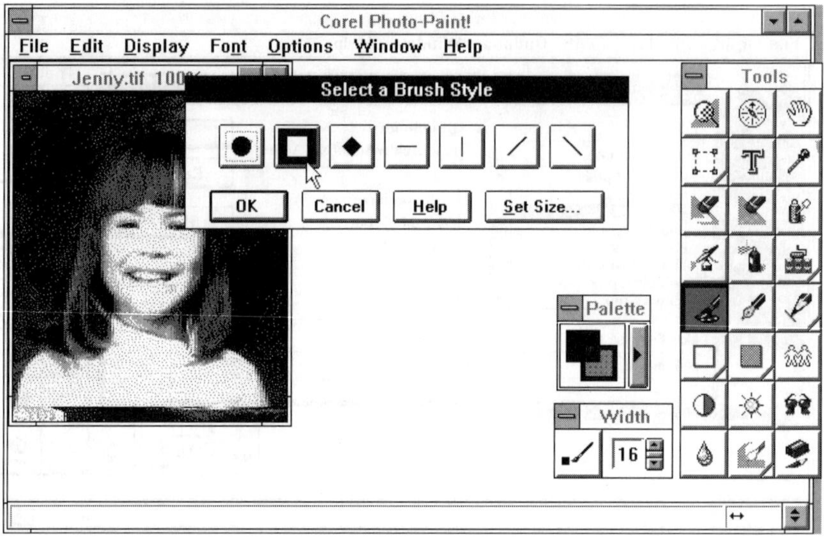

and width of the fountain pen exactly as you set the shape and width of the paintbrush.

Line

The line tool draws a straight line in the shape and width of the fountain pen. Place the line tool at the place where you want the line to begin. Press the left mouse button and drag to where you want the line to end. When you release the mouse button, the line will appear.

If you want to draw a polyline instead of a line, click with the right button. A line will be drawn from the most recent termination point to the current mouse location. Note that the line tool icon has a folded corner. Clicking on the folded corner gives you access to another tool—the curve tool.

Curve

The curve tool provides a Bézier curve instead of a straight line. Figure 11.6 shows the control points (circles) and end points (squares). Dragging the control points affects the curvature of the line. Once you click away from the line, the line is drawn with the current pen shape and width. Right-clicking causes a new curve to be drawn from the most recent end point to the current mouse position.

▼ *Figure 11.6. The Control Points on a Curve.*

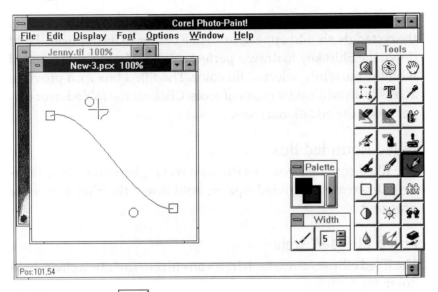

Hollow Box

The hollow box draws a rectangle on the screen. Simply drag where the rectangle should appear, from one corner to its opposite. Hold down the Shift key to draw a perfect square. The hollow box icon provides access to an additional menu of tools. Click on the folded over corner to see the additional tools.

Hollow Rounded Box
The hollow rounded box tool draws a rectangle with rounded corners. To create a rounded square, hold down the Shift key while dragging.

Hollow Ellipse/Circle
The hollow ellipse/circle tool draws an ellipse. To draw a circle, hold down the Shift key.

Hollow Polygon
To draw a polygon, select this tool and then click on the painting where the corners of the polygon should be. When you create the final corner, double-click and the polygon will automatically be closed. To limit the lines created to multiples of a 45-degree angle, hold down the Shift key while drawing.

Filled Box

The filled box draws a rectangle on the screen. Simply drag where the rectangle should appear, from one corner to its opposite. Hold down the Shift key to draw a perfect square. The box will be filled with the currently selected fill color. The filled box icon provides access to an additional menu of tools. Click on the folded over corner to see the additional tools.

Filled Rounded Box

The filled rounded box tool draws a rectangle with rounded corners. To create a rounded square, hold down the Shift key while dragging.

Filled Ellipse/Circle

The filled ellipse/circle tool draws an ellipse. To draw a circle, hold down the Shift key.

Filled Polygon

To draw a polygon, select this tool and then click on the painting where the corners of the polygon should be. When you create the final corner, double-click and the polygon will automatically be closed. To limit the lines created to multiples of a 45-degree angle, hold down the Shift key while drawing. When the polygon is finished, it will fill with the current fill color.

Clone

The clone icon is a little hard to understand. It essentially colors one image another. Say you have two images like the ones shown in Figure 11.7.

Just right-click on the image you want to clone, move the mouse pointer to the location where you want to clone the image, press the left mouse button, and proceed to draw.

TIP

Use a wide brush for cloning. It will make your work quicker and easier.

▼ *Figure 11.7. Two Drawings, One Being Cloned into the Other.*

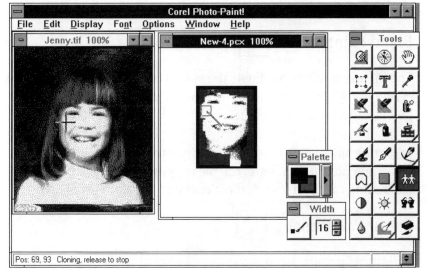

Contrast Paintbrush

The contrast paintbrush allows you to increase the differential between adjoining light and dark areas. Light areas will be made lighter and dark areas will be made darker. To adjust the sensitivity of the contrast paintbrush, click on the button in the Palette toolbox. Adjust the slide bar to the right to increase the contrast and to the left to reduce the contrast. Positioning to the left of center will actually cause the graphic to become less sharply contrasted where the paintbrush passes.

Brighten Paintbrush

The brighten paintbrush uniformly increases the brightness of any area you run the paintbrush over. To adjust the brightening power of the brighten paintbrush, click on the button in the Palette toolbox. Adjust the slide bar to the right to increase the brightness and to the left to reduce the brightness. Positioning to the left of center will actually cause the graphic to be *darkened* where the paintbrush passes.

Tint Paintbrush

The tint paintbrush paints a transparent color over the image. It's similar to using an ink wash.

Blend Paintbrush

The blend paintbrush adjusts the colors of pixels so that there is a gentle transition from one to the other. If you have a block of black pixels and you use the blend paintbrush, you will end up with a black blob with gentle gradations of ever lighter gray until the color turns white. Use the palette to adjust the effect. With settings at the right end of the palette, the blend will be its smoothest. If you use settings at the left end, the blend will be relatively sharp.

Smear Paintbrush

The smear paintbrush has the same effect as rubbing tissue paper on a charcoal drawing, except that by smearing from a light area into a dark area, you will cause the light area to smear over the dark (sort of like using an eraser on charcoal). You can see the smear effect in Figure 11.8. Note that this icon has a folded corner. By clicking on the folded corner, you can access the smudge paintbrush.

Smudge Paintbrush

The smudge paintbrush randomly mixes up pixels from all over the area of the brush. You can see the smudge effect in Figure 11.8.

Sharpen Paintbrush

The sharpen paintbrush sharpens edges. The palette is used to adjust the filtering.

Darkroom Software

Darkroom software is a specialized area of paint software designed for working with large palettes or large ranges of gray scales in highly detailed images. In some of the figures in this chapter you've

▼ *Figure 11.8. Smear (Left) and Smudge.*

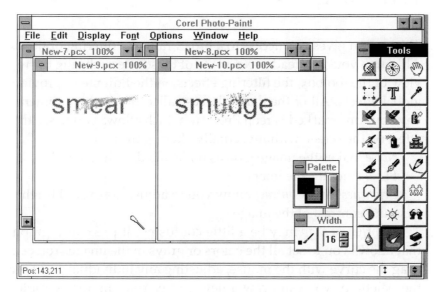

seen an actual scanned photograph that I use for examples. Although no real difference exists between a darkroom program and an ordinary paint program, the brightness and contrast controls are particularly useful for editing color and gray scale images.

Loading and Saving Your Image

The file-handling options of *CorelPHOTO-PAINT!* are the same as those within *CorelDRAW!*.

Converting a Drawing

You can't use all of the tools on all kinds of drawings. For this reason, or for reasons of your own, you might want to change a drawing from color to gray scale or vice versa. In that situation, select Convert from the Edit menu. You can convert between gray scale, 24-bit color, 8-bit color (called 256 color), and black and white (which calls up a submenu that allows you to choose line art, printer halftone, or screen halftone).

Filtering

This option gives you access to a broad range of filtering options. Although you've already seen some of these effects during the review of the toolbox, the filtering effects on the Edit menu provide global effects. All of the dialog boxes called up on this submenu have buttons marked Screen Preview, which allows you to see the effect on the screen without actually altering the image.

Noise makes the image look as if it is filled with "snow."

Blend smooths the image.

Brightness and *Contrast* allow you to adjust the overall brightness and contrast of the image.

Color/Gray Map may be a little confusing. It presents a graph that allows you to set all the colors or grays in the image. You can drag the curve with the mouse, adjusting any individual point on the palette or you can draw a new curve. You can, for example, draw a line from the upper left corner to the lower right (the default is for the graph line to run from the lower left to the upper right) to create a photo negative of the image. It's fun to play with, so dig in and try it. Click on Screen Preview to see the effect of your changes.

Diffuse makes the image look as if it's being viewed through pebbled glass.

Edge Detect outlines the edges of colored areas and then fills the areas with the color you select in the Color option.

Emboss has a very interesting effect as shown in Figure 11.9. Clicking on the arrows shown in the figure determines the direction of the light rays that appear to be striking the embossed image.

Equalize affects the amount of highlight and shadow in the image.

Posterize adjusts the level of detail in the image. Adjusting the posterization actually pixelizes the picture, turning it into ever-larger rectangles of color or gray. In Figure 11.10, you see the same image without posterizing (left) and at maximum posterization (right).

Motion Blur makes it look as if the camera was in motion when the picture was taken. You can adjust the direction of movement and the speed.

Remove Spots removes noise from the image.

▼ *Figure 11.9. The Embossed Image.*

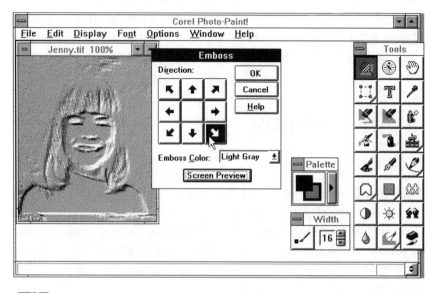

TIP

Remove Spots is a good option to use to make an image trace better in *CorelTRACE!*.

Sharpen turns dark grays black and light grays white.

▼ *Figure 11.10. Posterization of an Image.*

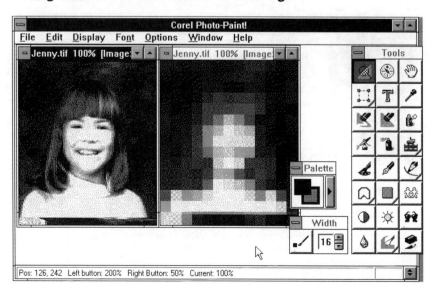

TIP

Sharpen will make an image print better on a low-resolution printer. These printers don't do well with grays, so sharpening the picture will allow a printer to do a better job printing continuous gray scales.

Transforming

You can perform other global changes with the Transform option on the Edit menu. You can flip horizontal (mirror the image left for right) or vertical (mirror the image top for bottom). You can invert the picture, turning it into a photo negative. Outline finds and fills a color area. Rotate 90 degrees makes the image rotate 90 degrees. The really fun part of the Transform is Area. Select it and you will see the dialog box in Figure 11.11.

Using this dialog box, you can resize an image, proportionally or not, you can flip the image, rotate the image in 90-degree increments, or rotate the image in up to 5-degree increments left or right with Deskew.

▼ *Figure 11.11. The Change the Selected Area Dialog Box.*

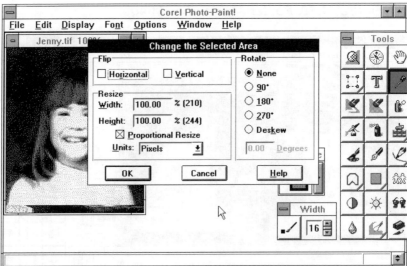

Multiple Windows

Although the purpose of the locator tool may not have been instantly obvious, we'll discuss its utility now. If you are working on an image in high detail, it might be difficult to tell where you are in the picture. If you load up an image and zoom in on this image until you can see individual pixels, it will probably be difficult to figure out where you are in the image.

To use the locator tool:

▲ Click on the locator tool and click on an area in the unzoomed image. The zoomed image will change. What you see in the zoomed image is the area you clicked on with the locator tool.

QUICK SUMMARY

Task	Procedure
Undo change	Alt-Backspace
Ctrl-1	Unzooms an image
Ctrl-F	Toggles maximized window
Ctrl-A	Toggles toolboxes on and off
Ctrl-W	Toggles Width toolbox
Ctrl-P	Toggles the Palette toolbox
Ctrl-T	Toggles the toolbox
Ctrl-D	Duplicates image
Ctrl-S	Saves the picture

PRACTICE WHAT YOU'VE LEARNED

For this practice, use one of the images in the CORELDRW\PHOTOPNT\SAMPLES directory.

WHAT YOU DO

1. Select Open from the File menu and select CORELDRW\PHOTOPNT\SAMPLES\PAINTWAY.PCX.
2. Select New from the File menu. Click on OK in the Create a New Picture dialog box.

WHAT YOU'LL SEE

1. The indicated file will be loaded into a window on-screen.

2. A new, blank window will appear on top of the first window.

WHAT YOU DO	**WHAT YOU'LL SEE**
3. Place the mouse pointer on the move bar of the new window and drag it to the side. Click on the arrow button in the Palette toolbox.	3. The palette will appear.
4. Right-click on red, left-click on green.	4. As indicated in the Width toolbox, the foreground color will be green and the background color will be red.
5. Draw a filled rectangle in the new window.	5. The outline of the rectangle will be green and the inside will be red.
6. Click on the clone tool. Right-click on the PAINT-WAY.PCX image, then drag the mouse pointer around inside the rectangle you just drew.	6. The area on which you right-clicked will be duplicated wherever you draw in the new window.
7. Click on the window that contains PAINTWAY.PCX. Pull down the Edit menu and select Color/Gray Map. When the dialog box opens, drag the mouse pointer through the graph from top left to bottom right. Click on Screen Preview.	7. The image will be a photo negative of itself.
8. Click on Cancel.	8. The dialog box will disappear and the image will return to its original condition.
9. Pull down the Edit menu again and select Convert. The Convert menu will appear. Select Black and White. Another menu will open. From it, select Line Art.	9. A new window will open displaying the same image in stark black and white.

CorelCHART!

Figures are difficult to understand at a glance. Charts help you to display information that can be conceptualized easily. But until computerized charting became available, making charts was tedious and difficult work, often requiring an artist and lots of transfers. With the advent of computerized charting, a chart became a simple addition to any spreadsheet. More and more programs include charting among their features and several important charting programs have become best-sellers. A charting program is simply a graphics program that can plug data into a graph. In this chapter, you'll learn about:

- ▲ **Choosing the right chart for the job**
- ▲ **Importing data**
- ▲ **Data orientation**
- ▲ **Colors**
- ▲ **Common errors in charting**

Choosing the Right Chart for the Job

As you will see shortly, getting data into *CorelCHART!* is easy. Deciding which kind of chart to use is the hard part of using *CorelCHART!* (or any other charting software) because there are so many specialized kinds of charts.

CorelCHART! charts can be broken into five general types:

▲ Text charts, which aren't really charts at all and won't be discussed here (the best-known text chart is the famous eye chart found in optometrists' offices)

▲ Charts that trace changes over time, such as sales over years, quarters, or months

▲ Charts that reflect proportions of a whole, such as a pie chart that indicates the percentage of each dollar of income that goes to taxes, rent, food, and so forth

▲ Charts that plot two values on a grid to give a graphic representation of a trend, such as a scattergram that shows IQ scores on one axis and GPA on another axis

▲ Simple tables

Take a look at Figure 12.1. If you start up *CorelCHART!* by double-clicking on it and then select New from the File menu, this is the screen you see.

The list of charts down the Gallery list box represents your options when it comes to charting:

Bar
Line
Area
Pie
Scatter
High/Low/Open/Close
Spectral Maps
Histograms
Table Charts
3D Riser
3D Scatter
Pictographs

▼ *Figure 12.1. The New Dialog Box within CorelCHART!.*

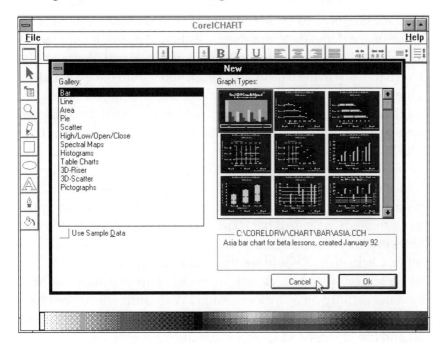

As you click on these options in the Gallery list box, you will see representations of the available chart styles in the Graph Types example box. To select a graph type, simply click on it and you will be taken to the *CorelCHART!* main screen. We'll take that step in a moment, but let's talk a little about the use of different kinds of charts.

Bar and line charts, histograms, and 3D risers are all charts used to chart changes in a dependent variable over changes in an independent variable. Generally, the independent variable (the one you have no control over) is time. The dependent variable is the one that some control can be exercised over, such as profit, expenditures, hours worked, and so forth.

A bar chart and a histogram are very similar charts. Bar charts indicate the value of the dependent variable by the height of the bar and each bar represents a unit of the independent variable, such as a month. Histograms are usually oriented horizontally and each bar in a histogram usually indicates a category rather than a value of a variable. For example, you might use a histogram to indicate the sales of beef versus mutton. A histogram can be oriented vertically. Click on Histogram in the Gallery to see the types of histograms available to you. A pictograph is similar to a histogram, but it uses pictures instead of bars to indicate values.

Line charts are used in the same way as bar charts, plotting the value of the dependent variable by its height above the horizontal axis at regular points along the horizontal axis. If you drew a line between the tops of the bars in a bar chart, you would have a line chart. Line charts are useful for comparing dependent variables. You might chart rainfall and incidences of forest fire with two different lines in a line chart to see whether they rise and fall at the same time. The line chart is particularly appropriate for this task because lines generally don't interfere with each other. You can easily see three or four lines on the same chart. Plotting multiple values on a bar chart is more confusing, though it can be done. The 3D riser allows you to use a three-dimensional bar chart to plot multiple dependent variables in a way that prevents them from being confused with one another. Click on 3D Riser to see the options available to you.

A high/low/open/close is a special chart that indicates with bars the activity on a stock exchange. With different colored bars, it indicates the open and close value of a stock or other item traded and the highest and lowest value during a given day.

Area and pie charts tell you the proportion of a whole that was used for different purposes. A pie chart is static in time, giving a snapshot of conditions at one point in time. To reflect changes in the proportions over time, you can use either multiple pie charts or an area chart, preferably the area chart. Multiple pie charts are used to compare the proportions in two different areas. You might use multiple pie charts to show how the typical family budget is broken up in Taiwan, Ohio, and Helsinki. By not comparing absolute values but only proportions, these charts avoid arguments about exchange rates and family income.

Scattergrams (identified simply as "scatter" in the Gallery) and 3D scattergrams ("3D scatter" in the Gallery) are used to chart two dependent variables against one another. The classic case is test scores as charted against grades. Generally, if you get good SAT scores, you will also get good grades in school. A school psychologist might plot a scattergram to identify a test that has no validity as a predictor of grades or to identify a student who tests poorly but performs well in class or who gets good test scores but performs poorly in school work in order to get special help for these students.

Tables are exactly what they sound like: an organized presentation of raw data.

Importing Data

To select a chart type (and enter data):

1. Click on **Bar** in Gallery.
2. Click on the sixth example (the last graph type in the second row) and click on **OK**. A tiny spreadsheet will open up. It doesn't have the capabilities of Excel—it's only intended for entering numbers that *CorelCHART!* will then turn into a chart.
3. Type 125 and press the right arrow key, and the number will appear in cell A1. Note that you can move around from cell to cell with the cursor keys.
4. Enter 138, press the right arrow, and enter 145. That is the first series of numbers.
5. Press the down arrow and press the left arrow twice to return to A2, the first cell in the second row of cells. Enter 132, press right arrow, 142, right arrow, 150. Press down arrow.

In the same position as the toolbox in *CorelDRAW!*, there is a toolbox in *CorelCHART!*. The top item in this toolbox looks a little like a chart. This item switches you back and forth between the spreadsheet view and the chart view.

6. Click on the toggle item at the top of the toolbox to go to the chart. Note that there are two series of bars, one (red, unless you've changed the color palette) representing the values 125, 138, and 145; and the other (orange) representing the values 132, 142, and 150.

The window behind the spreadsheet—identified in Figure 12.2 as Untitled-1—is the chart window. If you don't want to toggle with the icon, you can simply click on this window where it sticks out from the spreadsheet. That's all you need to do to create a chart. The finished chart can be seen in Figure 12.3. You don't know just by looking at the chart, however, what the numbers mean. That's why it's important to provide a legend.

▼ *Figure 12.2. The Spreadsheet.*

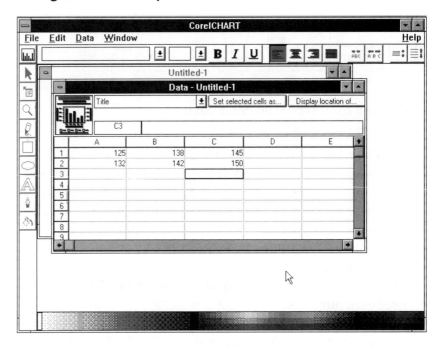

▼ *Figure 12.3. The Finished Graph.*

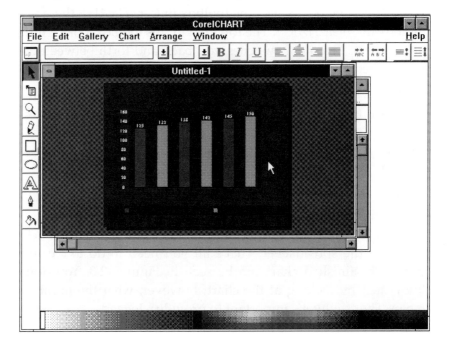

You can also copy data into the chart:

1. Start up your spreadsheet program—Excel, for example.
2. Drag a rectangle including all of the cells you want included in the chart. Pull down the Edit menu and select **Copy**.
3. Start up or switch to *CorelCHART!*.
4. Select **Paste** from the Edit menu to copy the cells into the *CorelCHART!* spreadsheet.

     This will simply copy the data into the cells in *Corel-CHART!*. But you can do more.
5. Select **Paste Link**.

Paste Link copies not the information but the spreadsheet itself into *CorelCHART!*. If you want to return to the spreadsheet from which the figures came, just double-click on the cells in *CorelCHART!*. If you change the values in Excel, the values will automatically be changed in *CorelCHART!* as well.

To import a spreadsheet:

1. Select **Import Data** from the File menu.
2. Use the resulting Import File with File Type dialog box to locate the spreadsheet you want to import. Excel is the default, but it will import most file types.

Filling in the Chart

To fill in a title, subtitle, legend, and row headers on your chart:

1. Return to the spreadsheet by clicking on the toggle at the top of the toolbox.
2. Click on any cell that doesn't already contain data and type the title you want to use for your chart. We'll use Profits as the title.
3. Pull down the list box at the top left of the spreadsheet window. It says Title in Figure 12.2 because this is the default. But note that when you pull down the list box, you can specify Subtitle, Footnote, Row Headers, Column Headers, axes titles for however many axes you are using, and Data Range. Select **Title**.
4. Make sure that the cell containing the title is selected (has a heavy border) and click on **Set selected cells as....** That will tell *CorelCHART!* that the text in the selected cell is the title of the chart.

5. Perform a similar task to create a subtitle. Enter 1991 Versus 1992 in a blank cell and select **Set selected cells as...** to tell *CorelCHART!* this is the subtitle. If you care to, enter additional cells for a footnote, row headers, and so forth.

6. When you have entered all of the information you want to appear on the chart, click on the toggle to see the chart. Note that the options on the main menu change.

7. Pull down the Chart menu and select **Display Status**. You will see the dialog box shown in Figure 12.4.

8. Click on the button marked **All Text**. That will make the title and subtitle (as well as anything else you have entered) appear on the chart. Click on the **OK** button.

9. Pull down the File menu and select **Save**. Enter a filename. This will preserve the information and settings you have made. Once a file is saved, it can be reloaded. When you start up *CorelCHART!*, instead of selecting New, you can select Open to open an existing chart file (all chart files have the CCH extension).

▼ *Figure 12.4. The Display Status Dialog Box.*

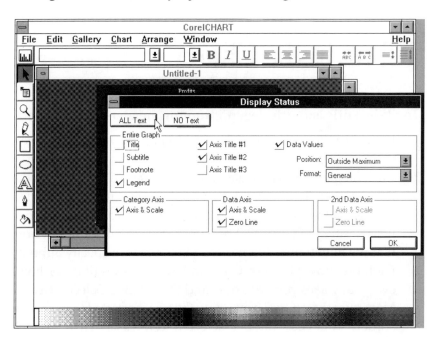

To adjust the size and other attributes of everything in the chart:

1. Click on the pick tool and click on the title. Note that a selection rectangle appears around the title.
2. Drag a corner handle to make the rectangle larger. The title will be proportionally larger.

You will note that many of the tools are the same in *CorelCHART!* as they were in *CorelDRAW!*. Click on the text tool and then click on some text, and an I-beam cursor will appear so you can alter the text. Click on a bar in the bar chart and click on the fill tool. Change the color or enter a gradient fill and all the bars that represent that series of data will take on that color or gradient fill.

But not all of the tools are the same. Just beneath the pick tool is a tool called the pop-up menu tool.

3. Click on the pop-up menu tool. Your cursor will change to a special shape that looks like a menu.
4. Place this special cursor on one of the bars in the chart and press the right mouse cursor. A special menu will appear featuring Bar Thickness, Bar-Bar Spacing, Marker Shape, Data Reversal, Data Analysis, Axis Assignment, Base of Bars, Display as Line, and Emphasize Bar (as shown in Figure 12.5).

Using these commands, you can alter the appearance of the individual parts of the graph. In short, *CorelCHART!* brings most of the powerful tools of *CorelDRAW!* into a graphing package.

Common Errors in Charting

The most common error in charting is creating charts that are difficult to read. Assuming that you understand the principles behind charting and that you have created a chart that contains the information you want to display, the last hurdle is to make sure your graph is readable. Many charts can contain numerous series of information. Too many series will confuse the viewer.

Keep your colors under control. The default colors are good. They're selected for slide presentations. A rule of thumb is to use dark background colors and bright element colors (bars, text, and so forth) when doing slide presentations. If you're printing with a black and white printer, limit your colors; bright green and bright

▼ *Figure 12.5. The Menu Called Up by the Pop-Up Menu Tool.*

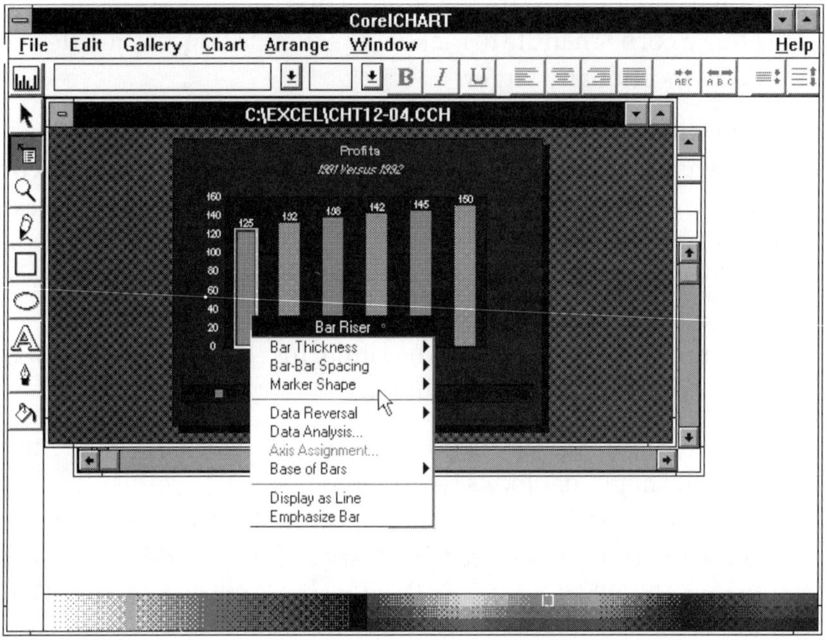

red will look vibrant and contrast beautifully on the screen, but on paper, they will look almost exactly the same.

QUICK SUMMARY

Task	Procedure
Open a chart	Ctrl-O
Save a chart	Ctrl-S
Print	Ctrl-P
Undo	Alt-Backspace
Duplicate	Ctrl-D
Cut	Shift-Del
Copy	Ctrl-Ins
Paste	Shift-Ins
Clear	Del

PRACTICE WHAT YOU'VE LEARNED

We'll create a three-dimensional bar chart.

WHAT YOU DO	*WHAT YOU'LL SEE*
1. Start up *CorelCHART!* and select 3D Riser.	1. The selection of 3D riser charts will appear in the Graph Types area.
2. Make sure the first chart type is selected and click on OK.	2. You will go to the spreadsheet data-enter area.
3. Enter the following values in series 1: 23, 52, 35, 23; enter the following values in series 2 (beginning with cell A2): 24, 42, 44, 51; enter the following values in series 3 (beginning with cell A3): 25, 28, 18, 10. Click on the toggle at the top of the toolbox.	3. You will be taken to the chart, which will be displayed in a three-dimensional form.
4. Pull down the Chart menu and select Show 3D View Menu.	4. A dialog box will open with the tools necessary to adjust the orientation of the graph.

WHAT YOU DO

5. One of the problems with the graph as it stands is that the column farthest away is also the smallest. You can't even see it clearly. Therefore, we need to "tip" the chart so you can see the back columns more clearly. Click on the downward-pointing arrow in the sphere area until the chart stops changing appearance (about 10 times). Click on Redraw, one of the buttons in the dialog box.

6. Let's have some fun now. Click on the right face of one of the columns. We're going to change its fill.

7. Click on the fill tool and select the fountain fill option. Click on the Start button and when the Palette dialog box appears, change the start color to black. Click on OK. Click on the End button and when the palette appears, select white and click on OK. Click on Apply in the Fountain Fill Effect dialog box.

8. Press Ctrl-S.

9. Save the chart as CHT12.05-CCH.

WHAT YOU'LL SEE

5. The chart will be tipped forward so you can see all of the columns.

6. Just the face you click on will be selected. Its outline will stand out.

7. All of the columns in the series will fill with a fountain.

8. The Save As dialog box will open.

9. The new name will appear in the name bar of the window containing the chart.

CorelSHOW!

In this chapter, we are going to create a presentation. It will be brief, but it will use most of the capabilities of *CorelSHOW!*. You'll learn about:

▲ **Creating a slide show presentation**

▲ **Editing a script**

▲ **Special effects**

▲ **Saving and printing a script**

Creating a Slide Show Presentation

In this section of the chapter, we will create a slide show.

To create a new presentation:

1. Start up *CorelSHOW!* by double-clicking on its icon. When the program begins, a dialog box opens asking whether you want to work on an existing presentation or start a new one.
2. Click on **Start a New Presentation** and click on **OK**. You will see the screen shown in Figure 13.1, except that *CorelSHOW!* is maximized by default.

We must define a background for our presentation. In the toolbox at the left side of the screen, you can see the pick tool with some other tools beneath it. The grid pattern immediately beneath the pick tool calls up a dialog box filled with backgrounds. Click on the select background icon. If no backgrounds appear in the dialog box, click on Change Library and in the resulting dialog box, go to the CORELDRW\SHOW\SAMPLES directory and select

▼ **Figure 13.1. The CorelSHOW! screen.**

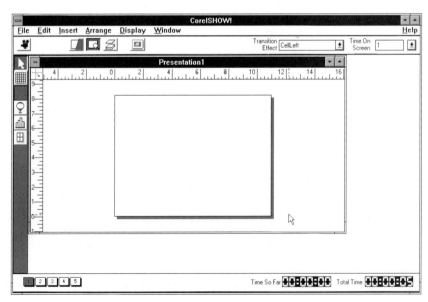

MASTER.SHB. Click on the first background (unless another one strikes your fancy) and click on Done to close the box. The background that appears on the screen will be the background for all the slides in the show (Figure 13.2).

To place an image in the background:

1. Click on the balloon tool in the toolbox and drag a rectangle on the first slide (the rectangle at the center of the *CorelSHOW!* window). *CorelDRAW!* will be started up.
2. Within *CorelDRAW!*, click on the text tool and type SAMPLE SLIDE SHOW, pressing **Enter** after each word.
3. Click on the pick tool and the words should be selected. Click on the yellow color in the palette at the bottom of the screen. Click on the outline tool and then on the palette icon in the outline tool menu. Change the current color to a yellow color.
4. Pull down the Edit menu and select **Copy**. Minimize the *CorelDRAW!* window by clicking on the downward-pointing arrow at the top right corner of the window. *CorelDRAW!* should become an icon at the lower left corner of your screen and *CorelSHOW!* should be visible again.

▼ **Figure 13.2. The Background Loaded and the Dialog Box from which It Was Selected.**

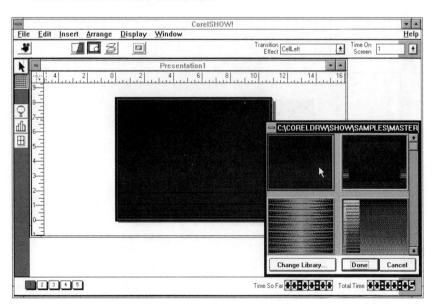

5. Within *CorelSHOW!*, pull down the Edit menu and select **Paste Special**. You will see the dialog box shown in Figure 13.3.
6. Select *CorelDRAW!* Graphic and click on **Paste**. The text will appear on the current slide. You can drag the handles around the text to make the text larger, smaller, wider, or taller, which I have done in Figure 13.4.

If you want to alter the text in some other way, double-click on it to call up *CorelDRAW!* again to make any necessary alteration in it.

7. Note the small rectangles along the lower left corner of the screen, numbered 1 to 5. These represent the slides in our slide show. Currently we are working on slide 1. We want to work on slide 2 now, so click on the second slide. You will see a blank slide.

We need to close down *CorelDRAW!* now, to reclaim its system resources.

8. Click on the *CorelDRAW!* icon. The system menu will open, though *CorelDRAW!* itself will remain minimized. Click on **Close** to shut down *CorelDRAW!*. You will be given the opportunity to save the file, but don't bother. Click on the **No** button.

▼ *Figure 13.3. The Paste Special Dialog Box.*

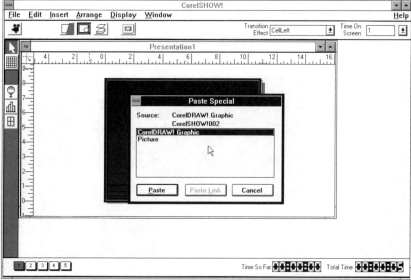

▼ *Figure 13.4. The Text Sized to Fill the Slide.*

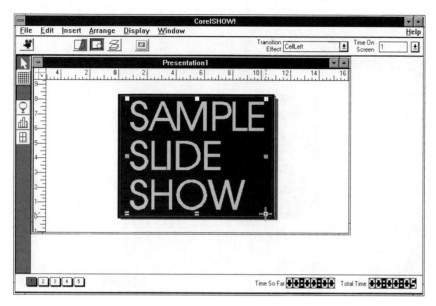

9. Click on the tool immediately beneath the *CorelDRAW!* icon—the *CorelCHART!* icon. Drag a rectangle in the slide. *Corel-CHART!* will start up. Load one of the charts we created earlier. Use the **Copy Chart** to place a copy of the entire chart on the Clipboard.

10. Close *CorelCHART!*. *CorelSHOW!* will be visible.

11. Pull down the Edit menu and select **Paste Special**.

12. Select *CorelCHART!* as the source of the paste and click on **Paste Link** in the dialog box. The chart will probably be far too large, but it is surrounded by handles. Use a corner handle to scale the chart so it will fit on the page, as shown in Figure 13.5.

Next, we will import a bit of animation. *CorelSHOW!* is shipped with a snippet of animation, but you can use any Autodesk Animator file or 3D Studio file. IFONLY.FLI is the file provided.

To import animation:

1. Click on the third slide.

2. Pull down the Insert menu and select **Animation**. In the resulting dialog box, click on **IFONLY.FLI**. If you want to see the individual cells of the animation, click on the slide bar at the bottom of the example box. When you are through selecting the animation, click on **OK**.

▼ *Figure 13.5. The Imported Chart.*

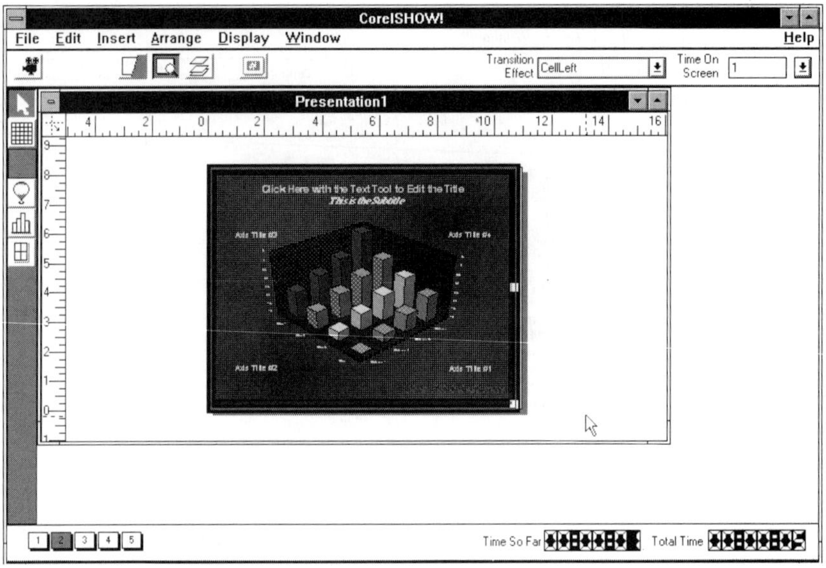

Now we have a brief slide show of three slides. Let's take a look at our presentation.

There is an icon that looks like an old-fashioned motion picture camera at the upper left corner of the *CorelSHOW!* window. A dialog box will open, indicating that *CorelSHOW!* is generating a slide show. Then a dialog box will open asking whether you want to see the slide show. Click on **OK** and sit back to admire your work. Pull down the File menu and select **Save**. Save the slide show as MYSLIDE.SHW.

Editing a Script

When you ran the slide show, certain things must have been clear to you. First, a slide was visible for a second and then the next slide appeared. Second, slides were drawn from the top and bottom toward the center. And finally, the slides were shown in a particular order. We will play havoc with each of these observations now.

To alter order of the slides:

1. Look at the icon bar at the top of the *CorelSHOW!* window. You will see the motion picture camera, then four more icons. Click on the first icon. This icon allows you to see the background of your slide show.
2. Click on the second icon. This allows you to see an individual slide—whichever slide was showing before you clicked on the first icon.
3. Click on the third icon. This icon provides a view that allows you to alter the order of the slides. You will see the screen in Figure 13.6.

Let's say that you want to see the animated slide first, followed by the one containing text, followed by the one containing the chart:

1. Place the mouse pointer on the slide containing the animation (it appears to be full of raindrops). Press the mouse pointer and drag until the area to the left of the first slide turns black. Release the mouse button and the order of the slides will be changed.

▼ *Figure 13.6. The Sorter Screen.*

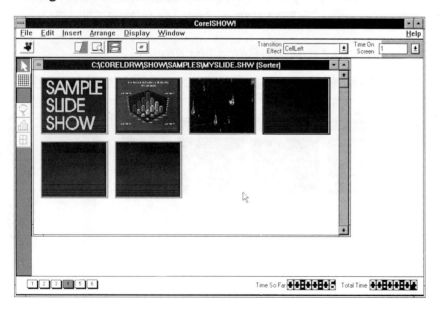

TIP

Another way to alter the order of the slides is to click on the fourth icon in the icon bar (it looks like a number sign). Little text boxes appear at the bottom of each slide. Click on the slides in the order you want them to appear. Then click on the number sign icon again. The slides will be reordered in numerical order according to the order they have been clicked upon.

To remove a slide, click on it and press **Del**. I have deleted the blank slides and pulled down the Transition list box in Figure 13.7. This box only applies to the currently selected slide.

2. Select **CellLeftDissolve** and run the slide show. Note how different the transition is.

3. Pull down the **Time** on Screen list box to pick a speed for the show. The number 1 is selected so that each slide remains on the screen 1 second.

TIP

If you are giving a talk, you will want to control when the slides change. Therefore, pull down the Display menu and select Presentation Options. Click on Manual Advance to Next Slide. This will

▼ *Figure 13.7. The Transition List Box.*

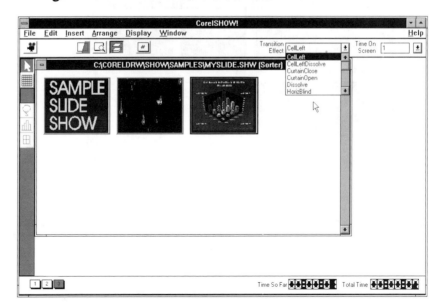

make the slide show wait for you to double-click your mouse before proceeding. Note also in this dialog box, you have the option of keeping the mouse pointer on the screen. This is useful if you are pointing to options on the screen.

QUICK SUMMARY

Task	*Procedure*
Run slide show	Ctrl-R
Open a slide show	Ctrl-O
Save a slide show	Ctrl-S
Print a slide show	Ctrl-P
Undo	Alt-Backspace
Cut	Shift-Del
Copy	Ctrl-Ins
Paste	Shift-Ins
Clear	Del
Insert a new page	Ctrl-N
Insert Animation	Ctrl-A
Move selected object to front	Shift-PgUp
Move selected object to back	Shift-PgDn
Move object forward one	Ctrl-PgUp
Move object back one	Ctrl-PgDn

PRACTICE WHAT YOU'VE LEARNED

I may have left you with the impression that you can only place one object on a slide. Not true. You can load up a slide with objects, if you want. That's what we'll do here.

WHAT YOU DO

1. Select New from the File menu to clear the screen and start with a fresh slide show.

WHAT YOU'LL SEE

1. You will see a fresh collection of blank slides on the screen. (If you are still in the sorter, click on the third icon, which looks like a magnifying glass over a rectangle.)

WHAT YOU DO	**WHAT YOU'LL SEE**
2. Click on the *CorelDRAW!* tool in the toolbox. Drag a rectangle on the slide.	2. *CorelDRAW!* will start up.
3. Draw some rectangles of various color in the *CorelDRAW!* screen. Copy them to the Clipboard and minimize *CorelDRAW!*. Then use the Paste Special to paste the *CorelDRAW!* object in *CorelSHOW!*.	3. The object will appear, probably grossly too large. Use the handles to resize the graphic.
4. Click on the *CorelDRAW!* icon again. Type some text in *CorelDRAW!*, select it, copy it to the Clipboard, and close *CorelDRAW!* to get it out of the way.	4. *CorelDRAW!* closes, but the text remains on the Clipboard.
5. Return to *CorelSHOW!* and select Paste Special. Select *CorelDRAW!* Graphic and click on Paste.	5. The text will appear in the *CorelSHOW!*.
6. The text should be in the foreground (in front of the rectangles you drew earlier) and it should be selected. Pull down the Arrange menu and select To Back.	6. The text will appear behind the drawing.

Appendix: Quick Keyboard Commands

About *CorelDRAW!*	Alt-H,A
Add New Envelope	Alt-C,N
Add New Perspective	Alt-C,P
Align	Alt-A,A
Align	Ctrl-A
Align to Baseline	Alt-A,L
Align to Baseline	Ctrl-Z
Alt-A,A	Align
Alt-A,B	To Back
Alt-A,C	Combine
Alt-A,F	To Front
Alt-A,G	Group
Alt-A,K	Break Apart
Alt-A,L	Align to Baseline
Alt-A,N	Back One
Alt-A,O	Forward One
Alt-A,R	Reverse Order

Alt-A,S	Straighten Text
Alt-A,T	Fit Text to Path
Alt-A,U	Ungroup
Alt-A,V	Convert to Curves
Alt-Backspace	Undo
Alt-C,B	Blend
Alt-C,C	Clear Envelope
Alt-C,D	Edit Envelope
Alt-C,F	Copy Perspective From
Alt-C,L	Clear Perspective
Alt-C,N	Add New Envelope
Alt-C,P	Add New Perspective
Alt-C,R	Copy Envelope From
Alt-C,V	Edit Perspective
Alt-C,X	Extrude
Alt-D,A	Auto Update
Alt-D,B	Show Bitmaps
Alt-D,C	Show Color Palette
Alt-D,F	Show Full-Screen Preview
Alt-D,G	Snap to Guidelines
Alt-D,I	Grid Setup
Alt-D,L	Guidelines Setup
Alt-D,O	Preview Selected Only
Alt-D,P	Show Preview
Alt-D,R	Show Rulers
Alt-D,S	Show Status Line
Alt-D,S,S	Snap to Grid
Alt-D,T	Show Preview Toolbox
Alt-D,W	Refresh Wire Screen
Alt-E,A	Select All
Alt-E,C	Copy
Alt-E,D	Duplicate
Alt-E,E	Redo
Alt-E,H	Character Attributes
Alt-E,L	Clear
Alt-E,P	Paste
Alt-E,R	Repeat
Alt-E,S	Copy Style From
Alt-E,T	Edit Text

Alt-E,U	Undo
Alt-F,A	Save As
Alt-F,C	Control Panel
Alt-F,E	Export
Alt-F,G	Page Setup
Alt-F,I	Import
Alt-F,M	Print Merge
Alt-F,N	New
Alt-F,O	Open
Alt-F,P	Print
Alt-F,S	Save
Alt-F,X	Exit
Alt-H,A	About *CorelDRAW!*
Alt-Return	Redo
Alt-S,A	Create Arrow
Alt-S,C	Create Pattern
Alt-S,E	Preferences
Alt-S,M	Merge-Back
Alt-S,X	Extract
Alt-T,C	Clear Transformations
Alt-T,M	Move
Alt-T,R	Rotate and Skew
Alt-T,S	Stretch and Mirror
Auto Update	Alt-D,A
Back One	Alt-A,N
Back One	PgDn
Blend	Alt-C,B
Blend	Ctrl-B
Break Apart	Alt-A,K
Break Apart	Ctrl-K
Character Attributes	Alt-E,H
Clear	Alt-E,L
Clear	Del
Clear Envelope	Alt-C,C
Clear Perspective	Alt-C,L
Clear Transformations	Alt-T,C
Combine	Alt-A,C
Combine	Ctrl-C
Control Panel	Alt-F,C

Convert to Curves	Alt-A,V
Convert to Curves	Ctrl-V
Copy	Alt-E,C
Copy	Ctrl-Ins
Copy Envelope From	Alt-C,R
Copy Perspective From	Alt-C,F
Copy Style From	Alt-E,S
Create Arrow	Alt-S,A
Create Pattern	Alt-S,C
Ctrl-A	Align
Ctrl-B	Blend
Ctrl-C	Combine
Ctrl-D	Duplicate
Ctrl-E	Extrude
Ctrl-F	Fit Text to Path
Ctrl-G	Group
Ctrl-Ins	Copy
Ctrl-J	Preferences
Ctrl-K	Break Apart
Ctrl-L	Move
Ctrl-N	Rotate and Skew
Ctrl-O	Open
Ctrl-P	Print
Ctrl-Q	Stretch and Mirror
Ctrl-R	Repeat
Ctrl-S	Save
Ctrl-T	Edit Text
Ctrl-U	Ungroup
Ctrl-V	Convert to Curves
Ctrl-W	Refresh Wire Screen
Ctrl-X	Exit
Ctrl-Y	Snap to Grid
Ctrl-Z	Align to Baseline
Cut	Shift-Del
Del	Clear
Duplicate	Alt-E,D
Duplicate	Ctrl-D
Edit Envelope	Alt-C,D
Edit Perspective	Alt-C,V

Edit Text	Alt-E,T
Edit Text	Ctrl-T
Ellipse tool	F7
Exit	Alt-F,X
Exit	Ctrl-X
Export	Alt-F,E
Extract	Alt-S,X
Extrude	Alt-C,X
Extrude	Ctrl-E
F2	Zoom in
F3	Zoom out
F4	Fit zoom in window
F5	Pencil tool
F6	Rectangle tool
F7	Ellipse tool
F8	Text tool
F9	Full-Screen Preview toggle
F10	Shape tool
F11	Fountain Fill
F12	Outline Pen
Fit Text to Path	Alt-A,T
Fit Text to Path	Ctrl-F
Fit zoom in window	F4
Forward One	Alt-A,O
Forward One	PgUp
Full-Screen Preview	F9
Grid Setup	Alt-D,I
Group	Alt-A,G
Group	Ctrl-G
Guidelines Setup	Alt-D,L
Import	Alt-F,I
Merge-Back	Alt-S,M
Move	Alt-T,M
Move	Ctrl-L
New	Alt-F,N
New Object Outline Color	Shift-F12
New Object Uniform Fill	F12
Open	Alt-F,O
Open	Ctrl-O

Page Setup	Alt-F,G
Paste	Alt-E,P
Paste	Shift-Ins
Pencil tool	F5
PgDn	Back One
PgUp	Forward One
Preferences	Alt-S,E
Preferences	Ctrl-J
Preview Selected Only	Alt-D,O
Print	Alt-F,P
Print	Ctrl-P
Print Merge	Alt-F,M
Rectangle tool	F6
Redo	Alt-E,E
Redo	Alt-Return
Refresh Wire Screen	Alt-D,W
Refresh Wire Screen	Ctrl-W
Repeat	Alt-E,R
Repeat	Ctrl-R
Reverse Order	Alt-A,R
Rotate and Skew	Alt-T,R
Rotate and Skew	Ctrl-N
Save	Alt-F,S
Save	Ctrl-S
Save As	Alt-F,A
Select All	Alt-E,A
Shift-Del	Cut
Shift-F4	Show page
Shift-F9	Show Preview toggle
Shift-F11	Fill Tool
Shift-F12	Outline Color
Shift-Ins	Paste
Shift-PgDn	To Back
Shift-PgUp	To Front
Show Bitmaps	Alt-D,B
Show Color Palette	Alt-D,C
Show Full-Screen Preview	Alt-D,F
Show Page	Shift-F4
Show Preview	Alt-D,P

Show Preview	Shift-F9
Show Preview Toolbox	Alt-D,T
Show Rulers	Alt-D,R
Show Status Line	Alt-D,S
Snap to Grid	Alt-D,S,S
Snap to Grid	Ctrl-Y
Snap to Guidelines	Alt-D,G
Straighten Text	Alt-A,S
Stretch and Mirror	Alt-T,S
Stretch and Mirror	Ctrl-Q
Text tool	F8
To Back	Alt-A,B
To Back	Shift-PgDn
To Front	Alt-A,F
To Front	Shift-PgUp
Undo	Alt-Backspace
Undo	Alt-E,U
Ungroup	Alt-A,U
Ungroup	Ctrl-U
Zoom in	F2
Zoom out	F3

Glossary

Alignment   The placement of objects relative to one another. *CorelDRAW!* can center objects or align them along their tops, bottoms, or right or left sides.

Autotrace   A method for turning bitmap graphics into vector drawings. It looks for edges, where black borders on white or where colors or shades of gray border on one another and places a line at this border. There is a simple autotrace within *CorelDRAW!* and a more complete version in *CorelTRACE!*.

Backup   A spare copy of a program or other kind of file. Prudent computer users back up their software as soon as they purchase it and back up their data files once a week.

Bézier curve   A curve determined (or described) by a method developed by a French mathematician named Bézier. A Bézier is determined by its beginning and end points, its "launch angles" which show the angle at which the curve meets its end points and how much force or "stretch" is involved in its movement (these are represented by the control points in *CorelDRAW!*).

Bitmap   A kind of graphic that is, in essence, laid out on a grid. Individual points in the grid may be turned on (black) or turned off (white) or, in some cases, contain a number representing a color or a shade of gray. The grid may be very fine, even 300 dpi or higher, but the graphic is made up of points that don't adjust well when sized and have no relationship with one another, making editing more difficult. The alternative to bitmap graphics is vector graphics. Raster graphics is another word for bitmap graphics.

Button A device in a dialog box in Windows. The most common buttons are Cancel (which means "make the dialog box go away and don't take any action") and OK ("go ahead and take action based on the settings in this dialog box").

CAD Computer-assisted design (or CAD) is the process of design with the mediation of a computer to take care of the simple tasks like file management and redrawing. CAD lets you use your imagination and never fear to make a change because it will mean redrawing everything. CAD output can then be used to operate machine tools to create real objects that match the drawing. This is known as computer-assisted machining (CAM) and you will often see these two acronyms together, as in CAD/CAM.

Check box A device you will find in Windows dialog boxes. When you click on it, it changes appearance to let you know the parameter it represents has been set.

Clear Means Delete in Windows parlance. No copy of the selected object is sent to the Clipboard. The only way to bring the object back is to select Undo from the Edit menu.

Clicking To click, press the left mouse button once and release it immediately.

Clip art Predrawn art that saves you time and effort when producing graphics. If you create the main part of the art, say, the house, you can decorate it with shrubbery and lawn flamingos from a clip art collection.

Clipboard A temporary storage area in Windows where graphics go when you select Cut and Copy from the Edit menu.

Close box The box in the upper left corner of all windows is known as the system menu or the close box because clicking on it once calls up the system menu and double-clicking on it closes the window.

Closed object   An object whose outline is complete: The beginning point is joined to the end point. Only closed objects can be filled with patterns and colors.

Control panel   A program within Windows that is used to make settings in Windows. You will most often use the control panel to change the printer or printer orientation.

Control points   The handles used to manipulate Bézier curves. The distance of a control point from the end point is an indication of the strength of its influence on the curve. The angle of the curve from the end point is shown by the control point's literal angle from a line that might be drawn to the other end point of the curve.

Copy   This term, as it is used in Windows, means that a replica of the currently selected object will be sent to temporary storage on the Clipboard.

Curve   Anything that is not a straight line is a curve. Curves take more memory and other resources than straight lines.

Cut   This term, as it is used in Windows, means that a replica of the currently selected object will be sent to temporary storage in the Clipboard and the original is eliminated from the screen.

Deselect   Clicking away from all objects will deselect all objects.

Dialog box   A box full of options that will appear on the screen. Some of the selections on the box may call up other dialog boxes. When you see an ellipsis (...) in a menu or a button in a dialog box, that means the item will call up a dialog box.

DISKCOPY   A DOS command that literally copies every piece of information from one disk onto another, including the arrangement of files on the disk (which is not an action performed by COPY or XCOPY).

Double-clicking   An action that involves rapidly pressing and releasing the left mouse button twice.

Dragging   An action accomplished by placing the mouse pointer on an object, pressing and holding the left mouse button, and then moving the mouse pointer to a new position.

Duplicate   A command in the Edit menu that creates a copy of whatever object is selected; the copy is placed on the screen rather than in the Clipboard. The duplicate is placed very near the original, but at a slight offset. You can set the off-set with the Preferences command in the Special menu.

Ellipse tool   A tool that creates an ellipse when it is selected and the mouse is dragged within the *CorelDRAW!* window. By holding the Ctrl key down while dragging, you can create a perfect circle.

Em   The width of the letter M in a font. It's the widest letter and therefore the standard width to use for measuring kerning and word spacing.

Fill tool   A tool used to fill objects with patterns and colors, or to remove the fill.

Font   Sometimes loosely referred to as a typeface; a group of characters that share certain attributes, like weight (thickness of lines), serifs, and others.

FORMAT   A DOS command that causes the computer to prepare a disk to receive data. Once a disk is formatted, it need not be formatted again, but a disk fresh out of the box must be formatted or it cannot be used.

Fountain   A gradual gradation of color or shading across an area.

Grayed menu item   Items that appear grayed in menus (rather than black) are not available at the current time for some reason. Clicking on these items has no effect.

Grid   A set of fixed points on the screen that allows you to easily place objects at regular intervals.

Guideline   An extension of the ruler. You can place a guideline anywhere on the screen to indicate alignment, for example. A guideline is obtained by placing the mouse on a ruler and dragging it.

Handles   When an item is selected and the pick tool is in use, the item will be in the middle of a selection rectangle with eight handles, or tiny rectangles, around it.

Justification   A term that refers to the alignment of text. Full justification means that both the right and left margins are even. Some people refer to fully justified text simply as justified text. Others refer to right-aligned text as right-justified and left-aligned text as left-justified.

Keyboard shortcut   A quick way to enter a command on the keyboard that might be entered more slowly with the mouse. The appendix of this book contains many keyboard shortcuts.

Ellipse tool
▼
Object oriented

Line   Anything that isn't a curve in a drawing. Lines have no control points, so they represent a savings in memory and other system resources over equivalent curves.

Maximize   A window is maximized when it fills the entire monitor screen. Maximize is a command on the system menu.

Menu   A list of options. Good programming practice dictates that the items on a specific menu should be related to each other or to the same class of actions. Thus, all the commands having to do with disk access are available on the File menu.

Menu bar   The most important menus for a program brought together at the top of the window in a line.

Minimize   A window that has been reduced to an icon is minimized. This doesn't mean that the program is shut off. In Windows, minimized programs can continue to operate, though they are not generally given 100 percent of the system resources. Minimize is a command on the system menu.

Mouse   An input device used to closely mimic the movement of the human hand on the desktop. It's about the size and shape of a bar of soap and, generally, is connected to the computer by a cable that transmits information to the computer about your movements.

Move bar   The move bar is the same as the title bar of a window. It contains the name of the operating program and often the name of the document or drawing currently in memory. If the window isn't maximized, you can place the mouse pointer on the move bar and drag the window around by it. Double-clicking on the move bar will maximize or restore the window, depending on its current state.

Nodes   The curves and lines of an object's outline are terminated by nodes, also loosely referred to as end points.

Object   An individual item on the screen. Objects can be grouped or combined to make more than one object into one object.

Object oriented   A drawing program that constructs objects and then manipulates these objects to create drawings is called an object-oriented drawing program.

Open object   An object whose outline is not completely closed. An open object cannot be filled in *CorelDRAW!* unless it is first closed.

Outline tool   A tool used to perform node editing and bitmap clipping, and for working with the character attributes of text.

Page area   The central area of the *CorelDRAW!* window that is partially filled with a representation of a sheet of paper.

Paint program   Programs that manipulate screen memory. They are not object oriented and produce bitmap graphics. *CorelPHOTO-PAINT!* is a paint program.

Palette   A collection of colors for use in a graphic.

Paragraph text   Text that is entered in a block format. It is the only kind of text that can be fully justified in *CorelDRAW!*. Paragraph text makes use of a property called *word wrap* to limit the length of individual lines. If the text is too large to fit in the paragraph block, the excess will simply not appear on the screen or in the printout.

Paste   An item on the Edit menu that brings information back from the Clipboard and places it on the screen. The information remains on the Clipboard, so it can be pasted more than once.

Pencil tool   The tool used for autotracing and freehand drawing.

Pica   A unit of measurement equivalent to approximately ⅙ inch.

Pick tool   The primary tool used for selecting and manipulating objects on the page. It's the arrow-shaped tool at the top of the toolbox.

Pixel   An individual dot of light on the monitor. It is the smallest unit of graphic information available on the monitor. Paint programs manipulate individual pixels, using them to paint a low-resolution picture.

PostScript   An interpreted language for describing pages. In whatever device it is used, it will drive that device to create a graphic at its maximum resolution, whether it is a 300 dpi laser printer, a 1200 dpi typesetter, or a 72 dpi monitor.

Precedence   Precedence determines the order that objects are drawn on the screen.

Preview   A screen that shows an approximation of the graphic as it will appear on paper.

Program group   Windows 3 and higher organizes its programs according to tasks in special windows called program groups. When *CorelDRAW!* is installed, all the associated programs are placed in a special program group called Corel Graphics.

Program item   The individual programs in a program group. They are icons that represent the programs.

Radio button   Certain items in dialog boxes are called radio buttons. They are like check boxes, but checking one box unchecks any other radio button that is already selected.

Raster   The beam of electrons a monitor uses to brighten the pixels on the screen. Since the pixels are, in effect, individual units of the raster, paint programs are referred to as raster (as opposed to vector) graphics.

Rectangle tool   The item in the toolbox used for creating rectangles and squares.

Registration mark   A tiny cross used to position a piece of paper or a film negative.

Restore   A screen size between maximized and minimized. It is one of the options on the system menu.

Ruler   A literal measuring device that can be turned on at the top and left side of the *CorelDRAW!* window.

Selection rectangle   A rectangle that can be dragged with the shape tool or the pick tool to enclose items you want to have selected. Any items not enclosed completely in the selection rectangle won't be selected. Once an item is selected, the selection rectangle is represented by the positions of eight tiny black handles that can be used to distort or rotate the selected block of items.

Shape tool   The tool used for node editing. It's the second item in the toolbox.

Skew   If you picture a rectangle being forced under pressure into the shape most people associate with the word "parallelogram," you have a pretty good idea what skew is. When you skew an object, the side you are skewing moves parallel to its opposite side, which remains stationary. The other two sides "lean" to accommodate the action.

Status line   A region just beneath the menu bar at the top of the *CorelDRAW!* window that tells certain information about the selected object and the position of the mouse pointer in the window.

System menu   A small rectangle at the top left corner of all windows, also known as the close box. Click on it once to see a menu of system actions for sizing the window.

Text box   A rectangle within a dialog box where you can type information. Generally, if there is text in a text box, you can double-click in the box to select the information completely. Then, when you type your information, the information that existed when the box was called up will automatically be deleted.

Text tool   The tool in the toolbox that shows the letter A. It's used to place strings and paragraphs on the page area, as well as symbols from the symbol libraries.

Title bar   The part of any window that contains the name of the operating program and usually the name of the currently open document; also called the **Move bar**.

Toolbox   A kind of supplemental menu bar that runs down the left side of the *CorelDRAW!* window.

Trace   See **Autotrace**.

Type size   A measure of the height of a letter in points (a value approximately equal to $1/72$ inch).

Type style   A term that usually refers to roman, italic, bold, or bold-italic.

Typeface   A term often loosely interchanged with the word font, although its actual meaning is not quite the same. A font is a typeface (like Times-Roman) in a particular point size and in a particular style, like roman, italic, bold, or bold-italic. Typeface refers to all of these at once. This distinction is rarely made in desktop publishing.

Vector   A line drawn from one point on the screen to another without reference to the raster. Oscilloscopes use vectors. The idealized way vectors trace objects on the screen is similar to the way PostScript describes them to the printer engine of a laser printer and the way *CorelDRAW!* saves its graphics. Therefore, *vector graphics* is used to refer to drawn images, as opposed to painted raster graphics.

Windows Areas of the screen controlled by a single program. Windows contain menus, close boxes, move bars, and other features not typically found in dialog boxes.

Wireframe The bare bones of a drawing, including nothing but the outlines of objects.

Wrap Wrap or word wrap is when text will automatically break at the end of a line and return to the left margin.

Zoom tool The tool in the toolbox that looks like a magnifying glass used to take closer looks at objects on the screen.

Status line
▼
Zoom tool

Index